Out of th

Philip Sean Coogan

Out of the Flames

Matador
9 De Montfort Mews
Leicester LE1 7FW, UK
Tel: (+44) 116 255 9311 / 9312
Email: books@troubador.co.uk
Web: www.troubador.co.uk/matador

ISBN 978-1848760-585

A Cataloguing-in-Publication (CIP) catalogue record for this book
is available from the British Library.

Some names have been changed for reasons of privacy.

Typeset in 11pt Book Antiqua by Troubador Publishing Ltd, Leicester, UK

Matador is an imprint of Troubador Publishing Ltd

Printed by the MPG Books Group in the UK

AUTHOR'S ACKNOWLEDGEMENT

My thanks to people in the medical profession, and a friend, who, on hearing of my journey, suggested that I should write and tell my story. Now, years later, I have put pen to paper. I am very grateful to John Parker of London, a journalist and writer who edited my manuscript in a helpful and friendly manner. Thanks to our very close neighbours, friends and family members, who helped over the years, many of whom are now deceased. Finally, but not least, my gratitude to those around me who suffered and endured; my wife Patricia for keeping the family together, our three young children, all standing shoulder to shoulder with me during the darkest years of my life, being ill and of little help to antone. Be assured all are constantly in my thoughts.

Philip Coogan, 2009

7TH DECEMBER 1971

The evening began just like any other. The children had their tea, laughing and squabbling, just like all children, with my wife Patricia keeping loving order over the proceedings. We were a happy family and happy families, as Tolstoy observed, are much alike the world over. When tea was done it was time for a little television before bedtime. On such a bitterly cold night with the wind blowing in from the north and hearing the sea close by us churning up angry waves that battered the shore it was a comfort to snuggle down in the warmth of the bungalow. However my own custom at that time was to return to the petrol station after our evening meal and do an hour's work, looking over the books and preparing things for the next day's trade. As anyone who's tried it knows, running a business is not a nine-to-five job. My own business – a garage and motor repair operation – was doing well, and I had plans to expand further to include a restaurant, supermarket, a club house and leisure facilities. But nothing comes from idleness. Only by putting in the extra hours of work had we come this far in making a good living for ourselves, and I knew that only by continuing the hard work could I take myself, the business and the family on to further success and prosperity in our community. This example had been set me by own father, as straightforward and industrious a man as one was ever likely to meet.

This particular evening there was a Western showing on TV, and kids being fond of the kind of harmless shoot-ups, rolling wagon trains and simple heroism you find in these films, my three young ones were sitting eagerly in front of the set as the opening titles came up. I can't remember if it was one of the old John-Wayne yarns or maybe a series – the High Chapparel perhaps – but the children were glued to that screen and just waved me off absently as I said goodbye and got up to leave for the garage. It was just as I was about to close the front door behind me that Patricia came running after me into the hall.

'Oh quick Philip – can you spare a minute, the picture's gone.'

This was a common problem with TV sets in those days. For no obvious reason the screen would roll or go fuzzy, and various knobs at the back of the set would need to be adjusted to restore the picture.

'Can you not fiddle with it?' I asked.

'You know I can't make head nor tail of it' replied Patricia, 'Aw, c'mon it won't take you a second, the children are awful keen to watch this film.'

Hearing the kids echoing their mum's plea, and reluctant to leave the family in any kind of unhappiness, even over a TV show, I made my way back to the living room and began twiddling the knobs on the set. Eventually the snowy lines disappeared and a lovely sharp picture returned to the screen. The children cheered with pleasure and looked on in anticipation as the gunslingers dismounted from their horses and strolled menacingly up the street. These were obviously the bad guys. Often it was the other way round and it was the sheriff's men who were dirty, but whichever the case, in Westerns you could always tell the good guys from the bad guys. Before long no doubt the Indians would come whooping into town and there'd be a real old fracas with all onto all. I found myself getting drawn into the action and sat back in the armchair to enjoy a little more time with the family. With the weather so bitter I'd have put off going out at all but for the fact a petrol delivery was on its way. The tanker was due around mid-evening and someone had to be on site. Also, tomorrow was the Catholic Holy Day, regarded as the start of the Christmas festive season. To mark the occasion I'd rigged coloured lights across the forecourt and wanted to go in and set the electronic time switch to bring them on early. Outside the wind howled, inside on the TV the guns began to crackle and, sure enough the Indians soon arrived waving their tomahawks. Suddenly Patricia sat up on the settee, her ears cocked like a retriever.

'What was that?'

'What was what?' I said.

'I thought I heard a bang.'

'Sure – the injuns have got hold of some dynamite, look.'

'No, outside.'

Patricia remained upright, listening intently.

'Probably the sea – it can make an awful row when it's angry.'

'Philip, it sounded like an explosion so it did.'

'In Donagahdee?' I said. Hearing explosions in Belfast was not a surprise at that time, but our little seaside town was well out of earshot of the city. After watching the film for another ten minutes I forced myself from the armchair for the second time, kissed my wife and went out to the Mercedes. I was just about to turn the key in the ignition when Patricia appeared at the front door again. This time she was waving her arms. It seemed there was someone on the telephone for me.

'It's Maria' said Pat (short for Patricia) as I came back into the hall and took the receiver.

'Maria?' I said as I came in and took the receiver. Maria worked in the shop attached to the garage and lived close by. I listened for a few seconds and then turned to Pat.

'They've bombed the garage – c'mon get in the car, and bring the kids!'

They say that in moments of crisis the brain moves faster. Like a computer, it works things out instantly, without your having to think about them. Perhaps that's why, on that fateful night, without consciously thinking why, I took my family with me. My mind had already told me: if the garage has been hit, something else may be. Bombs, like all troubles may come not as single spies but sometimes whole battalions. With the family by my side at least I knew where they were. My mind grasped something else in the few minutes it took me to drive from the bungalow to the garage – that bombs are intended not only to tear apart concrete and metal and glass. My regular routine of returning to finish off work in the evenings was easy for anyone to have observed. On any other night I'd have been in the inner office when the explosion occurred. Whatever faceless devil under cover of darkness had placed or thrown some device just thirty minutes earlier – this was about when Pat said she heard the bang – must, must, have known or expected a certain human being to be there. For how could anyone have foreseen that tonight of all nights a faulty TV and a cracking old film would make me reluctant to leave the house? As I raced the Mercedes the few hundred yards up the road my mind, like a steel door guarding my sanity shut out any further implications of this thought.

When the garage came in sight the flames were already licking up several feet into the night sky, accompanied by crackling noises and periodic bangs. It must be the cars I thought. A fire engine and the RUC were already on the scene. Two firemen armed with axes were attempting to break open the front doors to the offices. I jumped out of the car and shouted, waving my keys in the air. I then led the fire brigade to the rear of the building and unlocked the back door to let the officers in. Another entrance up the side alley had already been forced open. Inside I could see a number of cars already on fire and minor explosions were occurring. I was now in a frantic state. My immediate impulse was to get the cars that were so far untouched out of the building. I opened the door of the nearest saloon, took off the handbrake and steered it towards the exit and out across the forecourt. The firemen repeatedly shouted through the commotion for me to move away from the building now. Ignoring them I returned, picked up a fire extinguisher and directed it through a hole in the floor at one of the burning cars in the basement. I could see the fire crew below spraying the floors of the basement, beneath which lay the petrol storage tanks. At this point a fireman took me firmly by the arm and escorted me outside. I saw Patricia and the children standing speechless on the roadway. I walked towards them in a daze and put my hand on Pat's shoulder to steady myself. An army patrol had also arrived now, and quite a crowd of local people. Together we stared at the blazing building, our faces lit up in the flames. Like the scene at some macabre bonfire night, everyone had gathered to witness the act of destruction. There was now an intense heat coming off the burning garage and thick black smoke had begun to disgorge from the roof, doors and shattered windows. As the wind changed several people covered their faces and stepped back as noxious fumes hit their nostrils. There is no other smell quite like burning rubber. Again I thought of the cars – my stock, my livelihood, everything I'd worked long and hard for was in that building. If I could just get the rest of the cars out…As if reading my thoughts Pat gripped my arm as I strained forward. But nothing, not common sense or the wishes of my family could stop me now. I was a man beyond reason.

'Philip no – don't be stupid…!'

'Stay here Pat – hold on to the kids!'

In the instant I entered the front door of the garage again the heat hit me like a smack in the face and my eyes began to sting with pain. Floundering helplessly amid the black smoke and falling debris, suddenly I could no longer breathe.

PART ONE

1

Spirits of My Ancestors

'Here's a little treat for you young man' my grandfather James Foy says kindly, dipping his hand in his pocket and offering me some chocolate or other sweet thing. He is like a fellow out of a picture book, with a round black hat and sporting a large, protruding moustache. I reach forward and take the gift from his hand. I look up at him, and he smiles at me. There is trust between us.

I always looked forward to our family trips by motor car from our home in Tyrone to visit Grandfather and Granny Foy at their two-storey house and farm in Cloone, County Leitrim. As kind-hearted an old couple as a young boy could wish to have as grandparents, the Foys were my mother's parents, and the family had farmed in Leitrim for several generations. In the early 1900s I imagine they would have been considered wealthy, as they were said to have kept racehorses as well as cattle on their land. Fortunately they had not been uprooted during the Irish insurrection. Only when a little older did I understand the historical facts about the 1916 rising, which had forced so many families to flee their homes, piling everything they could onto the back of a truck or a cart, often never to return. Such was the story on the paternal side of my family. My father, called Patrick, was born in 1913 in King's County, now known as County Offaly. His father was Colonel Owen Coogan, a serving officer of the British Army and as such, deemed a sworn enemy of the Nationalists. The civil unrest following the Easter rising thus obliged Colonel Coogan and his large family to abandon their estate on pain of death, and in 1917 they migrated north to Cooneen near Fivemiletown, County Fermanagh where with modest savings they bought a very small farm. Although my father's parents died before I was born, I came to know them in a sense through my own father's memories, and also by an early and fond acquaintance with the place where they had lived. For, when on route to the Foys we would often stop off at the old Coogan family farm, which my Uncle Jim had continued the running of. In fine summer weather my mother and father and I and young brother Pat would make the few hours journey from the shores of Lough Neagh to stay for a week's holiday and help out our Uncle with work on the farm.

Cooneen being a mountainous region, most of the pasture lay on the slopes of the hills which rose up high above the holding and fell to the glen below. At the bottom of the valley flowed the River Coonen, which was a plentiful freshwater trout stream. This enchanted place, with its rich, silvery treasure flashing hither and thither in the sunlight, had to be a fisherman's paradise! Many were the happy hours I idled away watching the wild rainbow trout scurrying in abundance through the clear, shallow water till disappearing into the larger holes of the riverbed. In haymaking time, my brother Pat and I would eagerly help with the work, indeed as soon as we could walk we were told, we'd be out there with the men, gleefully pitching the golden stalks into the air. Many years later my father told me of an incident that took place between my brother and I. One morning, seeing our mother and father and Uncle Jim working with pitchforks to make the hay, Pat and I as usual race over to join in. Grabbing a spare pitchfork each, we begin lifting and tossing the heaps of hay and having a high old time of it. Our parents, on seeing our antics, call over to be careful, as pitchforks are dangerous for larking around with. From then on we take our task seriously, working furiously to each get the biggest pile of hay we can. And, as boys do, we each of us want to win at the game. An argument then breaks out between Pat and me as to whose heap of hay is the highest. Our childish quarrel grows so heated that Pat finally runs over and sticks me in the side of the head with the pitchfork. I can still remember nothing of what happened immediately afterwards. This is not to be the last time my memory will be affected, in one way or another, by untoward events.

Life on the farm isn't all work. There is always time in the evenings for talking long and unhurried over the events of the day. At sunset the neighbours who've been helping each other with the harvest call at Uncle Jim's homestead and gather around the open turf fire. Whenever the conversation pauses and the kitchen is quiet and still you can hear crickets chirping among the ashes at the back of the hearth. Above the fire is mounted an iron crane, from which hangs the large black kettle for making the tea. The crane can be adjusted according to the height of the fire at any particular time. As the water slowly heats and the home-made soda bread (always a little over-salted) and butter is prepared, Uncle Jim, my parents and the neighbours discuss the day's events. Whether it is the bringing home of the hay, the rounding up of the sheep from the hill or the cursed changeable moods of the weather, it is all examined and ruminated over in amiable detail. Sometimes there is talk of the following day's tasks – plans for going to the bog and saving some turf or leaving early to take some sheep or cattle to the local fair. As the evening wears on and the embers glow red as we huddle round the big black kettle, someone will begin a yarn, a local tale handed down from long, long ago. Some of these stories are repeated each time we stay on the farm, yet whenever I hear them I sit enthralled, welcoming the retelling, wanting to revisit the magical, sometimes disquieting pictures they conjure in my mind. Tonight's is a famous local legend of weird goings-on not far from where we sit in Uncle Jim's kitchen. The tale concerns a certain cottage in the Cooneen neighbourhood whose occupants have suffered great anxiety from believing the place to be haunted. The various manifestations of this haunting always both thrill and terrify me in equal measure, for whoever is telling the tale will themselves speak in a low and ghostly voice as they describe crockery on the dresser being rattled by invisible hands, chairs moving unbidden into the air and certain parts of the old parlour of the cottage becoming abnormally cold whenever the spirit is present. Sometimes the occupants hear running footsteps outside, together with a frantic panting of breath and the drumming of horses' hooves. On opening the cottage door however the lane is empty and deathly quiet. Talk among the locals draws the conclusion that the ghost is an unquiet spirit from the Civil War of Cromwell's time, a man likely killed in a terrible manner, without last rites. It is further believed that some guilty secret had been on the man's conscience at the moment of his death and that this knowledge, laying for centuries like an iron weight upon his soul, has condemned him to pace the floorboards of the old cottage for eternity unless he can be freed from torment, laid to rest, and his poor phantom horse put out to heavenly pasture. When prayers and special masses held at the local church fail to do the trick, a young priest calls at the cottage in person. The Father prays for several hours, accompanied by the family and neighbours, all gathered together in the kitchen. After a while they feel the eerie and unmistakeable chill come into the room, one or two folk whispering fearfully "It's the ghost!" The young priest walks slowly from one side of the kitchen and back again, and it seems to those assembled that the patch of chill air moves with him as he does so, yet still no-one can see this spirit whose presence is felt so palpably. The priest, having the power and the faith within him asks for a cork and bottle, still praying all the while. He then requests that all others should leave the room. From the other side of the closed door the family and their neighbours listen to the young man's incantations. There is then a loud noise from the kitchen, like a violent crash to the floor. The prayers resume for a few seconds, after which there is complete silence. Not a pin is to be heard dropping and a feeling of calm descends onto the cottage and all those present. After a moment the priest emerges from the kitchen. Grasped in his hand is the bottle, with the cork firmly in the neck. Looking steadily at his audience he quietly informs them that henceforward the ghost of Cooneen will trouble them no more. Sure enough from that day the family sleep sound in their cottage, hearing no more strange noises, horses' hooves or things that bump in the night, and the eerie pockets of chill air are no more felt around the home. As for the priest, the locals are sad when it is announced shortly afterwards that he is to leave the area. The reason given is poor health. This is surprising, as he has always been a robust and hearty type. A few months later news reaches the parish that the young man has unexpectedly died.

Occasionally my mother will recount memories of the Black and Tans and their brutal and indiscriminate attempts to root out rebels. The Black and Tans were mostly recruits returned from the Great War to an England no longer in need of heroes. After the execution by the British without proper trial of Patrick Pearse, James Connolly and other leaders of the Easter 1916 rebellion had turned these rebels from villains to martyrs in the eyes of many Irish people, the republican cause gained greater sympathy. At this time too the Royal Irish Constabulary could not cope with the frequent attacks on their barracks by both the Irish Republican Brotherhood and the IRA. The British Government therefore placed a newspaper advertisement for ex-servicemen who were prepared to "face a rough and dangerous task" in Ireland. Jobs being scarce on the mainland there were plenty of takers for the "King's shilling". The pay was in fact ten shillings a day, there was little training and because police uniforms were not sufficient to go round some of the volunteers wore their old military khaki – hence the name Black and Tans. Their brief was to make Ireland "hell for rebels to live in" and anyone who thinks their trigger-happy reputation was propagandist myth might consider the guidance issued by Black and Tans commander Lt Colonel Smyth to his men in 1920: "…you may make mistakes occasionally and innocent persons may be shot but that cannot be helped, and you are bound to get the right parties some time. The more you shoot the better I will like you, and I assure you no policeman will get into trouble for shooting any man." "Any man" would have included my grandfather at this time, and, even living in the remote countryside my mother and her family rightly feared any visit from the Black and Tans. Thus it was one evening that my mother, still being of school age, was about to sit down to tea with her parents and siblings when they heard a loud commotion on the narrow road just beyond their gate. Glancing through the window, my grandmother gasped that the Black and Tans were beating the shrubbery and on their way up to the house. I cannot say where my grandfather's political sympathies lay or indeed if he had any associates who were active republicans. Such facts would not have mattered one jot to the Black and Tans, as my family well knew. Bearing in mind they were likely to shoot him first and ask questions later, my grandfather made his retreat through the back door just as the men burst into the kitchen yelling "Where's your bloody Dad!" Nobody answered, and while one soldier held my poor grandmother at gunpoint beside the stairs the others ransacked the whole house, charging from room to room, overturning furniture and breaking crockery in their wake. My mother told me she was terrified all the while, hiding with her sisters beneath the kitchen table and crying out to the soldiers not to shoot their mother. Satisfied my grandfather was not in the house the officer in charge ordered his men to search the surrounding area. Knowing that he could not have got far in so short a time, my grandmother remained in fearful expectation of hearing shots at any moment. However it had now grown dark outside and also cold and her only slim hope was the men would abandon their search. Unbeknown to them, my grandfather had hidden in a deep drain at the back of the house, partly submerged in water and covered by thick bushes. When the Black and Tans departed he returned into the house shivering and glad to be alive. It later transpired there had been an ambush nearby earlier in the day and the culprits were being hunted. My grandfather would surely have been a welcome scapegoat had they found him, and the short period of discomfort in the freezing water almost certainly saved his life.

I was aware that the Coogan's former ancestral home in King's County had been, like Cooneen, plentiful in trout, in the Brosna river that flowed through the land. There had also been deer on the hill which roamed freely and came down to feed among the wild geese and mallard at the water's edge. The old

Georgian home had a coach house and outbuildings, there was an enclosed orchard to the rear and the estate was bounded by a high stone wall complete with ancient gate lodge at the entrance. This lordly abode was the birthplace of another cherished family legend of ours. It happened that my father's brother, my Uncle Philip, was an officer of the Royal Flying Corps during the Great War. One night whilst his master is away on active service, Uncle Philip's pet dog rises from the hearth and begins to howl pitifully at the moon. Not uncommon among dogs, but when the animal's distress continues thus for several hours the family become perplexed. Next morning a military man calls at the house to inform them that Uncle Philip has been shot down in a mission over France and his condition is unknown. The time given is exactly the hour at which his beloved dog had begun to cry out. The family have an agonising few days wait till word arrives that Philip has survived the crash, more or less in one piece. As soon as his injuries allow he does as heroic fighter aces did in those pioneer days of flying: he rejoins his squadron and goes "straight back up". The boys of the Royal Flying Corps were known as the "Twenty-Minuters" – as they spent on average just ninety minutes in the air before being shot down, and usually killed. However Uncle Philip continued flying missions till the war ended and lived to tell the tales. Many folk believe animals have second sight and other powers too. Doubtless to say, whenever Uncle Philip was in a dogfight with the Red Baron's crew, his own dog – snug by the old home fire, must have worked a lucky charm or two for his master.

2

A Schoolboy's War

When the Second World War started my father, like many Irish people, wanted nothing to do with the affair. Thinking the British Army might begin conscription in Ulster, he moved our family over the border to the Republic, which had remained neutral in the conflict. We settled in the county of Leitrim, taking a house by the long bridge over the Shannon at Rooskey. These were hard times for ordinary people in southern Ireland and a state of national emergency had been declared. With unemployment high and food scarce my parents would often be searching the house for an extra penny-farthing to take to the shop. However my father was an enterprising man and to bring in money he started up a dance band, playing both modern and Irish music, his own favourite instrument being the saxophone. In addition he began running a local taxi service, and between this and his music managed to earn a good enough living.

My brother Patrick and I were now of school age and I remember us rising early and making the mile walk, over the long bridge to the Roscommon side of Rooskey and through the village to the National school. Packed in our satchels we'd carry our lunch of a sandwich and a little bottle of milk, the neck stuffed with a cork or bit of brown paper to keep it from spilling. Such simple food has the taste of a banquet to a child, being the time when the senses are keenest, and all morning we'd look forward to break-time when we would tuck in to the soft bread and creamy cheese and guzzle down the refreshing white milk

On the way home from school we would often dawdle and play beneath the bridge, teetering along a narrow ledge which spanned the river. This was a dangerous manoeuvre and the kind of dare-devil game few boys can resist. In summer we'd watch the boats drifting up and down the Shannon, beguiled by the movement of the ripples on the sunlit water. I do remember these days in Rooskey as a happy time, whether in school, in our little house or playing in the fields and lanes.

There was however one incident which cast a brief dark shadow across my world. It was on the kind of afternoon described, a hot summer day it was, when after school Patrick and I, perched beneath the river bridge dreamily eyeing the boats caught sight of some people swimming not far upstream. Then, as we were watching them the scene suddenly changed. It was no longer a peaceful spot of bathing, for some sort of commotion had broken out. There were shouts and splashing and a couple of fellows were wading in fully clothed. A little crowd had gathered and there was a feeling of desperate agitation amongst them. Closer by us on the bank we heard a lady say again and again with anxiety in her voice 'There's someone in difficulties…' and crossing herself as she did so. Half a dozen or more fellows were hauling something up out of the river and onto the bank. We then saw that it was a body, which they then lowered, limp as a rag doll onto the grass. One man cried out 'Give him room, give him room please…' This man then knelt down as if in prayer, except he was bobbing rhythmically back and forth all the while. This went on for a long while, the crowd around him stiff as ninepins. Finally the man ceased his movements and sat up. A piercing wail was heard followed by an awful hush as the sodden body was carefully lifted and carried away. After witnessing this scene, a strange, unspoken sense of fearfulness came over my brother and me. Without a word to one another we scrambled out from under the bridge and ran for home.

We later learned that the drowned man had been a young priest. As children we did not really understand the meaning of death. But we did know it was some awful thing that happened to people, after which you never saw them again, which made everyone around them sad, and for such a thing to befall a man of the cloth seemed especially strange and unsettling. Along with everyone else in the village we were much more cautious of the river after this.

As the war in Europe intensified rationing was introduced and everyone was issued with a limited number of coupons for food and other basic requirements, including petrol. My father now found his business hard going, having insufficient fuel both for his taxi service and travelling out to dance-halls with the band. With a family to provide for, he was obliged to seek some other form of employment. Back in Northern Ireland, with the Americans having joined the war, there was now a large contingent of U.S. troops based at the Arboe aerodrome in Tyrone. These troops had with them a large fleet of vehicles, and word had it they were being prepared for a massive land invasion of Europe sometime soon. The jeeps and trucks obviously needed to be in first-rate mechanical order and my father, having the necessary skills, was fortunate to obtain a civilian post here, overseeing maintenance of all the military vehicles. Soon a bungalow was found close by the camp and the whole family moved up to Arboe.

Here, north of the border, our surroundings were very different to what we had been used to. After the sleepy village life in Rooskey, our new home seemed full of noise and excitement. Soldiers were everywhere and the roads were for ever busy with army lorries and jeeps speeding back and forth. Up in the sky we could see all kinds of aircraft taking off and landing, from fighter planes to the huge super-fortress bombers. Watching them from the edge of the airfield or from out my bedroom window I soon got to know the names of all the different aeroplanes. I learned to identify them not only by sight but by their engine noise, each particular plane having its distinct sound. Listening to the planes taking off at night I used to wonder in the morning how many had come back from their missions. Sometimes I'd try to stay awake and listen out for the engines on their return and try to make a count. But after a while I'd not be able to tell if the drones and rumbles were high in the night sky or deep in my head. Finally sleep would overtake me and I'd end up drowsy for school next day.

Walking to Mullinahoe School we had to be careful. Where the lanes were narrow and without a footpath there was a danger from the military trucks, which could appear suddenly on the bend, sometimes not noticing two little boys pressed against the hedge. When they did see us though, and were not in a hurry, the soldiers would stop and pass the time of day, asking us in a kindly way about our school lessons and giving us some American "candy". School in Arboe was not such a happy time for me. Back in Rooskey I had learned to write by natural inclination with my left hand and the teachers had not attempted to alter this trait. Here by contrast I was taken severely to task in the matter. The teachers, a Mrs and Master Ryder were frequently cross with me and whenever I was caught using my left hand to write with they would immediately wallop me across the knuckles. As these punishments went on I gradually found it easier to write with my right hand. Our home life however was largely happy. My father's position was now a very responsible one, and with the extra money coming in my mother purchased a large galvanised bath. It then became the custom that every weekend, in front of the fire, each of us would be washed. After a while I began to dislike this – a growing self-consciousness I suppose – and was eventually allowed to bathe alone.

Something else began to manifest itself at this time. It happened that some schoolmates and I were returning home along the winding lane one day, when we spied, lying lifeless by the hedge, a small bird. We surmised it had been hit by one of the army trucks speeding along. With the squeamish, insistent curiosity boys have for such things, we picked up the shapeless bundle of feathers. All agreed it was quite dead. When it was my turn to handle the creature I could certainly detect no movement whatever, though the little body was still warm. A sad feeling welled up in my heart for I saw that it was a little songbird, the tiniest thing, and the thought that it would no longer open its beautiful throat in melody seemed unbearable. That it had not fallen as nature intended but had been cruelly crushed by some brute machine of man made its fate painful to behold. I did not want to lay the bird down, and ignoring the teasing of my fellows, cupped my hands closer around the soft body. After a moment the strangest thing happened. I felt a slight twinge within my enclosed hands. Opening them slightly, I saw that the little bird was indeed moving. Amid the tangled feathers two small dark eyes suddenly opened. 'Look' I breathed in wonder, 'Look, its alive!' The others crowded around and watched as the bird struggled in my hands, summoning energy. I allowed my fingers to widen and as I did so the bird started to lift its wings. Instinctively I raised my palms to the sky. As I did so the bird gave a little shudder and suddenly it was airborne. It flapped its wings and, finding the breeze, glided gracefully up, over the hedge and across the fields. We watched till it became a tiny speck in the distance then vanished. This incident was repeated on several occasions, and whenever an injured or lifeless bird was found, I would be asked to work my "magic" as my friends called it. Then one day I was called over by some boys who'd found a sparrow by the roadside. Lifting it carefully and cupping the body in my hands as usual, I waited to feel some stirring within. However nothing happened and finally it was apparent that the bird was really dead. On seeing this, the other boys began to ridicule me and started chanting 'Philip's lost his magic, Philip's lost his magic...' again and again in a derisive tone. Amid the jeering and shouting I began to cry and ran off upset. Afterwards I felt I did not want to have such an experience ever again. Another time I opened the front door one winter's day to find a robin lying dead on the doorstep. Asking my mother for a box to bury the little creature, she said to throw it away. When this reduced me to tears mother quickly found a box. I then took a spade and cut through the icy ground, and only when the tiny robin was laid properly to rest was I able to depart sadly for school.

Our home in Arboe being very close to the military base, from our back garden we could often hear the men calling out and drilling. One particular day, when Patrick and I were home from school for some reason, we heard a voice calling from quite close by.

'Hey – ma'am!' it rang out.

This was followed by a powerful whistle, the kind you make by putting the fingers into the mouth. Walking further down the garden we peered over into the field. My mother, who was hanging out the washing, also looked round. Separating our garden from the base was a wide trench beyond which lay a spiralling tangle of barbed wire stretching around the entire perimeter. On the other side of the wire a GI was waving at my mother trying to attract her attention. Mother had also seen the soldier and was surveying him with a suspicious eye.

'Yes?' she called back guardedly 'What do you want?'

'Beg pardon ma'am, I'm from Dallas, how you doing. I was wondering ma'am if you'd consider selling us boys a few of your hens?'

The GI gestured towards the little shed and netting enclosure where our hens were scurrying about. My mother looked at him curiously before replying,

'Where would you keep them?'

'Aw they can just peck around the camp ma'am. We could sure use the eggs and we'll pay you.'

My mother thought for a moment, then said,

'I'm sorry no, we need the hens.'

As my mother was about to return to her pile of washing the soldier said,

'In that case, would you sell us some eggs or maybe you could you use some good fresh butter for your family?'

My mother looked interested at this. Butter, being strictly rationed, would be very welcome. A rate of exchange was quickly agreed and Patrick and I helped our mother gather up a few dozen eggs from the run and pack them in a box of straw. The soldier, now addressing Patrick and me said,

'Now how about you young fellers come along over here – we can fetch that butter for your ma and I'll show you round the base. I'll be sure and bring you back home safe. That be alright with you ma'am?'

This was a thrilling offer for Patrick and me as we had never seen inside the army base. My mother nodded her assent, told us to be good and to mind not to break the eggs. In no time we were over the little garden fence. In our excitement however we had forgotten about the ditch. It was both too wide and deep for us to cross. Our new friend however had already breached the barbed wire and found a sturdy plank which he threw across the gap. He first tested the plank's strength with his own body weight then reached out his arms to help us across.

'Oh be careful!' called mother, watching from the garden. When we were safely on the other side the GI took the box of eggs from us and lifted the wire off the ground so we could scramble under. With a wave to mother we trotted off towards the billets. There were row upon row of Nissen huts, each with soldiers sat at the windows or milling around outside. Entering our friend's billet we were introduced as his 'new pals' and greeted warmly by all the men. There must have been thirty to forty camp beds laid out in two rows, and about a dozen men in the hut. Some were reading or playing cards, others just lounging on their beds. A lively dance tune was on the record player, and one or two of the fellows were snapping their fingers to the rhythm. The butter was brought out as agreed and our box of eggs warmly approved. With great enthusiasm all the GIs then dived into their rucksacks and brought out part of their ration of sweets, chocolate, chewing gum and other goodies, which they pressed into our hands. As our pockets and arms were now full of sweets, the soldier carried the butter and we made our way back home. Mother took the butter into the house and Patrick and I said thank you and farewell to our friendly young American soldier. It had been a rare treat for my brother and I to be taken into the base, especially getting such a warm welcome from all the soldiers. We had felt that warm sense of comradeship among all the fellows there, and their generosity of spirit. To us kids they were all big tough men of course, but in truth most of them were probably teenagers, little more than boys themselves, all thousands of miles from home, many for the first time probably.

A few weeks after that, we began to see fewer and fewer planes taking off from the base. The army trucks no longer jammed the narrow lanes on the way to school and there were no more American sweets in our pockets. On the base the Nissen huts were suddenly all empty, our friend from Dallas and his comrades were no longer lounging on their beds chewing gum, listening to Glenn Miller and enjoying the eggs we'd given them. Instead, they were preparing to make the voyage across the English Channel, crouched in invasion barges heading for the French coast where, hidden in the sand dunes of Normandy, thousands of German machine guns lay silently in wait.

With the war almost at an end, the family began to visit the farm at Cooneen once again. From my child's sense of time it seemed another life since I'd romped around the old place and it was a joyous experience to return to those fond-remembered Fermanagh haunts of what seemed to me so long ago. The stream at the foot of the glen was exactly as I'd recalled it, every stone and pebble in the clear, deep pools unchanged in my absence. Now I was old enough, my father and Uncle Jim were of a mind to teach me how to fish. The overhanging trees and bushes meant plenty of shady places, from where we would watch quietly till one of the big lazy trout came up to the surface of the water to snap at a fly or other insect unfortunate enough to slip off a branch. First I was shown the delicate art of tickling trout with the bare hand dangled in the water and after some moderate success at this was given a rod and line. My early attempts at casting caused Uncle Jim and my father much hilarity. This was chiefly due to the spirited way I would raise the rod above my head only to catch the end of the line firmly in a tree branch. 'The young feller caught three twigs today' Uncle Jim would tease when we got back to the farm. It wasn't long before I had the hang of it though, and could land a trout as good as any man, a skill they all agreed would prove useful enough in a hungry family. However, a phase of my life was about to begin which was to affect not only the pleasures of fishing but much else besides.

3

The Dark Tunnel

It was while staying at the farm that I first started to experience the breathing difficulties. The general opinion seemed to be that there was nothing seriously wrong with me. Mild bouts of asthma were not uncommon in children and were usually cured with plenty of fresh air and exercise. It was something one 'grew out of'. When the wheezing symptoms became more acute however, the doctor diagnosed a severe chest infection. I was therefore ordered to stay off school and rest until fully recovered. A week went by then another and still I was coughing, short of breath and showing no signs of improvement. I had also begun sleeping for longer and longer and coming downstairs, even briefly, left me fatigued and listless. After I think the third week the doctor was summoned again. This time, on re-examining me, he made a new diagnosis – that I had contracted tuberculosis.

On hearing this news my family were extremely worried, and had good cause for their concern. Tuberculosis, or TB as it was known, was taking the lives of many people in Ireland. The disease was one to strike fear into any family, not only from the high rate of fatalities, but from the unsightliness of its effects on the body. The old name – consumption – was an apt description for the drastic loss of body weight experienced by the sufferer. In Ireland at that time TB was also called "The White Plague" by virtue of the ghostly pallor inflicted on the complexion. A likely cause of spreading the bacteria through the air was thought to be the habit of spitting in public. Among men, this was a perfectly acceptable thing, pipe smokers being especially prone to regular expectoration and every drinking establishment having a spittoon conveniently placed for the purpose. Such was the prevalence of TB that some employers, particularly in more sought-after professions such as banks or the civil service, would not engage a person without a clean bill of health – which meant authenticated x-rays from the hospital. There was not only a shortage of hospital beds to take TB sufferers, but the current medical wisdom was against putting sufferers in with other patients for fear of transmission.

Whether this was the reason I remained at home after my diagnosis I do not know. All I remember is that gradually I grew weaker and soon had neither the strength nor will to get out of bed other than for the call of nature. Some days I would rally and get dressed, only for the familiar dizzy breathlessness to force me back into the womb-like comfort of my blankets. Sometimes I slept around the clock – more often I was in a perpetual half-sleep, in the daytime my eyelids flickering at the drifting clouds through the window or at night conjuring strange dreams from the shadows on the wall. When one is ill for a long period, the everyday structures of one's routine disappear. I was no longer getting up in the morning, walking to school, seeing my classmates and coming home at a set time and having tea. Neither the ordered dictates of the timetable, the boisterous stimulation of my friends or the rhythms of the home was I any longer a part of. Instead I languished mostly in a dreamy half-world, often only aware of the time or date when my mother informed me. The only tangible realities of the outside world were night and day, and for much of the time even these polarities could become blurred, just as my waking thoughts and my dreams now swirled around one another, showing me bright, exotic visions – occasionally passing through dark and disturbing images. Such was the vast and boundless sea that now made up my ever-shifting consciousness as I lay prone in my bed, oblivious to the hours, devoid of will. The weeks turned to months, the seasons unfolded. Through the bedroom window I watched the buds on the trees unfurl into green leaves and grow larger as the sun rose each morning higher in the sky. Outside I could hear the sounds of a ball and games being played – whoops and cries and high spirits to match the height of the summer sun. Then, with the school holidays over it became quieter during the day again. Gradually the air cooled and sometimes the sky was leaden and overcast, sometimes a cold piercing blue. All the leaves turned a fierce shade of red and gold, as if the trees had caught fire, but a beautiful, living fire, like the burning bush in the Bible. After the trees had shed their leaves the smell of wood-smoke often drifted up from the fields. Winter descended. I slumbered on.

I did not know what time or day it was when I became aware of someone in the room with me. My senses, shrouded in the heavy cloak of sleep, were first aroused by the sound of a voice. What made me take notice was the fact it was not the voice of my mother, or indeed any of the family, who had been wont to peer solicitously if cautiously around the bedroom door at me from time to time over the last months and whisper a few words of loving sympathy for my poor sick soul. What I heard now was the voice of a stranger, that of a man, speaking softly and rhythmically. Though the voice was unfamiliar the phrases being uttered were not – at least the rhythms were not, I knew those cadences well – but my befogged mind could not as yet place their source. Thinking the sounds may be in my imagination, I opened my eyes and saw a shadowy figure standing a little way off towards the curtained window. Nearby, on the little bedside table had been placed a white cloth, upon which stood a small bottle of oil and a solitary lighted candle. As I stirred a little the figure moved closer, and when my eyes had focused more, the shape at the end of the bed became clearer. I could not see a face nor discern it as any person known to me, but from the garments and demeanour I realised that it was a priest who was in the room with me. Now I recognised the words too – "In Nomine Patris et Fillis et Spiritus Sancti" – in the name of the Father, Son and Holy Ghost, the first prayer of the Rosary. I do not clearly recall my feelings on discovering a priest in my bedroom, making the sign of the cross and praying – I suppose in my feverish state it may not have seemed strange. My eyes drooped again and soon I felt something cool on my forehead and hands. I realised that the priest must be anointing me with the oil. I had sometimes seen priests perform the ritual of Extreme Unction to sick and elderly people in church. Did this mean I was dying? Another prayer was being said now, and I was transported in my mind to the atmosphere of the service, which had always enriched my senses and uplifted my spirit – the aroma of the incense from the swinging thurible, the choir singing and the stained-glass depicting the great dramas of Christ's martyrdom and the splendours and glory of the heavenly afterlife. Then, as the priest began to recite the Lord's Prayer, I thought I heard other voices joining in softly and made an effort to look around the room. My weakened body would not allow this however, and as the priest reached "The Power and the Glory…." I fell again into a swoon. It was then that I had a most extraordinary experience. To call it a dream would not convey the remarkably vivid nature of the sensations which now completely overtook my body and soul. The first impression was of passing through a dark tunnel. I was not however walking, or indeed upright at all. Rather it was as if I were flying at great speed through this hollow space, my body rapidly tumbling and turning as I did so. I felt giddy and nauseous, as in those dreams one has of falling, in which there is nowhere to fall from or to, merely an incessant plummeting forth. What light there was served only to illuminate a host of small, black, creatures which flew past me in all directions as I pitched headlong through the tunnel. These creatures, winged and bat-like, seemed both repulsive and dangerous, and I felt instinctively compelled to swerve my body to avoid them. This helter-skelter journey seemed to have no beginning and no end, and I had a weird, doom-laden feeling that I had, for some unexplained reason been condemned, and was now destined to remain trapped in the dark tunnel for eternity.

Although time was impossible for me to gauge, it seemed I had been hurtling in the tunnel for many hours when at long last, there came a feeling of slowing down. The winged creatures had become fewer and soon they disappeared entirely. The sense of being thrust along was replaced by one of floating, and ahead of me where there had been only darkness I now saw a tiny pin-prick of light piercing the gloom. This pin-prick grew larger as I approached, swelling to a bright glow until all at once the tunnel walls had gone and the darkness lifted. It was like the blackest night had now broken out into a glorious summer morning, with sunlight flooding my eyes and the sound of birdsong in the air. I was in a beautiful meadow or garden and all the sensations of nature now greeted me – from the sight of perfect green trees and fields to the aroma of pollen and freshly cut grass. Above all I became filled with a deep sense of peace and tranquillity. I felt a happiness and joy entirely untainted by guilt or concern of any kind. I had reached a new place in my life – some point of entry or door through which I had passed into a new and miraculous world, a place of both innocence and fulfilment. My soul rejoiced and I felt an abiding and absolute certainty that here was where I belonged. Opening my eyes I saw that I was now alone in the room. On the bedside table the oil and white cloth had gone, though the candle, now burnt low, remained snuffed out. Through the drawn curtains I could make out the first glimmerings of dawn.

The sense of peace remained with me after the dream. My first thoughts were to thank Our Lord and the Blessed Lady Mary for helping me to come through the dark tunnel and out into that wonderful garden and restoring my soul. As well as feeling immediately revitalised spiritually, I also noted that my physical strength was beginning to return. Later that day I was able to sit up in bed and talk with my parents. Seeing such a sudden improvement in my health, they notified the doctor who soon allowed me to get up. Within a couple of days I felt well enough to take a short walk into the village, marvelling as I did at the freshness of all the colours of nature. Everything my eyes lighted upon seemed full of infinite and wondrous detail – the bright painted windows of the houses, the rag-tag fences and walls and the friendly winding lanes. It was the first time I had been out of doors in a whole year.

The following week I made the journey to the Tyrone

Hospital in Dungannon, where X-rays of my chest were taken. The results showed the tuberculosis was still present. It was however much reduced, and taking my renewed vitality into account, I was judged to be on the way to a full recovery. The prognosis proved correct and in no time at all I was out playing football and, strange as it might seem in a nine-year-old boy, looking forward to returning to school. When term did begin, being amongst other children again was certainly a welcome change after my long year of isolation, yet that absence had also left a gap in my learning, and I struggled to apply myself.

Also at this time there was about to arrive, a milestone in my young life which since the illness and the vivid and compelling nature of my dream, had I felt begun to assume a deeper significance for me. This was my Confirmation service, due to take place at our local church on the 9th May 1946. For Catholics, the Confirmation is the ritual sacrament during which the young person affirms their commitment to Christ and the teachings of the church. If baptism is seen as the young child's introduction by their family to Christ, then the Confirmation is the time when that same child is old enough to demonstrate their own religious understanding, and in the presence of others, take the sacred vows binding them to Our Lord. I was sure I was old enough and, because of the dream, though I had spoken to no-one of it, felt I'd had some fleeting glimpse or clue at least of what heaven and hell and purgatory might all mean. I do not think I could have explained the dream – the dark tunnel and the frightening bats and the beauty of the garden and the exquisite sense of peace – and would not have cared to for it felt too deep for explanation, and the essence of the experience would be lost, or worse sound foolish in the telling. There were certain things I would have to show knowledge of before my Confirmation though, since everyone had to sit an examination testing them on Bible facts and other theological points. Time being short I feared I would have to work hard in order to pass.

In the event the exam went well and on the appointed day my family and I joined the great crowd gathered from early morning at The Church of the Blessed Sacrament to greet the arrival of Bishop O'Callaghan, who would be conducting the Confirmations. It seemed like hundreds of people were milling around outside the church gates where several stalls, some selling religious items and others refreshments, lent an air of festivity. The day was long, as a number of young people were being confirmed and it was late in the afternoon before we all left the church. After the service my parents bought me a prayer book to commemorate the occasion.

That same night, lying in bed and listening to the breeze gently moving through the trees, I was reminded again of the presence of God in all things around us and thought of the prayers I had said earlier in the church service. They had already been familiar to me, yet now, today, at this special hour in my life, they carried a meaning that had not been there before. I heard again in my head the words of The Act of Contrition and realised for the first time the person speaking them was myself: 'Oh my God, I am heartily sorry for having offended thee, and I detest my sins above every other evil because they displease Thee my God, who, in Thy infinite wisdom art so deserving of all my love. And I firmly resolve with the help of Thy grace never more to offend Thee and to amend my life. Amen.'

As the shadows fell across the room and the long, momentous day began to close, my mind revisited the question that had nagged at me ever since my return to health. I thought: today in Church I was anointed by the Bishop, as I was also anointed in this bed by the priest when I lay gravely ill. Had I indeed come close to my end during those languorous months? No-one could answer that with certainty. But if I had been through the valley of the shadow of death, and the Lord had seen fit to spare me, raised me up like Lazarus, was this not for some purpose? Earlier that day in the presence of my family, of our community and of God himself I had made the solemn promise to reject evil and to amend my life. How I wondered might I achieve these things – fulfil such vows, such high ideals absolutely? My dream of the tunnel and the garden was still so vivid. It felt like a sign. Perhaps now there was only one way I could truly serve Our Lord and devote my life and soul to him.

4

The Call

'...and I am here today to make that appeal. Remember that the work will be hard, the earthly rewards few. Nevertheless I say to you 'come and join us' and you will be welcomed with open arms. Look within your hearts. If there are any young people in this congregation who feel the calling to spread Christ's message and to help the poor people of the world to find eternal salvation, would they or their parents please make themselves known after the service'

The Father was of course addressing me, or rather God was. Such was my immediate thought as I stood in church that day with my family and listened to the visiting priest make the announcement from the pulpit. There is an urge in boyhood for us to define ourselves, and on that definition rests our whole and glorious future. We do not yet understand about change and development, failure and doubt and the often divided nature of human beings. We are desperate to be complete, continuous and unblemished. This youthful urgency to find our real selves is universal, and though its expression may differ according to time and place, its purpose is consistent – to declare to ourselves and the world what we shall be 'when we grow up'. The timeless chant of 'Tinker, tailor, soldier, sailor...' expresses the fascination with destiny, to select for ourselves the right and particular role, cast in iron for the life-sized, adult world that lies ahead. A child pictures the future as if the story of their life is already written. Perhaps it is. Since we cannot literally turn the pages of any book to see what happens in the chapters to come, we must eternally look within ourselves and ask 'who am I, where am I going…?' 'I am Father Philip, a mission priest'. In my mind's eye I was already in the robes, dispensing wisdom and doing good works, showing kindness to the high and the low, the rich man in his castle and the poor man at his gate, God's children and deserving of grace one and all. I would travel the seven seas and heal the sick, spread the word of the Lord and bring the Good News to benighted souls in jungles and deserts, and god-forsaken ghettoes from Tokyo to Timbuktu.

My sudden burning desire to enter the priesthood at the age of nine was not I suppose wholly unusual. There used to be a saying among the English that every Irish family contained one priest among their number. With a tradition of large families and a dearth of other employment in the 1940s, it was not at the time so great an exaggeration. The priest, along with the teacher and the policemen, were the three figures the community looked up to, a holy trinity of local authority. Priests commanded a particular respect. Some may have trod softly but all carried a big stick, literally so when chasing loitering children off the streets. The priesthood was nonetheless viewed as noble and selfless, the most absolute of vocations for a good Catholic boy. Of the priests I knew, though many could be stern and bad-tempered on occasion, one never questioned their goodness. And having the ear of God, they were in much part feared, especially by the young. The intensity of my long illness and the vision of the tunnel and the garden had put me in search of a spiritual road. After the Father's appeal for recruits my road now lay open. When I told my parents I wished to become a mission priest, they listened carefully, any reservations they may have had outweighed by a dutiful determination to respect my intentions. My father obtained the relevant leaflets and registered my name with the church. After this I began to receive communications on the good works being done abroad and was encouraged by the mission office to keep faith with my desired vocation. The wheels were turning, and a grand adventure seemed to be in store for me. It should not be forgotten that this was a time when only the rich travelled to foreign parts, unless you counted sailors. To a nine-year-old, the possibility of journeying around the world to China or India, South America or even the colourful countries of Europe, was like opening a story book and taking a ride on a magic carpet.

Meanwhile there was still school work to attend to. There were also my duties at home to fulfil, which as the eldest child in a large family were necessary and expected. Though time spent on the latter would often affect my scholastic attainments, I was obedient in my chores and errands and would always have them completed in time for the family rosary. However performing a task is one thing – doing so with initiative and an alert mind is quite another. I was to appreciate this distinction when one day my mother gave me some money and a note to take to the butcher's van which stopped at Arboe Cross between 12 noon and 1pm. I arrived, handed over the money and order and the butcher read the note. He then put a large quantity of sausages into a bag and gave me some change. It wasn't till I got home I realised a mistake had been made and the butcher must have read my mother's one as a seven. Irate, my mother ordered me to return the excess sausages and retrieve the correct change. I raced back the half-mile to the Cross and arrived breathless and dripping with perspiration, only to discover the van had left. Perhaps I should have known we didn't want seven pounds of sausages and that I'd given away a large amount of change needed for other household purchases. On my abject return my father had heard about the matter. I protested that on mother's note the figure one could be read as a seven. My father's wrath already roused, he gave me a swift slap across the face. Still I pleaded my innocence. This questioning of parental authority merely inflamed my father's anger. He fetched his stick and proceeded to wallop me across the legs and backside, my sister and brothers cowering in terror as the blows rained down and I yelled for mercy. Finally it was my mother who restrained him, saying anxiously she thought I had "had enough now". Looking back I think my father must have had some remorse for the severity of the thrashing, for it was to be the last time I was beaten at home.

They say the hardest lessons of life are only learned through our mistakes, one such being the serious nature of money and how a fool and it are easily parted. The beating from my father made this lesson a memorable one. Though I felt unfairly treated in the matter all round I thereafter developed a habit of checking facts and figures. Mistakes – and the blame for them – could, like rain fall on the righteous and unrighteous alike. This incident did not make me cynical – for it was unlikely the butcher had deliberately swindled us – but I did become more aware of things from then on. It instilled in me the necessity of being watchful on occasions, both for my own well-being and that of others. It was incidentally around this time that I became conscious of the particular divide within our community in the North. I was not allowed to play with children who called us "Fenians". Likewise many of the "Prods" families forbade them to mix with us.

Slip-ups with sausages and beatings at home were one thing, and all part and parcel of growing up at that time. If I was going to be accepted for training in the priesthood however, I could not afford such incompetence. My future vocation depended on adequate knowledge of my Bible texts and prayers and having a sound grasp of Catholic theology, better so than other boys. I'd already had my first confession heard. It had been 1945. How long ago that seemed now! I still recalled the occasion very clearly though, since I'd been so nervous. When the day had come for my first confession I did not know the priest who was to hear it. This added to my general anxiety when I entered the ornately carved wooden closet and sat amid the silence and smell of wax polish, looking up at the ominous grille. I waited in trepidation for the priest on the other side to issue some instruction. A chair scraped and the sonorous disembodied voice began speaking. As soon as I was asked to recite the Act of Contrition I felt more relaxed. I knew the words of this prayer by heart and was confident I would give a shining rendition. Yet as I began to recite, sensing the priest's ear focused so intently on my voice and it seemed, on my very soul in all its raw, unformed eagerness to please a strange affliction descended upon me. In my desperation to do well, I began to stumble on my words. Each time I did so the priest would quickly prompt or correct me. Whether his intention was to assist or admonish me I could not tell, but the abruptness of his manner each time I hesitated only made me more anxious and confused, until there was no room in my mind for anything but flight. Like an actor with an attack of stage-fright I had utterly dried up and wanted to run away and hide. The priest erupted in fury. He bellowed at me to go home at once, take hold of my prayer-book and learn the Act of Contrition. I scuttled timidly from the church, thankful to escape with so light a penance.

Despite the poor performance at my confession, I hadn't been excluded from going to Mass, and my empathy and affinity with all that the service entailed had grown stronger. The sumptuous colours and textures of the church and its vestments, the shadows and candlelight along the pillars and arches, the soft gleam of silver and gold from the altar and the silken sheen of the priestly robes all stirred the flame of religious emotion deep within me. As the congregation intoned the rhythmical affirmations and responses I felt caressed and inspired, assured yet again of some truth that existed beyond time and place, yet a truth that was nonetheless present in our little parish church, touching and knowing me and understanding me. Kneeling to take the host and wine there was a sense of acceptance, of being made whole again each time the holy ritual was enacted. As the Trinity was invoked and the priest made the sign of the cross while the incense breathed amongst those gathered in prayer, my soul was taken in thrall, drawn closer to the heart of a mystery, yet a mystery which even as one approached it would grow deeper and infinitely more extraordinary, the mystery that was Christ.

My parents, though willing for me to join the church, had certain apprehensions about my ambition to work in foreign climes. Their worries concerned mainly my health. Although I'd fought off the dreaded TB, my asthma still troubled me. I also had a tendency to stammer, and since an accident some years

35

earlier I would often feel overcome amongst a large crowd. With the uncongenial aspects of life in far-flung places – strange diseases, extremes of climate and rudimentary conditions – both my mother and father felt I would not be robust enough for the work. It was true I did get sick quite frequently, yet I felt perhaps this was a divine test of my resolve. If I gave up because of physical infirmity then I would also be proving my spiritual inadequacy. However one day when both my mother and I had severe colds, she made us up a potion of milk with a little iodine mixed in I think it was. Mother then went outside and I followed her, after which each of us was violently ill. Amid confused arguments I just remember my father being very angry with my mother about the whole incident. It sticks with me chiefly as a reminder of my "sickly" status, and a reinforcement of the parental wisdom that I should not join the missions. With sadness I came to accept their judgement in this, and slowly reconciled myself to the fact I would not after all serve overseas. If this was God's will then so be it. But if foreign work was not my destiny, I concluded God must instead desire me to serve him elsewhere and why not in my home country. I therefore spoke again to my parents, informing them of my desire that on leaving school I should go to a seminary and train to become a priest here in Ireland. Again they listened with a solemnity matching my own earnest sense of vocation, nodded and said as one that we would all 'have to see'.

Seeking to improve my constitution, it was arranged one day I should visit a certain Father Gethin, a healing priest who resided in the Grand Monastery at Enniskillen. The Father saw me in his small room, gave me healing and talked at length about prayer and how it could help in all manner of things. He was a kind man with a great aura of peace and goodness about him, and I left the monastery feeling much stronger and replenished in faith. Determined now to pursue my plans for the priesthood, I would spend whatever spare time I had in thoughtful preparation for the religious life. In the long summer holidays I would take long walks in the countryside, reading my prayer book and marvelling at the great world religion into which I had been born and in which I would one day take Holy Orders. I felt sure enough in my faith, yet being of an enquiring mind certain factual discrepancies began to nag at me. This was nothing to do with the inner rituals of the church such as transubstantiation for example being the body and blood of Christ, which I fully believed. My questions were about what people did outside the walls of the church. In particular I was increasingly puzzled by the cold hostility between our families and those of the Protestants around us. God had decreed we should love our neighbours as ourselves: why then were Protestants not included in this commandment? Was it that Prods didn't love us and we were therefore excused from loving them? The Bible did not seem to carry any such rider to this effect. And besides the Prods would claim that it was the Catholics dislike for them which had caused their own antipathy. Like a childish argument it seemed to boil down to "who started it". I felt an explanation must lay somewhere and that if I studied and thought hard enough I would find it.

However, such temporal problems were soon to pale into insignificance. For it was during one of my long, meditative walks in Arboe, that I experienced a phenomenon that would take such a hold of my thoughts and feelings, indeed my very soul that, just as with the vision of the hellish tunnel and the beautiful garden during the delirium of my sickness, all other considerations would vanish from my mind.

I was walking, prayer-book in hand, by the now disused airfield close to our home. It was one of those dry summer days, with the sun high in the sky and the grass bleached yellow in places. A few clouds hung motionless above and there was very little breeze. Everything seemed very still. It was as I approached the empty Nissen huts that something made me stop and look up from my book. In the middle of the field was a patch of short grass which looked greener than usual. I walked a little closer to this area, and when I was a few yards from it the scene altered. A kind of mist seemed to be forming a few feet above the ground. This mist, which was light grey in colour, then began to expand, reaching a width of about six to eight feet. At first I thought perhaps some underground pipe had burst and a jet of steam was escaping into the field. However this could not be, for the mist was not dispersing as steam would quickly do. Furthermore it was not emanating from the earth but seemed to have materialised in a space several feet clear of the grass. Here the mist continued to hover, its shape shifting and slightly in motion, yet maintaining its position in mid-air. This in itself was remarkable enough, what followed was infinitely more so. In the centre of the mist there appeared the figure of a pretty lady. She was elegantly dressed all in white, her face sweet and serene with an abundance of kindness. Amid this luminosity of white the only other colour was a hint of blue about the lady's dress. Beneath her feet however had now sprung three lovely red rose bushes in full flower, the most luscious blooms I had hitherto seen. After the first shock at apprehending this vision I closed my eyes tightly in an attempt to clear my head. Clearly I was hallucinating, and from the powerful descriptions in the prayer book and the heat of the summer sun my mind had stoked a mirage. I looked again. The patch of mist was still there, the beautiful lady floating within its halo. She made no sound or movement, but looked steadily and directly at me. I closed my eyes again and this time I began to pray. After a few moments I opened my eyes once more. The grey mist, the gorgeous rose bushes and the beautiful lady in white had all gone. There was no doubt as to the identity of the person who appeared before me. It was Our Lady the Blessed Virgin Mary. Breathless with excitement I ran home to tell my family.

My mother, busy with some washing in the kitchen, listened with one ear and a fond, absent smile as I gabbled out the story of what I had witnessed up by the old airfield.

She made no expression of disbelief, neither however did she stand spellbound as I'd hoped she might and ask me to go over the details of my experience. Such proved the case with the rest of my family and others to whom I related the tale. Some said plainly they didn't belief me, but most, perhaps remembering how 'Philip lost his magic' with the songbirds, seemed uninterested. After a few weeks I stopped telling people that Our

Lady had materialised in spectacular fashion before me. Though I never spoke again of what I had witnessed, I knew it to be true, and kept the experience present within myself.

In the months that followed I took up a new pastime. It was introduced to me by a friend who happened to be a Protestant. He was a good-natured young fellow who'd visited me regularly throughout the year of my illness and ever since been welcome at our home. This friend, whose father had been in the army, one day brought his air-gun and box of pellets around and began teaching me to shoot. After a few weeks observing my target practice with the airgun, my father allowed me, with the proviso I kept to a safe area, the use of his .22 Winchester rifle. That winter of 1947 saw heavy snowfalls, which for several months rendered the roads impassable and forced the schools to close down. With travelling difficult it was a blessed release from boredom to tramp the few yards out from the house and blast away at icy tin cans or little piles of snow on the fence posts. Spending a couple of hours each day with the rifle I quickly became an excellent shot. With supplies cut off by the weather food was in short supply, equally so for my beloved song-birds, who tapped their beaks on the impenetrable snow and ice in vain search of a worm or grub. After each meal I would gather any leftovers from our table and take them into the garden where the little feathered heads would gratefully receive. For months the hedges and fields remained covered in deep snow. Tree branches drooped low under the accumulation of repeated falls and the view from our house resembled that of a Christmas card. Over hills and valleys the snow seemed to go on for ever, as if a seamless white blanket had been laid over the world.

Then one morning the sky which for so long had been a dull metallic grey, brightened. The sun had finally broken through and slowly the air grew warmer, bringing with it that feeling of joyful uplift which comes with a thaw, especially after such a long and freezing incarceration. As the temperature rose the trees began to shed their burdens, the packed snow sliding and flopping from the branches in large heaps. Hanging from our roof, the long icicles, tapered like daggers, began to creak and moisten before crashing to the ground. Green was now visible across the landscape as the hedges came back into view. Not only evergreens, but the white-thorn, which must have been busily preparing during the long months buried under the snow, showed new leaves and flowers already in bloom.

Though my siblings and I were now able to attend school again, the return to routine was to be short-lived. Early in the spring my parents announced they had decided to leave Arboe and we would soon be moving back to County Fermanagh. Though I was apprehensive about leaving behind friends and familiar surroundings, the prospects of being close to the lake scenery of County Fermanagh and the trout fishing at Cooneen were pleasant ones. And the move need not interfere with my grand design of joining the priesthood. Shortly before we departed from Arboe I broached this subject again with my parents. As before, my words were treated with a degree of seriousness appropriate to the subject. It was then explained that a great deal of money would be required to fulfil such a goal, and that I would need to spend years away at college before I could be ordained. Was this to be a yes or a no? I was left unsure how the matter stood. Were such comments simply a setting out of the facts, or a kind way of saying my dream was impractical? Perhaps, as with my health, I was once again being tested.

5

Border Incident

'Be careful Philip – make sure you're home before dark' called my mother as I pedalled off on my sports bicycle. The bike was a present from my father, and a finer item he could not have given me. With multiple gears and drop handlebars it could pick up a rare speed and I had already enjoyed many grand days out exploring the countryside around our single-storey cottage by the two bridges overlooking Lough Erne Upper and near to Lisnaskea. The move had also brought us close to Belturbet in the Republic. In Belturbet lived our cousins, and it was my plan that day to meet up and have some fun with them. I was also curious to see along the border.

The afternoon was fine and it was a pleasant ride, with a warm sun on my back and the breeze about my face. However approaching the south the road surface deteriorated, much of it covered by sand, slowing my progress considerably and delaying my arrival in Belturbet. My cousins were nonetheless pleased to see me, and together we took a rowing boat out on the River Erne that flowed close to the town centre. I was then invited back to the cousins' home where we all tucked into a fine tea prepared by my Aunt Esti. By the time the meal was done it was already late evening and Aunt Esti suggested I should stay the night. I thanked her but said I'd promised mother not to be late. Mounting my bike I waved goodbye and headed off back north. After about half an hour the light began slowly fading and I switched on my rear and front lights. About a mile later I arrived at the border. As I rode up to the checkpoint a British customs officer stepped out and raised his arm.

'Have you purchased or obtained any goods?' he asked.

'No' I replied.

'What was the reason for your being in the South?'

'Visiting family.'

The officer walked slowly around my bicycle then undid the small saddlebag at the back and looked in. There was nothing but some spanners and a puncture repair kit.

'All right, you can proceed' he said.

As I pedalled swiftly away, the night seemed to gather all of a sudden about me, my front light offering but a feint glow in the surrounding darkness. I was still some miles from home and, remembering my mother's words on setting out and knowing she would be worried by now, I put on a spurt. However the rhythmic cycling and tranquil night soon lulled me to a slower pace and I pleasantly recalled the day's events while riding happily along. Being in this tired and dreamy state I was paying little attention to the darkened road. So mentally disengaged was I that when an indiscernible shape sprang into my path I was taken utterly by surprise. It happened so abruptly I had to pull hard on my brakes to avoid careering into whatever the obstacle was. Stopping so sharply very nearly shot me over the handlebars. Peering into the gloom I soon realised one thing – this time it was not Our Lady that had materialised in front of me. I made out a tall figure, dressed from head to foot all in black. With a stab of alarm I saw that the man was carrying a rifle. Almost at once another figure appeared. This man had a rifle strapped on his back and carried a powerful flashlight which he proceeded to shine directly into my eyes. The two were quickly joined from the surrounding hedges by yet more armed and black-clad men. With horror I saw that some of them also had their faces blacked up. One of the men spoke,

'Where have you come from?' he rasped.

'Belturbet' I stammered.

Clutching my bicycle, I stood terrified as the group surrounded me and aggressively fired questions from all sides: Where was I going – what had I been doing – what was my name and address – what identification did I have….!

Reduced to a fearful state I was unable to give proper answers. I fished in my pocket and found some scraps of paper which I hoped might bear my name. These were snatched and scrutinised by my interrogators, whilst one of them searched my saddle bag. When the flashlight was taken off my face for a moment I saw the men more clearly, and from their uniforms and caps now realised that I was in the custody of the B-Specials. I knew something of these men, and it explained the degree of stealth with which I had been apprehended. The B-Specials frequently operated in silent foot patrols in order to stalk their quarry with the utmost element of surprise. They had been known to hide out in bushes along the dark country roads, often all night and in torrential rain, waiting to snare any suspected IRA member or Republican sympathiser who happened along. The B-Specials were quite different to the RUC, and were zealous volunteers, committed to the defence of their homeland whatever that might entail. The questions were still coming at me thick and fast – what was my age – had I purchased any free-state goods – where did I go to school. This last information was a way of finding out my religion of course. Finally deciding they could not hold me as either rebel or smuggler I was sent on my way and the black-clad figures melted back into the night as silently as they had appeared.

Arriving home I found my anxious parents sat up burning the kitchen lights. On seeing me cycle up the path they ran to the door in relief. They were also angry, and after hearing the whole story of what had happened gave me strict instructions never to cross the border again so late in the afternoon or be out after dark. Naturally my brothers and sisters wanted to know all about my adventure – had I been scared by the B-Specials – what did they say etc. We also discussed in grim detail what might have happened if I'd ridden past the patrol or had something I shouldn't in my saddle-bag.

The consequences of defying the B-Specials in the dead of night were that I could have been shot. I knew the damage a .22 rifle could do. Though still too young to be granted a firearms licence, this had not stopped me sneaking out with my father's gun, and Northern Ireland being armed to the teeth it was not long before I'd been shown how to rub the lead nose off a bullet along a brick wall or flatten it by cutting the top off. This gave the bullet much greater killing power. Not that I was thinking of taking pot-shots at the B-Specials. The large pike that swam among the tall reeds of Lough Erne provided good enough sport, and on bright sunny days they could be seen clearly in the shallow waters close to the shore. If you scored a direct hit the pike would turn upside down and float to the surface where it could be retrieved with a long stick if you didn't want to wade in. These secret hunting trips I restricted to certain occasions only, for getting caught at unlicensed shooting by the RUC would mean serious trouble both for me and my family. My father had some inkling of what I was up to, mentioning there was about to be a new law to make pike-shooting illegal. Shooting wild duck and widgeon was a different matter. For this I used my father's shotgun and, as these were edible prey, he and my mother turned a blind eye so long as I was careful. Going out on a winter's day I would usually manage to bring home a duck or two, pluck off the feathers and clean them ready for dinner. Having by this time five brothers and two sisters these contributions were always gratefully received. Sunday shooting was forbidden by law in Northern Ireland even for those with a license. If seeking something for our family pot on the day of rest I had to be quick to bag up my quarry in case the RUC had heard the shots. Having two good gun dogs, as soon as they had retrieved the wild fowl from the field I would hurry home. On the way I would often see a police car arrive on the bridge trying to see who was breaking the law. Being a strong Nationalist area, my foraging activities never reached the ears of the authorities.

It was about this time my youngest brother was born. Although I was still a schoolboy, the local priest allowed me to become the little fellow's godfather, which felt a most important honour. This title did not absolve me from household chores as eldest, though my brother Patrick was now helping out by going to the well for spring water, a twice-daily job for our growing family. Likewise my sister was now of an age she could help our mother in the busy kitchen. When my parents were out though, I was still responsible as head of the house. This was also the period when, in addition to field pursuits and sports, I began to develop an interest in the arts. Reading and music drew me into imaginative worlds, and painting and drawing offered new forms of self-expression. Whenever I could find peaceful surroundings I would disappear with a sketch-book and try to capture and interpret colour and form, recreating the moods of the sky and the trees, or some fresh or half-remembered fond vision of my own on the blank page. Nurturing these creative talents brought both great satisfaction and several school prizes for artwork.

My eye for colour was not unappreciated outside art class either. My father now had a motor business, and by my early teens I had begun to help out at the garage. Mixing the paints for body repairs it was soon apparent I could achieve a near-perfect match on a damaged vehicle. Re-spraying was of course only one aspect of motor repairs, and mostly it was mechanical faults which brought customers into the garage. One day I happened to call at the premises while my father was away on business. I was then aged about thirteen. Talking to the staff was a builder who had just been on route to work with his crew when their van had broken down. I asked if I could have a look at the vehicle, and walked along to where it had stalled, up by the RUC barracks. Lifting the side bonnet and noticing damp on the coil and plug wires, I dried them with a cloth. Still the van wouldn't start. I then took off the distributor cap and saw that the points were burned and bunched up. I asked the builders for a screwdriver and used it to break the burned parts off and adjust the points. This time the engine turned over and the driver revved up. The builders gave me a ten shilling note for my trouble and I felt like a millionaire. I told the gentleman to call at the garage soon and get a new set of points to avoid further problems. A few days later he did call in, and in front of my father praised my abilities at some length, which made me very embarrassed. It must have been about a year later that I was to help out in a rather more perilous situation. I was doing some odd jobs at the garage while my father, his head and upper body hidden, worked away intently beneath the chassis of a car. At a certain point this calm scene broke into a commotion when my father cried out suddenly in pain and shock, his legs kicking about under the vehicle. The other men began shouting and there was a general panic. I must have realised there had been a short circuit and my father had literally received a shock, for I instinctively hurried to the wall socket and pulled out the extension lead that trailed beneath the car. My father was helped to his feet, a little shaken yet otherwise unscathed from the incident.

Another accident at the garage was not so short and by no means sweet. It occurred as a result of the road outside being dug up to repair the sewers. One certain thing about sewers is the prevalence of rats, and in this sewer one particular rodent, finding his habitat disturbed sought refuge in Dad's garage. Once the rat was spotted no-one could relax and get back to work till it had been chased away, so everyone began beating the concrete floor to drive it out. Finally my father had the animal cornered and attempted to steer it to the door. Rats naturally gravitate to dark tunnels and this one, unhappily for my father, mistook his trouser-leg for such a bolt-hole. With quick-thinking my father, to stop the rat reaching more delicate parts, clamped his hands around his trousers, whereupon he received a sharp bite on the leg. Though painful it didn't seem too serious and ointment was applied to the injury after which my father returned to work. About two weeks later however a sore developed where the rat bite had been and the doctor, having given an injection, advised complete rest in bed. When the doctor next visited there was distressing news. My mother was informed in hushed tones that gangrene had developed and, to avoid even greater danger to his health my father's leg may have to be amputated. On hearing this a nauseous feeling hit me, and I wept bitter tears of pity and sorrow for my poor father. The horror at the thought of anyone having to suffer in such a way was simply awful. For my dear father to be permanently disfigured by the intrusion into our family of such a malign and poisonous creature as a rat, was the stuff of nightmare and simply unbearable. The age-old symbol of the rat as harbinger of doom brought up dark pictures which resonated in my imagination. If the powers of medicine failed to cure my father in time to save his leg then all we had left was prayer. Hearing of our plight Cannon Donnelly of whom I was very fond and who always asked for me if his car gave trouble, called at the house. While the good Cannon prayed at my father's bedside the rest of us bowed our heads downstairs. It was a few days till the doctor was able to visit again, and we waited with tense faces till he emerged from the bedroom. His report was one of amazement at the improvement in the condition of my father's leg and his prognosis that of a full recovery. The opinion proved correct, and within a few weeks my father was back at work as fit as ever. After that I reckoned I owed both the doctor and Cannon Donnelly a free service on their cars.

By this time I was almost fourteen years old, and with my last day at school also fast approaching, I had now to think seriously about my future.

6

Crossroads

A round the age of twelve a boy's interests begin to change. Things perceived as childish are put away as the awaiting world expands before him and the gates of manhood beckon. For myself I felt no sudden crossing of the threshold from boy to man. Before the age of fourteen shooting and fishing were already taking up much of my spare time, though I was increasingly keen on the Gaelic football too, playing in regular matches and attending training sessions. Alongside such energetic pursuits my fondness for painting and drawing had continued, both at home and school, and my abilities in this area had come to the attention of one particular teacher. She took me aside one day and made the recommendation that I should take the offer of an art scholarship at Queens University in Belfast. I felt excited by the possibilities this might open up. Going to university would be a fine thing. To be selected was recognition of one's talents and potential, an elevation in life. I had been chosen from on high to join the great and the good, and my mind fizzed with thoughts of the new world that lay in wait among the dreaming spires of Queens. Lofty conversations over supper about line and colour, my canvases praised and exhibited to wild acclaim not least from my proud family, and a glittering career as a world-famous artist. Seductive as these images were, they did not obscure the immediate practical aspects of embarking on such a course. I knew that Belfast was too far to travel in each day and I would therefore have to leave home. For lodgings and living expenses in the city I would require money, and there were now eight of us children at home to feed and clothe. If I became a student it would mean a big draw on the already over-stretched family purse strings. On the other hand if I began earning a wage on leaving school my contribution to the household bills would alleviate a lot of the financial worries that burdened my parents. I felt the pain of the dilemma. Added to this was the matter of the priesthood, an ambition I had still not abandoned and which even now stirred deep emotions. Three desires thus fought for control of my life – should I pursue what might be a thrilling opportunity in the arts world or a lifelong vocation with the Church, or ought I to think instead of my mother and father's well-being? Oscar Wilde maintained that 'each man kills within himself the thing he loves' and when I considered forgoing both the priesthood and the scholarship it was with a sense of smothering some inner flame. Yeats' lines about not letting people tread on our dreams might also have applied to my situation. However fighting with my parents was out of the question and to be fair they tried their best to be neutral and encourage me as much as they dare to think of my own future. Therefore the only person who could tread on my dreams was me. Likewise Wilde's grim observation about sacrificing one's hopes could be interpreted in more ways than one. I may have been in love with the idea of being a priest or becoming an artist, but if what I truly loved were my parents, should I not act in their best interests rather than my own? I decided, finally, to do just that.

And so it was my destiny on leaving school to follow the same path as countless other young men down the centuries – I went into the family business. I was to become a full-time mechanic in my father's garage, and when the matter had finally been decided a pair of men's overalls was purchased for me. This seemed a fitting rite of passage into adulthood, until it was discovered the garment did not in fact fit, and my mother had to turn up the trousers to the length of my legs. For the time being I was not the sheep in wolf's clothing but the boy in man's dungarees!

At first I was strictly speaking an apprentice with much to

learn still. But having worked alongside my father in the summer months I was a useful enough employee and was straightaway left alone to complete simple repairs. I greatly enjoyed the job, and from the first day thought little about the priesthood or the university. Perhaps it was the absorbing nature of the work. Just as the medieval monks devoted themselves entirely to the infinitesimal detail of illuminated lettering, so the intricacies of the internal combustion engine excluded all other thoughts from my mind. Maybe there is holiness in any honest toil, not that I reflected on it in a pious way. With my head under a bonnet I simply became self-forgetful and happy. There is a great challenge in dismantling a faulty engine, diagnosing the problem and then reassembling the whole thing in working order once more. As a young lad I also derived great pleasure from taking the cars out for a test drive after I'd repaired them, and basking in the compliments of the satisfied customers when they told me what an excellent job had been done. After a while I learned to do crash repairs, undertaking the panel beating and spray painting to resurrect mangled vehicles and bring them up to a gleaming finish. When I did have time to think back on how things had gone after leaving school, it was not without an element of resentment over what I might have lost out on. But I could not be angry with my family for holding me back. The only other person to blame was God. I realised that deep down I had been expecting him to take care of my future and by some miracle transport me to those higher realms of the priesthood or the privileged world of the university. Maybe my cure from TB and the vision of Our Lady had given me the notion I was special. If so it was an impious presumption, yet it served to turn me somewhat away from the Church and God at that time.

Meanwhile my additional skills in crash repair meant the opportunity of earning extra money, and after paying for my keep at home, I found for the first time I had spare cash in my pocket. I had already started attending dances, all across County Fermanagh and sometimes over the border in Cavan. Learning the various steps and getting on the social circuit I soon began to make lots of new friends. For a young man in his mid-teens the opportunity of meeting and dancing with a wide variety of girls was of course high on the agenda of new-found delights. On the day I attained my great new wealth I planned immediately to go along to the forthcoming Ceilidh dance in our local St Ronan's Hall. Such events are greatly enjoyed by anyone who loves the Irish music, and when the night arrived every dance and tune seemed just perfect. Evidence of my new fortune jingled in my trouser pocket as I wheeled around the floor and everyone was smiling. As usual, any reveller who fell out of step was helped along by the more experienced dancers. At the end of these evenings the Irish National Anthem was always played, even though it was officially banned in the North. Usually the RUC or "peelers" as they were known would turn up outside the hall to observe who was breaking this law or shouting out Nationalist cries.

Life for me had settled into a routine, working at the garage by day and during the football season of spring and summer, spending my evenings and weekends training or playing. Most Sundays there would be a football game, and sometimes it would be alongside a Feis celebration. This was like an open-air Ceilidh, a gathering of young and old, with Irish dancing, singing, seven-a-side tournament and other activities going on throughout the day. The event would usually be held in a field well away from residential estates in order to avoid any friction between Unionists and Nationalists.

It was at a County Fermanagh Feis in Newtownbutler in the very early 1950s that I had my first taste of sectarian animosity on a large scale. The field chosen for the Feis was some way off the public roads, and this particular Sunday being bright and sunny a large crowd of all ages was in attendance. There were ice cream vans and stalls selling sandwiches, sweets, minerals and the traditional "Yellow Man". On the slope running down from the field sat dozens of young families enjoying a peaceful picnic as the Ceildih music drifted across from loudspeakers set on the back of a lorry. Troupes of young boys and girls, dressed in colourful Gaelic costume were keeping time to the music. There were competitive events for singers and dancers and each group, after months of practice, was today hoping to qualify for a place in the final and the chance of winning a medal or cup. On one truck a rostrum had been constructed, from which rose a tall flagpole. At the top of the pole, billowing gently in the afternoon breeze was the green, white and gold of the Irish Tricolour. It was an innocent enough scene you would think. I was with my team-mates near the top of the slope waiting to play our match in the Minor group, when we spied a group of uniformed RUC men approaching below us. As the officers neared the top several of the senior football players and the Feis stewards, seeing what was happening, moved towards the dancing, which was in full swing. As the music played on the police slowly advanced, drawing their batons as they got closer. Then, ignoring the fact there were elderly people and young children, they began to push their way through the crowd towards the rostrum bearing the tricolour flag. On seeing this, my team-mates and I ran over to join the stewards and spectators attempting to stand firm between the rostrum and the advancing RUC men. The music had by now trailed away and a confused stalemate ensued, with the officers unable to move any further through the sea of bodies. Under British law it was illegal to display any Nationalist emblem or flag, yet having insufficient force to remove the offending article from the flagpole, the RUC quietly retreated from the field. The stewards then quickly got the music started again and the seven-a-side football tournament kicked off. Although the light was now beginning to fade, a good crowd still remained to carry on the festivities.

Those who had departed for home after the RUC incident however were to have their predictions borne out, for about an hour later the police came back. This time it was a much larger force, probably three dozen officers, some with batons already drawn as they arrived. They made a charge up the hill and behind them came two fire tenders. Scuffles and fighting broke out and water hoses were turned on the older performers, ruining their fine costumes. Anyone getting in the way was drenched, including the elderly and parents with young children. There was a malicious energy in the way the RUC carried out this assault on a peaceful celebration. At one point an officer had his revolver drawn as the Tricolour was torn down to cries of 'Black and Tans' from the crowd. 'Watch yourselves you Fenian bastards!' came back from the RUC. There were a few arrests made and charges brought for disturbance of the peace and flying an unlawful flag. As we drifted off the field a rumour went round that Eamon De'Valera had been invited to the Feis that day but been refused entry at the border. It was alleged that as the Northern Ireland Prime Minister Lord Brookborough had not invited him, De'Valera had been attempting to "interfere" in a foreign country. The all-Irish Ceilidh that had been planned to round off the day did still go ahead in the local hall, though with an understandable note of sadness in the air. At the end of the night the Irish National Anthem was played and as we made our way outside everyone was expecting to see a large RUC presence, but it was very quiet, with just a single police car parked some way up the road.

That Sunday I was just one among many to feel the intolerant hand of the forces of law and order in Northern Ireland. It wasn't till some time after that things got more personal for me you might say. In the meantime I discovered it wasn't only the Protestant Ascendancy who sought to enforce harsh and petty rules. Keen as I was on the Gaelic football I also enjoyed watching soccer and one day travelled with a group of friends to a top division match. A few days later I was informed by the Gaelic Athletic Association that my attendance at the soccer match was a breach of GAA rules. As a consequence of this misdemeanour I was suspended from playing Gaelic football for several games afterwards. I remembered that several of the friends I'd gone to the match with happened to be Protestant, and wondered whether this had been the real reason for the GAA censure. No doubt 'fraternising with the enemy' had compounded my crime in someone's eyes.

Happy as I was working at the garage, it was around this time I began to feel the need for a change, perhaps a new role in life. Two friends, Frankie Cahalane who was Protestant and John Rogers, a Catholic, had recently gone off to train for the RUC.

Now although I'd seen the unpleasant face of the Ulster Constabulary, the fact that a lad from each side of the community, pals of mine, had just been taken on together, somehow suggested its intentions were those of an honourable institution. Bad apples in the barrel and bad laws could be changed. There was a certain glamorous appeal in wearing the smart military-style uniform with the shining leather belts, in being clean-living and disciplined and treating everyone equally. Like the priesthood it was more than a job, and there was a sense of nobility about it. There were also family connections as my father's brother, my Uncle Owen, had served in the RUC in Belfast for some years. I therefore submitted an application and received some study material and test papers to prepare me for the entrance exam.

One winter's day shortly before Christmas, I had taken time off from work and decided to go out hunting in the afternoon. The law against discharging a shot from one hour prior sunset to one hour after sunrise had now been passed and I therefore assured my parents before setting off that I would be home early. I drove over to Lough Erne, parked my car in a little lane and taking the shotgun from the boot, picked my way over the fields to a small hillside overlooking the water. Here was a shooter's paradise with all manner of wild fowl. My father and I were familiar with this spot, having obtained written permission from the farmer to shoot there. This was incidentally a privilege we shared with the Prime Minister Lord Brookborough among others, though we never saw him. The farmer, who also owned a hotel and happened to be a Unionist, was both a customer and good friend of my father. Hunting can require much patience, spending often hours crouched in reeds or flattened against the earth watching, waiting for the chance of a shot. Stillness and silence are all. Usually this is repaid but sometimes one passes the time in vain. This particular day fortune was not favouring me. Having concealed myself for over an hour without so much as the sound of a wild duck or goose, I emerged from the bracken, my limbs stiff and cold. I decided to concede defeat and get back to the car before dusk fell. I replaced my gun in the boot and was about to close it when I heard footsteps behind me. Turning I saw two uniformed RUC constables. One of them I immediately recognised as having called at the garage on occasion. The other I vaguely knew by sight. Both men looked stern and officious.

'Why were you wild-fowling at sunset?' demanded the man I'd seen at the garage. Though he clearly knew me his tone was immediately hostile.

'I've come from over the fields' I explained. 'It's taken me twenty minutes to get back.' This was true.'

'What's your name and address?'

I gave them the information.

'I've had no luck anyway' I said, 'I've not fired all day. Please look at the gun if you wish.'

My suggestion was ignored. I then took it they'd heard no shots and knew full well I was telling the truth.

'Show me your gun licence' demanded the second man. 'And your driver's licence and motor insurance' Again there was aggression in the voice. I found the documents in the car and handed them over. After examining them for a few moments the officer returned them and said 'I must inform you that prosecution will take place for being on reserved ground and for shooting after the hour of sunset. You'll hear further.'

It seemed useless and unwise to protest. Yet I felt angry and apprehensive, as the men seemed bent on pursuing the matter. I wondered how they had found me in such a remote spot, since I had made no noise all day and my car was parked off the road. A few seconds after they walked away it was obvious what had happened, as their own vehicle suddenly reversed out of a clearing in the trees and drove off past me. Like me they had been lying in wait for their quarry. They however had been luckier.

Arriving back home I found we had visitors. It was my cousin Jackie from Belfast who was serving in the Royal Navy and with him his father, my Uncle Owen, a sergeant in the RUC! We were delighted to see one another, though when I related what had just occurred Uncle Owen was understandably embarrassed. It was decided that the next day my father would produce the written authority which permitted us to shoot on Lord Brookeborough's Hill as it was known locally. I then told Uncle Owen I was thinking of joining the force myself, to which he replied plainly that he would not advise anyone to do so. This puzzled me and I wondered if perhaps his remarks were for some reason prompted by hearing about my encounter that afternoon. However I later learned from my father that Uncle Owen had mixed feelings about the RUC, having years earlier passed his exams for rank of inspector, yet never received promotion. Uncle Owen was of course a Catholic.

Unnerved by my run-in with the RUC, I had no inclination for wild-fowling for the rest of that season. A few days later a constable had called at the garage and handed me a summons for shooting within an hour of sunset, though the trespass charge had been dropped. Some weeks after, I appeared before the magistrate and paid the fine of ten shillings, a good deal of money in the1950s. The payment was recorded in the court ledger and I was given a receipt. I had paid the penalty for a crime I did not commit, but what else could I do.

Christmas came and went. Spring began to unfold with daffodils and crocuses showing white, yellow and purple through the grass. Bird-song in the early morning gladdened the heart as the sun rose early each morning. Many birds were already nesting, fluttering around in search of twigs and fluff to line their new homes among the branches. Spring is always a time of possibilities and this year was especially so for our local Minor football team, each man regarding it as 'our year' when we could win a County Medal. Training had begun in earnest, and with my suspension well out of the way I was delighted to be back in the team. With all this excitement about the matches, and the fine weather opening up, it felt good to be alive that spring.

7

Arrested

One thing you learn about life is that it's unpredictable and you never quite know what's around the corner. Fate gave its first warning of just such a turn for me in May of that year. I had returned home from the garage for a spot of lunch when there was a knock on the back door. My mother opened it and was confronted by two RUC constables demanding to see me. Hearing mother's protests that I was at the table I went anxiously to the door. One of the officers asked my name, on confirmation of which he began to read out a long statement. It was a warrant for my arrest, the charge non-payment of a fine. A uniformed arm reached out to take hold of me.

'Hold on – what do you mean…?' I said agitatedly.

'Crumlin Road jail – it'll be seven days for you – now come on!'

Across the road I could see a waiting police car.

'The fine was paid!' I protested, 'Ten shillings – for shooting within an hour of sunset. It's already paid I tell you…'

Ignoring me the officers stepped across the doorway.

'I have the receipt" I said, "I'll fetch it.'

At this they hesitated.

'We'll be back shortly.'

Twenty minutes later there was another knock on the door.

'A mistake has been made and therefore you will not be arrested for the time being.'

The words were formal and authoritative, without trace of an apology. For the time being – what did that mean? I assumed it was just an attempt to intimidate me, keep me unnerved. I realised that the officers must have been annoyed at their failure to make an arrest. They had lost face and been obliged to back down. To some men, especially those used to giving orders, this is very hard to take. Like most people in the neighbourhood, particularly the Nationalists, I was always careful to abide by the letter of the law, driving a roadworthy car, fully taxed and insured. With checkpoints and random stops from both the RUC and B-Specials one could not afford to give them any excuse for accusation. That didn't mean they couldn't invent one if they felt like it. I felt angry and distressed about this sudden rude intrusion onto my own doorstep, and paced moodily in the house for a while before returning to work.

Though I remained resentful over this incident for some weeks, there were plenty of distractions to take my mind off it, not least being the all-consuming passion of football. The season was well under way and excitement had been mounting since our local Minor Team reached the league final. Having won this match all eyes were now on the County Championship Final in a few weeks time. Talking with my team-mates about the recent attempt to arrest me led us to some general conversations about the state of affairs in our community. A number of the fellows said they were considering leaving to seek their fortunes and a fairer crack of the whip either in the Republic or overseas. Certain of my football pals, who were also customers at the garage, lent a particularly sympathetic ear regarding my encounter with the RUC. Aware my feelings still ran high over the affair, one among their number approached me with a suggestion. It was their custom he said, that on a couple of evenings a week he and his friends would travel across the border to southern Ireland to a remote spot near Clones in County Monaghan. I asked him for what purpose these trips were made. He replied that in a secluded area they engaged in small-arms fire, target practice and the like, together with what were described as 'training exercises'. Their hosts on these occasions were the Irish Republican Army.

My father as I have said was an enterprising man. The

garage gave us a good enough living and employment to others, but he always had his eye open for additional opportunities. Both the dance-band and the taxi service had provided an honest supplement to the family income and now my father had come up with a new idea. Every so often he would go down south, buy up crashed vehicles and bring them over the border, paying customs duty at the British point of entry. Back in the garage we would repair the cars and sell them on for a profit. The viability of this operation was enhanced by the lower amount of duty paid on a vehicle in damaged condition. For some months, during slack times I had been working on a red Hillman my father had bought in Dublin. It was badly wrecked and hence the customs duty had been minimal. The car's condition presented quite a challenge. The roof was buckled, the windscreen and rear window broken and a door and other panels damaged. Though mechanically still sound, the bodywork was likely to be one of the most difficult repair jobs I had yet undertaken. My Uncle Jim, who by this time had sold the family farm at Cooneen and moved up to Enniskillen, was now a regular visitor to the garage. Though like us a Catholic, Jim had acquaintances among the Orange Order and Freemasons (he adamantly told my father that though it wasn't possible for Catholics to join the Orange Order unless they converted to Protestantism, they could in certain circumstances be elected to the Masons) and it was through such connections that people could advance in their business and careers in the North. Uncle Jim would recommend our garage among his circle and sometimes find a purchaser for one of the restored vehicles. One of his friends was a wealthy farmer who, like Jim owned horses and enjoyed race meetings and point-to-point. It was to this farmer that the red Hillman, when I had lovingly completed its repair, was sold.

Uncle Jim's friend was very pleased with his purchase, and it was gratifying to see the car go to such an appreciative new owner. I didn't imagine I'd see much of that dear old Hillman again. I had played my part in its life and never predicted it might return to play a part in mine. Like I said, you never know what's round the corner.

Through visiting Dublin my father was building up good relationships with others in the motor trade there, often staying over for a few days to conduct business and socialise. Such was his affinity with the city that he and my mother began to discuss the possibility of us all moving there. In fact it was my younger brother Patrick who took off. Having gone along with father sometimes on his trips, Patrick had been much drawn by the free and relaxed atmosphere of the south, and when his schooling ended he left home and went to live in Dublin. Being only a year apart Patrick and I had been good pals, playing Club and Minor football together, and I felt the loss of his company. I thought of Dublin's fair city and the wider world of opportunities that might be lying in store for me out there somewhere.

When my father was away I was now put in charge of the business, and one day during his absence two men called at the garage and asked to see him. They did not give their names or any message. On his return my father said they must have been from the revenue. A few days later the two men returned, this time however they came up to the house and spoke to my father in the driveway. He confirmed they were Customs and Excise officials. The following day my father left again for Dublin and I carried on working as normal. The two Customs men called yet again and asked for my father. This went on for a while – the men would appear, and each time my father would seem to have avoided them.

A few weeks then elapsed during which time I thought again about my future. The repair work was greatly satisfying in itself but I felt restless to be independent of the family, as Patrick now was, and wondered if I should pursue my idea of becoming an RUC officer. It was while I was driving out a newly-repaired car and musing on such things that I recognised two local policemen walking slowly in front of the garage. Shortly afterwards a car crawled past with two other faces I vaguely recognised. After it had gone I remembered the faces as those of the two Revenue men. Though this seemed a coincidence I did not sense anything ominous about it.

That same afternoon around four o'clock, one of the

policemen I'd seen earlier came into the garage. Behind him were the two Revenue men. They asked if my father was in and I replied that he was not. They then put the same question to our two other mechanics, who affirmed that my father was not there. At this point I noticed the police officer was shadowing me. Without further explanation the Revenue men then said they were arresting me on the charge of illegal importation of a Hillman car. I listened in a state of absolute shock. Giving me no opportunity to talk to my colleagues, I was summarily marched outside, put into a waiting police car and driven off. Only a short while ago I had been thinking again about joining the RUC, but not in this fashion. I was already fearful. We arrived at the RUC station where I was taken to an interview room and questioned. Here the revenue men confirmed who they were and continued to insist that I had smuggled the car over the border and that I had better confess to it now. It was an extremely frightening ordeal. I was seventeen years old, alone in a police station surrounded by hostile interrogators. All I could do was tell the truth, that the Hillman had been a wreck when we bought it and full duty had not been required. But it was useless. All they wanted was to hear me admit the offence. After several hours at the Lisnaskea station I was taken under escort to Enniskillen where shortly after nine in the evening I was placed in a holding cell and the door slammed shut on me.

That night through the bars of the cell window I looked up at the moon and listened to the rippling waters of the Erne flowing close by. So near and yet so far – I knew now what that meant. I had a single coarse blanket for warmth, but I did not sleep. Instead I lay deep in thought, angry at everything the British establishment stood for. They say you don't know what you have till it's taken from you, and liberty is one of the most precious possessions, to walk around as a free man – it's something we take for granted. My only desire that night was to have that liberty back, to be out of this nightmare and back at home drinking tea in the kitchen or out by the river with my rod and line. To kick a ball about with my team-mates would be sheer bliss at that moment, even stuck under the bonnet of a car and covered in oil was a picture of heaven – anywhere so long as I had my freedom. I thought of my brother Patrick again and the relaxed way of life in Dublin, where you didn't have to keep glancing over your shoulder or feel your heart miss a beat every time a policeman looked at you. I also reflected on the offer made some months earlier by my football friends to train with the IRA. At the time I had declined, but events can make a man think again. I was certainly now of the opinion that whatever one tried to do in the name of peace and however law-abiding you were, if the ruling classes – in these parts the Protestants – didn't like you, your good intentions were simply spat on. The charge against me was entirely false, as it had been when I bit the bullet and paid the shooting fine. In the eyes of my captors I was just another Catholic, a Republican and a Fenian, and hence a threat to the deep-rooted Unionist culture of Northern Ireland.

That night in the cells was a long one, the only human contact a policeman who looked once at me through a peep-hole in the door. The dawn came slowly and after finishing some breakfast in the cell I was immediately informed that I was now to be taken to the Crumlin Road jail in Belfast. I said I did not understand what was going on, and was told I was now being remanded and sent for trial in a few weeks. I could barely believe what I was hearing. Remanded? Sent for trial? I was innocent! My dazed mind reeled at the terrible prospect of spending weeks in the notorious Crumlin, let alone what might happen after that. I was handcuffed and escorted outside to a police car. However the driver did not head out of town. Instead he pulled up outside the Enniskillen railway station. Here I was taken onto the platform, still handcuffed to the officer. Weary from my sleepless night I gazed up the tracks, trying vainly to make some sense of what had happened to me in the past twenty-four hours. What I saw next made me shrink back in horror. For standing close by were a group of my friends, boys and girls of my age whom I knew well. I turned my face away hoping they had not noticed me. But it was too late. Already they were looking curiously in my direction and speaking to one another in quiet tones. I dared not acknowledge them, yet my silent disregard seemed further confirmation of my guilt and I burned with shame. If ever I wanted the earth to open up and swallow me it was now.

When the train arrived I was helped into a seat, the officer I was chained to sitting next to me, the other opposite. Other passengers, on seeing the policemen, moved away along the carriage. My friends from the platform appeared to have got on some way ahead. The train pulled away and began to pick up speed. I stared from the window as the hedges and ditches, mills and cottages of Enniskellen hurried by. After a few minutes the officer sitting opposite leaned over and spoke to me.

'We'll take these off' he said, putting a key to the handcuffs and removing them. 'They should never have been used in the first place' he added.

I rubbed my swollen wrists gratefully. Though physically more comfortable and looking like less of a criminal, I remained tense with anxiety. My mind would not stop whirling, trying to grasp the situation and what lay ahead. We arrived in Belfast, bustling with people and traffic and transferred to another police car. Shortly afterwards the high walls of Crumlin Road jail arose into view. The gates opened and we passed swiftly inside.

8

Prisoner

'Get your clothes off – and be quick about it!'
My pulse began to race as I hurriedly disrobed. Better not upset anyone I thought – better just do as I was told.

'Prisoner number….!' yelled out another man, from behind a high counter. He had piles of folded uniforms laid out waiting for the new inmates to collect. 'Number!' he repeated. I could not remember my number. Was I supposed to? Probably not, it was deliberately reeled off too quickly so they knew you wouldn't be able to say it back. It was just to put the fear of god into you that you'd done something wrong from the minute you arrived. There is something about nakedness which makes anyone feel very vulnerable – especially when those who have taken your clothes are barking out orders and have thick wooden batons which they swing menacingly close to your face and body. I instinctively flinched as the warders paced back and forth, looking me up and down. There were some comments, words of ridicule and hatred, a feeling you might get hit somewhere very painful any minute.

'Well, well look what we have here. Dear oh dear another little Fenian bastard been up to no good. What are we going to do with him eh?'

'Lock him up and throw away the key' said another warden.

'Mind you that'd be a waste of money and I don't think the little bugger's worth it do you?'

'No, still we can't be having an empty space in the cells now can we.'

'Not when there's Papists roaming around on the loose.'

'Come on, move along you Popish fucker!'

On and on it went, like a hammer beating remorselessly on my head as the paperwork and procedure of admitting the new prisoners took its relentless course Herded along corridors before a series of orderlies, warders, policemen and other officials of the state, I was being forced ever deeper into the brute efficiency of the penal system. Each rubber stamp stole another part of my identity, and with every turn of the corridor a little more of my dignity crumbled away. Prison is like a mincing machine for human beings. The remarks and the hate-filled looks and the threatening batons were I knew all intended to see me cower, make me afraid. We Catholics were seen as a mortal threat, and they sought to keep us subdued at all costs. My full name, address and religion were written in a book, my photograph was taken and my fingerprints recorded. Looking around me I was surprised at how many other men were coming in at the same time. Some looked a lot older than my own father and I appeared to be one of the youngest there. For some reason this made me feel even worse. When I finally arrived at my cell my heart sank even further as I realised I was to share with another prisoner. He was a much older man and looked suspiciously at me as I was shown in. I did not speak and lay straight down on the bed. Soon after that it was time for lights out, when sleep mercifully overcame me.

Over the next few days I kept my head down and spoke little to anyone. Inside I had painful feelings of despair and self-pity at what had happened to me. It was still like a bad dream, except that I knew it was only too real and I wasn't going to wake up. I knew however that I couldn't afford to weaken and had to try and put some sort of a brave face on. I concentrated as hard as I could on learning the ropes and fitting in with all the prison rules and routines. I just wanted to get through each day without stepping out of line or drawing attention to myself. The part of the prison I was in was well away from what they called the hard men, the long term criminals and violent characters. My cell-mate had made some attempts to talk, which had been rather unnerving, since some of his questions had a nasty edge to them, and I remained wary of the man. I had of course wondered continually about my family. I'd been told my mother had been informed of my arrest and I knew they would be doing everything they could to try to get some sort of legal representation for me. However they had by this time arranged to move to Dublin, and I wondered how my unexpected situation would affect their plans.

A couple of weeks went by and although trying hard to keep my head together, my nervous state was all too clearly showing the strain. I had begun stammering again quite badly, something I hadn't done since before my tuberculosis. Asthma was also giving trouble and I was becoming generally weak and run-down.

One day a warder came into my cell and said the prison governor wished to see me. The governor informed me that some phone calls had been received and as a consequence I was to be seen by the prison doctor. After a brief medical examination I was returned to my cell only to be hauled out again after a few hours. It seems I was to be moved to another part of the prison. Though relieved to get away from my hostile cell-mate I was also thinking better the devil you know, and concerned about where they might now take me. On arrival though it appeared I had been transferred to a kind of hospital wing of the prison, since there were a number of inmates here who seemed less than fit. The conditions here were much improved. To my relief I found my new cell was a single one, and furthermore there was a Bible placed upon the table. The cell was also noticeably cleaner, although with no toilet there was still the ignominy of slopping-out. I was to find the food better with fresh salads alongside the meal, and each day there was an hour of exercise in the outdoor yard. I was not told who it was that had telephoned about my welfare but could only assume it was my parents. I therefore requested writing implements so I could send a letter thanking them and assuring them I was as well as could be expected. My request was granted, though I was told to leave the envelope unsealed as the letter must be examined by the prison authorities before posting.

A few days afterwards I met a person named John Grimes, who was from Pomeroy, twenty miles from Arboe Cross in the County Tyrone, where I had seen the vision of our lady some years previously. John walked with a severe limp due to some disablement, and like me was on remand, his own charge relating to the holding of "republican views" though in fact like me, he'd been arrested on some petty charge. John then had also experienced injustice as a result of simply being a Catholic, and over the next couple of months we became very good friends. John, being a little older than me, was able to offer much good advice, mainly that I should beware of everyone, especially the authorities. His moral support came as a great blessing in the harsh and lonely confines of the prison and I was pleased, being a non-smoker myself, to pass on my ration of one Woodbine cigarette each day to John.

My family had now arranged for my eldest sister to come up from Dublin to visit me. When the day arrived I was of course delighted to see her, and somewhat emotional. Shirley was only thirteen and it must have been quite unnerving for her to make the trip to Belfast and pass under the intimidating gaze of the prison authorities. However she told me that the warders had been courteous and considerate towards her, advising her to take particular care of her watch whilst there. She had brought some of my own clothes from home, which the governor had given permission for me to wear since my transfer to the hospital wing.

Following the excitement of my sister's visit, and all the memories of home which it had stirred, the long days in prison hung heavily with me. Aside from meal-times and the brief period of exercise there was very little to occupy the time or provide any diversion. I did however spend many hours reading the only literature available, the Holy Bible, reacquainting myself with inspirational passages and finding some that were new to me. I was thus engrossed one morning when the warder arrived at my cell and announced that two men wished to interview me. He said I was not obliged to see them or to sign any papers they may produce. As I had continually protested myself innocent of any charge I felt I had nothing to hide and so went along.

Following the warder I passed through a series of locked doors, and wondered if anyone had ever escaped from the Crumlin jail. It certainly struck me that day as the tightest place on earth. I was shown into a room where to my surprise were the very two revenue men who had arrested me in the garage all those months ago.

Together we sat down and the warder left the room. There then ensued a barrage of questions, much of them a repetition of what I'd been asked back in Enniskillen police station on the day of my arrest. I realised this was not an investigation to find the truth or to move my case forward. It was simply another attempt to induce me to confess to the crime I had consistently denied. As I gave the same answers to the same questions, the revenue men wrote down pages of notes. This went on for it must have been an hour, after which time I was handed the notes and asked to sign. Glancing through what had been written it seemed fairly clear it was not the truth and that I was being asked in effect to put my name to a confession of guilt. When I angrily refused to sign any such documents the revenue men became annoyed and then abusive. With raised voices they told me it made no difference whether they had my signature or not, as they would simply write it themselves. On hearing the shouts the warder returned, and relieved at his intervention I asked to be taken back to my cell. Returning along the corridor the warder told me that the revenue men had had no right to be so aggressive towards me and that I shouldn't let them get the better of me. Being upset I was grateful for the man's sympathy, but his advice was easier said than done, and I sat down in my cell feeling worried. Had the warder heard what they'd said, and even if he had, would he be prepared to take my side against the authorities? That would surely be more than his job was worth. He was probably familiar with this kind of corruption and though he may not approve was a helpless part of the system like everyone else. If the customs men did carry out their threat and sign a false confession how would I ever convince anyone I was innocent? And in theory they could frame me for anything that way, perhaps cooking up far more serious crimes than the mere illegal importation of a car. My mind reeled at the possible implications. John Grimes had been right to tell me to "beware". The long days and nights slowly passed, during which I continued to read from the Holy Bible, very often falling asleep with the pages open on my chest.

It was in June of that year 1954, that great excitement arose in my former home village of Arboe. The newspapers reported that Our Lady the Blessed Virgin Mary had appeared to two people, a John Quinn and Anne Hannal, and already a flow of pilgrims in coaches and buses had begun to arrive from all over Ireland and descend on the little village. The fact this was the very place where I myself had seen the vision of Our Lady seven years previously was both thought-provoking and a comfort to me in my prison cell. At the time of my own vision I had been but an innocent boy and no-one had believed me, wandering about the fields with my prayer-book and my dreams of the priesthood. How my circumstances had changed! Seven years on I was a man, no less innocent I hoped yet incarcerated behind bars, far from the caring warmth of home and family and facing an uncertain future. Apart from the friendship of John Grimes, the one constant guiding light for me now was the Bible. My faith may have wavered during the period of leaving school and going out into the world, and perhaps I had been a doubting Thomas, yet the words of the Lord were unaltered and had been an undeniable succour in my lonely cell. "Let us run with patience the race that is set before us" says the Bible. No priest had visited me in the prison, but with the Bible at my side and then hearing the news from Arboe I was reminded of my faith, and given the patience I so needed during those anxious, dreary days in the Crumlin.

A date for my court hearing was finally set, to be held in Enniskillen. On the appointed day, after an early-morning breakfast of porridge, toast and tea in my cell, I was escorted to the front entrance of the prison where a driver and two RUC officers with side-arms were waiting by a dark-coloured van. On arrival at the courthouse there was already a great flurry of activity – press reporters, lawyers and clerks all waiting expectantly for the proceedings to begin. My appointed solicitor, a Mr Murphy of Clones came over for a few words and introduced me to Mr Gerry Lennon of Armagh, who was the barrister my family had engaged to fight my case. Mr Lennon confided to me that he was confident the prosecution would not get far and may not even proceed to trial that day. This was music to my ears. The courthouse was now packed and as the magistrate called order I took my seat between the two RUC men and a great hush fell upon the room.

The hearing was opened with the Customs and Excise alleging illegal importation of the Hillman car. There followed a cross-examination by Mr Lennon, pointing out my consistent statements that the vehicle had been repaired since crossing the border as a wreck and the relevant duty paid. No attempt had been made to avoid the legal tariff. The customs then argued if such a repair had been carried out it would be obvious from looking at the car, which it was not. Mr Lennon asked customs to prove the vehicle had not been repaired, and as far as I could gather the argument then centred on the burden of proof and was swathed in lots of legal terminology, with each side hitting the facts back and forth like an angry game of ball. The magistrate, who was himself looking confused, finally called me to take the stand. I felt a little nervous but knew all I had to do was speak the truth. I was asked to confirm my name then the magistrate said,

'Did you in fact make a substantial repair on the vehicle in question?'

I replied that I did.

'And could you show the court exactly where on the car this repair was carried out?' Again I replied in the affirmative. Then the magistrate asked how old I was. I replied that I was seventeen. On hearing this the magistrate decreed that the case was to be adjourned for a maximum of six weeks and in that time the Customs and Excise must produce the Hillman at the courthouse so that he could view it for himself. He further added that 'this young man should never have been brought before the court'

And so it was to be back to the Crumlin for me. As the prison van sped along the country road out of Enniskillen I hoped and prayed that if the magistrate did get to inspect the Hillman he would be convinced of what I'd told him. This thought gave me some misgivings. The whole purpose of a good repair job is to ensure the owner can't see where the original damage was done. The Hillman looked almost good as new when Uncle Jim's farmer friend had bought it. Perhaps he would testify for me. But then again he had not seen the car prior to its repair. There were of course ways to show exactly where the repairs had been done. But would the magistrate allow me to do this, or would he take a cursory look at the Hillman and make up his own mind there and then? It was all beginning to seem quite ironic in a way – the thought that I could be convicted, indirectly because of my superb repair skills. Again the days in the prison dragged by, till late one evening I was informed that 'breakfast will be early tomorrow'. Back in the Enniskillen courthouse there was a feeling of 'here we go again' as the Customs and Excise hammered home their contention that the vehicle could not have been repaired. All my thoughts were of whether or not they had the Hillman. Finally, in response to the magistrate's question they conceded that the car 'would not be produced in court'. At this the magistrate got quite annoyed and shuffled his papers decisively. It appeared he was ready to make a pronouncement. As the courtroom went very quiet waiting to hear what the magistrate was going to say, I felt my pulse quicken a little as he cleared his throat. His verdict when it came was a simple one: the whole case was to be dismissed with full costs allowed against the customs. There was immediately a general murmuring amongst all present, above which the magistrate reiterated his opinion that the matter should never have come to court in the first place. I remained seated between my RUC escorting officers, uncertain what would happen now. There seemed to be a lot of serious discussion still going on among the clerks and legal officials. Finally one of the RUC men leant over and told me I was free to go. After thanking my barrister and solicitor I made my way past the customs men who sat with very long faces, and left the courthouse. I was free. It was a blissful feeling. Later that evening I got a lift to Lisnaskea and later went on to Clones where I picked up a train to Dublin.

9

Dublin

When I arrived at the Amiens Street railway station, my relations were delighted to see me. Naturally they were pleased at my release from prison, but also by the fact I had decided to join them in Dublin. We were to be a family once again, both at home and in business. During that period of the 1950s stock-car and motor racing was a great craze. My father was already renting part of a garage at Fairview Strand, together with a man named Charlie Norton. This garage, with its large yard out the back, was where I was soon to spend some of my happiest working hours, building the racing cars for the competitions at Phoenix Park. I also worked with an older, experienced fellow called Tony Power, and together Tony and I would form flat sheets of mild steel and aluminium into the bodywork panels. The cars would be fitted with Jaguar engines, and once assembled we'd spray them in metallic paint. The finishing touch would be to paint a large white competitor number on the bonnet. It was gratifying to attend the races and watch a car we'd built in action, particularly if it took the winner's flag.

Of course I'd known the atmosphere in Dublin would be more relaxed, but the changes took me a while to get used to. It was mainly the attitude of the authorities that was so different. In the North, the sight of a policeman would always give one a slight feeling of tension. Here, officers of the law did not regard you as an enemy, and unlike the RUC, the Gardai usually went about unarmed. They spoke to people on equal terms, and you did not have to think twice before answering their questions. I still had a tendency to stammer in my speech when I saw them however, a psychological legacy from my experience in the Crumlin. The stammer could surface in any social occasions, which could be embarrassing. Still, there were many attractions in Dublin – colourful shop windows, brightly-lit bars and pubs by the dozen in streets that seemed teeming with life after the quiet of Lisnaskea – which I hoped would help wash away the bad memories. I began to see some of my old pals, who had also moved down from Fermanagh in search of work, often meeting them at the dance-halls around Parnell Square.

I'd been living in Dublin for over a year, when my Uncle Jim from Enniskillen visited me with a request. The owner of the Hillman car, the very one that had landed me in prison, had been attempting without success to reclaim the vehicle from Customs and Excise. Unbelievably, they were still holding on to it after all this time. Uncle Jim wondered if I could help the man recover his lawful property, by giving evidence again at a hearing. I was immediately apprehensive at the thought of returning to Northern Ireland and getting involved in the whole unhappy mess again, especially after such a care-free time in Dublin. However I also felt justice should be done if possible for the man who'd bought the car, and was still out of pocket, and so agreed to accompany Uncle Jim to a special hearing for the case in Enniskillen a few weeks hence. Also, if I could help to prove the car had been repaired, it would also prove, once and for all my own innocence in the matter. In the event, after a long day of legal arguments, the hearing was adjourned for another three months. This would have been frustrating for me, but for one thing – the instruction by the judge that Customs must produce the Hillman in court at the next sitting. If Customs complied, and brought the car to court, I had already thought of a way of settling the matter with them once and for all.

The following weekend I met up with some pals, one of them from Lisnaskea, who said he'd read about the Hillman court case in the Fermanagh newspapers. We were at the Galway Arms in Parnell Square for the weekly ceilidh, and it was about half-way through the evening, gazing across at the assembled ladies on the other side of the room, that my eyes lighted on a tall, slender girl. She was indeed beautiful, with the face and figure of a fashion model. I made a few attempts to catch her attention, and several times crossed the floor as the music started. Each time I was too slow however, and she was partnered before I could offer the dance. I decided therefore to remain on the 'ladies side' of the room. The tactic paid off when an Irish dance was called, and together, the young lady and I introduced ourselves and took to the floor. She told me her name was Patricia, and she was a native of Dublin, though her parents were from the outskirts of Limerick.City, beside Clarina Castle. Patricia said she knew from my accent that I was from the North, whilst I hoped she hadn't also noticed my stammer, which I was endeavouring to control. Next to be called was an old-time waltz, which we also danced, remaining deep in conversation until the music had finished. We then parted, and returned to our respective friends on either side of the ballroom. There followed an Irish dance or two and in the following interval, as the dancers began to pair up again, I saw Patricia approaching in my direction. My hopes were not disappointed, as she walked straight up and asked me to dance. I gladly accepted, flattered and delighted to be taking the floor again with the most beautiful girl in the room. It was not the last dance we had together that night. Later on, Patricia introduced me to her sister and her friends, and after the Irish National Anthem had been played, we arranged to meet again the following week.

Friday soon came around again, and wanting to look as smart as possible for Patricia, my preparations drew the attention of my brothers and sisters, who were already guessing I had met a special girl. When I arrived at the Galway Arms, Patricia, looking as lovely as I'd remembered, was as pleased to see me as I her. We had a most enjoyable evening, talking intimately of my life in Fermanagh and hers in Dublin. Afterwards, everyone was scrambling to catch the last bus, but as I had my car I offered to give Patricia a lift. On the way I told her about the hearing in Enniskillen the following Friday. I explained I would be arriving back late in Dublin, but would still come and meet her at the Galway Arms again in the evening. As the last bus pulled up beside us, Patricia waved me goodbye and joined her friends for the short walk home. I knew it would be the last time I would see her before travelling to the North.

Over the intervening days, Patricia was much in my thoughts however. This helped to ease my mind a little regarding the imminent hearing. I told myself repeatedly I had nothing to fear, the judge having long before dismissed the case against me. But memories of the long months in the Crumlin would not go away. If false charges could be brought once, they could be brought again. However my mind was now made up to attend, and my own scheme for overturning the Customs, which I'd so far kept quiet about, was all prepared for. On the Thursday, my brother Patrick and I travelled up to Enniskillen, where we were to stay overnight at the Railway Hotel.

Uncle Jim greeted us and we were told the bill for our stay had already been settled. It was then I revealed my plan to Uncle Jim. When we were sat in a private corner together, I opened my case and took out two items. One was a small, hand-held blow-lamp, the other a box of matches. On seeing these, Uncle Jim's face went almost white, and he demanded to know what I was up to. I explained that if the Hillman were produced outside the court the next day, I could play the blow-torch over the damaged parts, causing the solder I had used in the repairs to melt and fall out. The magistrate, and everyone else, could then see for themselves that the vehicle had clearly been a major reconstruction job. The colour slowly returned to Uncle Jim's face. Perhaps when he'd first seen the blow-lamp, he'd thought I was planning to burn down the court house.

Next morning the court was already thronging when we arrived. There was Gerry Lennon the solicitor and Mr Pascal O'Hare QC, both of whom had been engaged by Uncle Jim to fight my case. The RUC were also present, together with several newspaper reporters armed with notebooks and pencils. The photographers' cameras were already flashing as more people turned up. I spotted the same two customs men who'd given me such a hard time before, and began to feel very nervous and intimidated. After some prolonged legal argument between Mr O'Hare and the opposing QC I was called to the stand as principle witness, where I was subjected to a gruelling barrage of questions by the customs' prosecution QC. Photographs of the Hillman in its damaged state were produced, and it was argued I could not possibly have transformed such a vehicle into the one that had been sold on. The latter it was maintained, was a different car, one that had been smuggled over the border. There followed further exchanges between Mr O'Hare and the prosecution, till finally the magistrate intervened to ask whether the vehicle was available to view, as he had previously instructed. The prosecuting QC confirmed that the Hillman car was indeed standing in the yard. The magistrate then ordered everyone to adjourn outside. On hearing this I was delighted. I gathered up my small bag containing the blow-lamp and matches and followed the whole crowd – clerks, solicitors, barristers, press men and all the various hangers-on – out into the yard. It was two and a half years since I'd seen the dear old red Hillman, but I recalled her every contour immediately. Patrick held the blow-lamp while I lit it, and when the magistrate had checked the chassis and engine numbers against his file, he asked me to show where and how the car had been repaired. I opened the door and proceeded to remove a small part of the head-cloth, then pointed to certain marks under the roof. The magistrate bent down to see. Patrick then passed the blow-lamp, which I played closely along the marks. The assembled crowd were craning forward, all trying to see inside the car, waiting for something to happen. In a few minutes the metal began to bulge, and a lump of solder dropped out. There was a murmur among the crowd, as those at the front reported back what had happened. I moved the blow-lamp to another part of the car, quickly producing the same result. The magistrate thanked me and said he had seen enough. Back in the courtroom, the magistrate announced there was now no doubt in his mind that the car had been skilfully repaired, and ruled that it should be returned immediately to its rightful owner, together with any costs incurred. With the case finally over, Uncle Jim's friend shook me warmly by the hand and thanked me for coming to Enniskillen to give evidence. It was now apparent to everyone that the original case had been wholly unsound and my false imprisonment the result of collusion. There was considerable excitement as the courtroom emptied, especially among those who'd turned out for the defence, my Uncle Jim and company, and our legal people. The press were eager to interview me, but I brushed past them, reluctant to get further involved in any story. The only thing on my mind now was getting back to Dublin in time to meet Patricia.

Life in Dublin thereafter quickly settled into a routine. I began to see Patricia quite regularly now, often meeting under Nelson's Pillar in the city centre, as was the custom of many a courting couple, before going off to a dance or a pub. My habit of stammering had unfortunately persisted, but Patricia was very patient and understanding about it, urging me not to rush my words. Playing Gaelic football took up much of my remaining spare time, and during the day I was still enjoying the work in the motor business with my father. After a few months though I developed an itch to strike out in a business of my own, and went to look at a garage premises in Newry, County Down. Though it was the North, with my reputation restored by the magistrate after the Hillman hearing, I now felt more confident of returning, and seeing if there might after all be greater opportunities in terms of business up there. Liking what we saw, my brother Patrick and I decided to rent the premises. As before with my father, we began importing and restoring crashed vehicles. With good workmanship, we found we could make a handsome profit on the cars, and business quickly took off. We both still spent our weekends in Dublin though, so I could continue to see Patricia. Over the next few months however, the province of Ulster grew rather tense, with an IRA raid on an army barracks in Armagh causing greatly increased security measures along the border areas, including Newry. Whether this accounted for the fact our premises was shortly afterwards put up for sale or not, I cannot say. All I know is, Patrick and I were asked to leave, and despite great efforts, were unable to find another suitable garage. The year was 1956, and another crisis, this time a long way off, now began to have an impact on all European economies. President Nasser of Egypt had seized control of the Suez Canal, the main shipping lane for oil tankers from the Middle East. This 'international situation' quickly led to widespread redundancies and a scarcity of petrol. I now just needed a job, and decided to try my hand in Liverpool, where I secured a position doing truck maintenance for a haulage firm. While away, I wrote regularly to Patricia, who would occasionally visit my family in Killester.

When the petrol crisis had eased, I returned to Dublin and started work in a motor manufacturers. I had been saving money for some time, and with a purpose in mind. I had already bought an engagement ring in Grafton Street, and was waiting for the 'right moment' to propose to Patricia. I decided that a summer evening would be as good a time as any to pop the question and the date I had chosen, 29th June 1957, was warm and balmy, perfect for the occasion. On meeting up I suggested to Patricia it might be pleasant to take a walk in Phoenix Park, and sit by the quiet pond, close to the wildlife. But she was keen to go to the cinema and see 'The King and I'. 'Can we not go and see it Philip, it's very good' she implored. Not wishing to disappoint her tonight of all nights, I willingly agreed, though wondered how I might make the proposal. I had been nervous all evening, and by now the ring felt like it was burning a hole in my pocket. After the film I parked the car outside her home and Patricia, clutching the remainder of the box of chocolates she always kept for the family, was just about to get out when I said 'Don't go yet'. She looked at me with a very grave expression and replied 'Philip, what's wrong?' I said 'Will you marry me?' For a few minutes she said nothing. She seemed shocked and more unsettled even than I was. She then made her reply. 'Yes' she said. 'I will' and held out her slender hand to take the diamond ring with its three stones I had been keeping all this time. It slid perfectly onto her finger. After that we sat in the car talking for a long time, before she became restless for us to go inside and break the news to her family. Patricia was now my fiancée. We agreed to marry the year after next, 1959, all being well. After our engagement I received regular invitations to Sunday lunch with Patricia's family, whom I soon got to know well. Her only brother Peter was a fine fellow, not least for his ability to produce tickets to all the big sporting events – football, rugby and horse racing! I was taken on the rounds of all Patricia's acquaintances, including a close friend who was a nun with the Dominican Order at Eccles Street, where Patricia had concluded her schooling. The sister confided to me that at one time, Patricia had nurtured serious thoughts of becoming a nun herself, but it now seemed clear her future lay with me. So the girl that once would have been a nun was to wed the boy who had longed to become a priest. It seemed fitting enough, and on 8th April 1959 Patricia and I were married in the Church of Christ the King, a mere stone's throw away from where we had sat in the car the evening I gave her the ring. We received a papal blessing from Pope John 23rd and at the reception there was a three-tier cake with all the trimmings, music and dancing and much fun and laughter.

Shortly after we moved into the bungalow we had purchased at The Rise, in Blanchardstown, County Dublin. There were three bedrooms and large grounds stretching right down the Tolka River which ran along the bottom of our back garden. We called our home 'St Anthony's', while on a more down to earth note, opposite the house was a large pub called the 'Greyhound Bar' and, literally down to earth and much appreciated, were the potatoes and other vegetables which Patricia's father came over and planted in our garden. Thus our basic needs were provided for. Furthermore, since we became engaged my stammer had gone.

10

Ambitions

In 1961 our first child was born, a little girl whom we named Aileen. After starting a family, many couples are inclined to stay put in their home. Patricia and I on the other hand, felt at this time the urge to spread our wings a little. Patricia's brother Peter, also now married, was living in London, and we decided we would follow on and see for ourselves what the life there was like. We found a nice flat in a quiet area just off the Edgware Road, though within easy distance of Marble Arch and the bright lights of the West End. There was no shortage of crash-repair work in London, with good, clean cars being in great demand. I was soon making excellent money, and with an eye to the future, I began studying at night-school for a Higher National Diploma in General Garage Management. In London our standard of living was high and we regularly went out socialising. We liked the buzz of the big city, seeing all the new fashions on show along Oxford Street and Carnaby Street, and enjoying the excitement of the endless shops and the varied nightlife.

Early one morning, Patricia received a letter from her family in Dublin. After all the local news, came the report that her mother was not very well. Over the next few months there was no improvement, and after some consideration we decided to close down the business in London and return to Dublin to be with Patricia's mother. Though we were doing well, there really seemed no alternative, and family had to come first. I arranged for my garage equipment to be shipped back home, and we obtained a rented dwelling at Firhouse in Dublin. Patricia's relatives had a great welcome laid on for us, but the underlying mood was inevitably sombre. Patricia's mother's health had deteriorated noticeably during the past year, with a substantial loss of weight and intensive chemotherapy having taken its toll. Patricia, being the youngest in the family, was particularly distressed. Shortly after the Christmas Day of 1963 Patricia's mother died. A few days later, Patricia gave birth to our second child, a son. One life on this earth had drawn to its close, another was just beginning.

We were now uncertain as to how our own lives should proceed. Patricia's father, after staying with us for a few weeks, had returned to his home. However, being now on his own, we were reluctant to leave him entirely behind and return to London, despite the fact jobs were scarce in Ireland at that time. The solution finally came with the offer of a position managing a repair-shop in Tralee, County Kerry.

We soon fell in love with this seaside area, especially our eldest girl, and in the summer we'd spend most of our evenings and weekends on the long, golden beaches of Banna Strand. Watching the Atlantic waves roll into Tralee Bay was a truly breath-taking sight. In wintertime though, the exposed position of the area required us to keep plentiful supplies of logs and turf for the living room fire. Indeed it was here in 1916, that Roger Casement had almost died of cold before his capture in McKenna's Fort. Patricia and I found the local people kind, good-humoured and always ready for sport and fun. We were very happy, and it was whilst living in Kerry that we had our third child, this time another girl. She was however born prematurely at home, and was in need of special care. Therefore the doctor drove us to the private nursing home we had booked some months earlier, while I sat in the back of the car and held the tiny baby during the journey. The doctor had phoned on ahead and the staff were prepared when we arrived, and placed the baby in an incubator. Both mother and child were very well looked after, but naturally, this was a worrying time. Patricia was allowed out after ten days, but it was several more weeks before our baby girl could leave the incubator and join us at home. For a while the child had a slight murmur on the heart, but with good medical attention the condition cleared up and she came through strong and healthy and we had reason to count our blessings.

One downside during our sojourn in Tralee was my own health, suffering as I did a severe bout of the mumps. This illness was to be the reason we did not have further children. However as I say, we counted our blessings and truly regarded each of our offspring as a gift from God. Fortunate as we were in our lot, I nevertheless felt at this time an urge to achieve more, to which end I became involved with a new political party which was just starting up at that time in Ireland. This party was broadly socialist in its aims, and for several weeks I travelled after work to meetings at the Limerick City Hotel and, along with my good friend Jim Kemmy and others on the steering committee, spent many hours working hard to get the movement off the ground. I was the only representative from Kerry to have a voice on the party's committee. Things came to a dramatic climax when the party leader was offered a lucrative position by the government of the day and most of the committee melted away. Possibly there were, or were believed to be IRA connections somewhere within the organisation. A few of the committee fought on and obtained seats on the Limerick council. My friend Jim Kemmy went on to become a TD, a seat he was to hold until his death.

After my involvement with politics came to an end I began to think again about where I might channel my general feelings of ambition. I was still in touch with a number of friends from the North, many of whom visited Tralee for their holidays, and when they were there we'd meet up in the singing pubs to enjoy the old Irish ballads and dancing. From these friends I gleaned the information that Northern Ireland was now flourishing, and with discrimination coming to an end, there were golden opportunities for hard-working Catholics and Protestants alike. By this time, Patricia's father had died, and in his will had bequeathed to her the family home in Dublin. We were now therefore in possession of some capital, and agreeing that it should be put to use for the benefit of our own growing family,

Patricia and I decided to look to the North for a suitable business to purchase. We soon found a most promising property called 'Rockview Motors', a garage and filling station with shop attached, the whole site having been closed for some time. The premises were situated at 23 Warren Road in County Down, on the main coast road from Bangor to Donaghadee. To the rear was a large slipway for boat access into the sea, which had formerly been used by the local lifeboat service. After buying the business there was enough money left to put towards a home, and so with a little extra from our combined savings and a building society loan, we were able to purchase a luxurious bungalow just a few hundred yards from the garage, overlooking the local golf course. Patricia was delighted with our new dwelling. In the driveway there were flowering cherry trees, encouraging all kinds of colourful birds and insects, and the mature gardens to the rear made a safe and pleasant area for all three children to play. Here they had swings and a slide, and a blue-painted pool to splash in during the warm weather along with our neighbours' children, with whom they soon made friends. The surrounding landscape of Donaghadee was one of real scenic beauty and in spring one could hear the crows from early morning building their nests in the tall trees. From the day we moved in everyone we met was so friendly and welcoming, lending the whole place a sense of tranquillity and well-being. Only six miles away was the popular seaside town of Bangor, with its golden sandy beaches extending around the Ards Peninsula, and from our house, looking out on a clear day across the Irish Sea, one could make out the coast of Scotland. We could also see the luxury cruise liners plying slowly across the horizon. At night, they would be all lit up, suspended against the dark ocean like silent ships in a fairy tale. All in all Donaghadee did seem a magical sort of place to raise a family. All we needed now was for the business side of things to take off. Once that happened, we could consider our new life truly complete.

11

We Open Shop

We opened our new premises for business shortly after Easter. We were helped no doubt by the fine spring weather, which, putting people in the mood to go out motoring for pleasure a little earlier in the year than usual, ensured us plenty of customers. Tourists visiting Bangor would extend their sight-seeing along the coast, and needed to fuel up. Donaghadee being as pretty a spot as any in the area made the perfect stop-off. Over that first year the car sales side of the business also expanded, as did the crash repair workshop. Naturally, the workshop was where I was mostly to be found, often staying till late at night to complete the work that was streaming in, and soon in a position to employ extra staff to meet the growing demand. We had made a very promising start to our new venture, and having a good income, were able to send our two eldest children to a small private school run by nuns on the other side of the town. I would drive them there each morning, stopping off first at the garage, where the girl in the shop would always give the kids a great welcome and have some chocolate ready to 'sweeten the day' for them before beginning their lessons.

Over in Belfast, civil rights marches had now begun, and families wishing to escape the tumult would leave the city and spend a peaceful day by the sea. On such occasions we always did a brisk trade in ice-creams and snacks as well as petrol. The Belfast demonstrations were intended to improve the lot of the underprivileged, and many were optimistic for progress in this respect in Northern Ireland. With unemployment among Catholics still more than twice the Protestant average, something had to be done. Advice centres had been set up throughout the city, and these would offer help to any citizen, regardless of their religion. The marchers' requests were for equality and justice for all, and they sought an end to discrimination in employment, housing and all other basic rights. These demonstrations were not always dominated by Nationalists, and Unionists who were sympathetic to the cause would often join in. As the Civil Rights Association attracted greater publicity however, Stormont, the Northern Ireland Parliament, began to fear the thin of a wedge which could endanger national security and destroy the Unionist way of life in the province. When, on the 6th October 1968 a march was organised for Londonderry protesting at the lack of council housing for Catholics, the authorities challenged the allegedly 'provocative' route, proceeding as it did from a Protestant area. In the event about 400 hundred demonstrators were in attendance, and were attacked by the RUC with batons and water-cannon. It was seen as a shameful day for Ulster loyalists, and one Irish TV cameraman who remained on the spot filming, showed the world the wanton brutality that some of the RUC were capable of.

Although the province of Ulster hit the world stage the year we moved there, we felt at a distance from the drama. Donaghadee was a peaceful and largely harmonious community where many Catholic and Protestant neighbours socialised together and indeed seemed oblivious of each other's religious identity. Thus the events we saw unfolding on television at that time, beginning with the awful violence of the Derry demonstration, seemed in no way a reflection of the part of Northern Ireland we ourselves lived in. By late November the Northern Ireland Prime Minister Terence O'Neil announced there would be major reforms in housing and local government. This split the civil rights activists, with some calling for a truce and others claiming the proposed measures were too little, too late.

In January of the following year seventy marchers were

violently ambushed by Loyalists just south of Derry, with the police escort doing little to intervene. As summer and the Protestant marching season approached Ulster grew increasingly tense. The RUC and the B-Specials were now on the streets in large numbers, and the Shoreland armoured cars mounted with heavy calibre Browning machine guns became a familiar sight. In Londonderry on August 12th, following an Orange Order parade, Loyalists attacked Catholic barricades in the Bogside area, which had been declared 'Free Derry', dropping the 'London' part of the city's name. It was during these attacks that the RUC fired CS gas for the first time in Ireland. The next day, the battle for the Bogside intensified, as over 700 RUC men, supported by B-Specials attempted to force their way in. However the Bogsiders now seemed immune to the CS gas, as they fought ferociously to defend their homes. The Nationalists of Derry appealed to the Irish Government in Dublin for help. After much debate it was agreed that direct intervention was not an option, but that field tents would be set up south of the border in Donegal, offering safe refuge to anyone fleeing. The violence was inevitably soon mirrored in Belfast, with Loyalists moving in on the Catholic community of the Falls Road. This began in an isolated fashion with threatening sniper fire here and there from suspected B-Specials' rifles. However when someone was injured by a bullet, a group of men rounded up some oil drums and set alight the disused building in which the sniper was positioned. When the fire brigade arrived they were stoned by a mob of youths, and only when the RUC turned out in force was order restored. As dawn broke the following morning the atmosphere was tense. Belfast was a powder keg primed and liable to explode at any moment.

It didn't take long. The 13th August saw hijacked buses and cars set alight and parts of the city reduced to a state of total bedlam. As the Nationalists dug themselves in around the Falls Road, the Loyalists were also consolidating, with many members of the B-Specials, armed with revolvers, rifles and machine guns coming onto the streets. By the 14th, a large Loyalist group was moving from the Shankhill Road in the direction of the Falls

Road. This war-like mob was petrol-bombing any Catholic houses in its path, beating up anyone who protested and shooting after fleeing residents. Approaching the Falls Road, the mob was met with stones and petrol bombs thrown from behind makeshift barricades. Some men were set alight, and a lone republican volunteer opened fire, leaving one of the Loyalist gunmen dead. Bringing up the rear , the RUC and B-Specials opened up heavy machine-gun fire from the fleet of Shorland armoured cars. Two Catholics fell dead; one a nine-year-old boy, the other a young man home on leave from the British Army. Many others were wounded as they dived for cover. As darkness fell the armoured cars with their heavy bull bars on the front tore through the barricades like knives through butter. Tyres and other material had been set alight by the residents, but the Loyalists, determined to reopen the roads, pushed through the smoke and flames regardless. That night the whole area erupted in violence, with the streets around the Falls Road being hardest hit. Dover Street was burned to the ground, leaving its entire Catholic population homeless. In all a hundred and fifty Catholic homes were gutted, leaving a hundred and sixty people injured and six dead, one of whom was a Protestant. Overnight, in the space of a few hours the Falls Road area of Belfast had become a war zone, and when daylight came the landscape was transformed.

Much of Northern Ireland was now lawless, with looting, violence and arson spreading throughout the province. After a further day of mayhem, when the death toll had reached ten and the number injured by gunfire over a hundred, Stormont and Westminster agreed to the swift deployment of British troops in the Catholic areas of Belfast and Londonderry. The soldiers were welcomed as saviours by the Nationalist population, who greeted them with cups of tea and gratitude. Certainly things were now peaceful, if still very tense.

The conflict in the city areas had not affected my business, which had continued to grow during that year. I had strong support from the honest, hard working Loyalists in our area, whose creed above all seemed to be live and let live. We did have a boycott of anything 'Irish' including butter at our local Co-op, but it was a short-lived protest. Perhaps it was the deflecting effect of the army in the cities which caused the trouble, when it did first arrive, to appear not within our own community, but from outsiders. When two Catholic pubs in Donaghadee were petrol bombed and the front of the Catholic church was set alight the blame was put on Loyalist gangs who'd been out drinking in Donaghadee and after carrying out the arson attacks, made their escape back to Belfast. In each case neighbours rallied round, along with many other locals of all religions, organising sales of work, cake baking and the like to establish a fund for repairs and other kinds of support. Our community it seemed was resolved to remain united against the forces of violence and discord.

Meanwhile trade at the garage continued to improve, and more staff were taken on. On the crash repair side, auto insurance jobs now constituted a high percentage of the work, and I had begun travelling regularly into Belfast, visiting insurance firms and other garages, covering territory from the Falls Road to the Shankhill in the line of business. One Monday morning I had arranged to meet a friend called Joe in Belfast, and Patricia was coming along in the car too. Having picked up Joe, we had just turned into Sandy Row when we spotted a group of UDA men stationed on the roadside up ahead. We were in a Loyalist area and liable to be stopped and questioned if they thought we might be Catholic. However our car gave no clue as to our religion. Or so I thought – for Joe suddenly noticed something we had not. After the church service the day before Patricia had left her Rosary beads in the car, and now they were sat in full view above the dashboard. Without a word Joe grabbed the beads and put them in my pocket. I drove slowly past the UDA men, trying to look neither in a hurry or too casual either. We all breathed a sigh of relief as soon as the Loyalists were safely out of sight. After an appointment at Marshall Watson's garage, where I had to pay for three cars and trade one in, then various other calls, I arrived at Greenan's Garage in Lesson Street, round the corner from the Falls Road, where I was to pick up a vehicle already purchased.

I had left Patricia and Joe in the car and was walking up to the premises when I felt a burning sensation in my eyes. One of the garage workers was already wise to what had happened. 'It's the CS gas' he shouted, 'Get out!' Squinting up the road I saw infantry running and makeshift barricades being erected. An RUC armoured car raced past, followed quickly by another. The crowds gathered across the road scattered as the vehicles approached them. More CS gas was being fired and the air was filling with smog-like clouds. I could see two cars and a bus already on fire in an attempt to block off the street. As a shot rang out from the nearby Clonard area, I realised there was no option but to retreat, and get myself, Patricia and Joe out of the danger zone. I just hoped the vehicle, which I'd already paid for, would still be in one piece when I came back. The garage man quickly gave me directions for the safest route out of the area, and I ran back to the car, where Patricia and Joe were waiting anxiously. I drove off, making my way via the Grosvenor Road as advised, though there were more troops on the street here. Next day I returned to the Falls Road with one of my employees, and found the area now quiet. The burnt-out vehicles had been cleared away, and with relief I saw the car I'd purchased was safe and sound. We drove off over large patches in the road where the fires had melted the tar the previous evening.

12

Internment

With the arrival of the British Army, being under surveillance soon became a feature of everyday life for the residents of Northern Ireland. In key parts of the city centre tall metal poles sprouted up, on top of which were mounted CCTV cameras to monitor civilian movements day and night. Still needing to make frequent trips into town on business, I remarked to friends that I must now be one of the most photographed men in Belfast. At the army checkpoints road ramps had been put down, one of them so high it ripped the exhaust clean off my new Mercedes on one occasion. The root of the ongoing tension and violence in the province was of course the sectarian divide between Catholic and Protestant. There were many individuals though who, through family circumstances, had a foot on either side of the fence, or in the case of my friend Roy, saw people as people, regardless of their faith. Roy was a spray painter who'd formerly been a British soldier and was now married to a Catholic girl, though he himself remained a Protestant. Roy lived near Sandy Row in Belfast, and one evening a group of men had arrived with the intention of burning out Roy's neighbours, a Catholic family with young children. Roy, a tall and broad-shouldered man, stepped out to reason with the group. When they refused to listen Roy went indoors, fetched his revolver and told them in no uncertain terms to leave and not come back. Thanks to his courage the family were not troubled again. One evening I was giving Roy a lift home through Belfast when we heard gunfire. It seemed we were in close proximity to a fire fight between the

Provisional IRA, now equipped with modern Armalite rifles, and a British patrol. RUC Land Rovers and the British armoured cars were swarming everywhere. Up ahead of us were some burning barricades and we passed both UDA and Provo units, who were flagging down drivers. Roy surveyed the threatening scenes around us. 'You can let me off here, I'm not far from home now' he said. 'But listen' he warned as he stepped from the car, 'don't stop for anyone other than the army'. 'Alright Roy' I said, 'thanks'. I wished him a safe journey home and pushed on. Approaching Newtownards Road I saw a large cloud of black smoke rising high into the evening sky. Suddenly a group of men came running towards the car, shouting and waving their arms aggressively. I felt my heart start racing. I'd heard the recent horror stories of drivers being randomly pulled from their cars and beaten, or worse. As the men drew closer I knew I had to make a decision. There was a side street just ahead, though there was no telling what I might find down there. I put my foot down and turned quickly off the main road. Seeing the street quiet and free from obstruction I breathed a sigh of relief, and was able from here to circumnavigate my way back onto the main road and get safely home to Donaghadee. It had been a nerve-wracking few minutes.

It was now approaching midsummer, and the local workforce was looking forward to the annual July holidays. The Donaghadee carpet factory, the largest employer in the area would be giving all its staff time off, and big crowds were expected to attend the speedboat racing in the bay. Come the day of the event almost a hundred boats from all over Ulster turned up. Steady streams of spectators called at the garage shop for refreshments, and we did a good trade throughout in sandwiches, drinks, ices and sweets. I had made an arrangement to sponsor the petrol and oils for the speedboat event and with the boats bobbing and skimming round the bay for several hours at a time our pumps were kept busy.

The success of the race day and seeing how the services of our shop and garage had played a part in so many people's enjoyment as they flocked to the nearby beaches made me feel more confident than ever about my future intentions regarding the business. My grand plan, which I had been mulling over carefully for some time was to redevelop the whole site, from the road frontage right back to the seashore which lay behind. The crash and mechanical workshops were to be relocated to a larger building near the old gasworks in Donaghadee harbour. This would free up space on the subterranean floor of the garage for additional used car sales, whilst the forecourt above could be rebuilt with extra pumps. I would apply for a 'VG Stores' supermarket franchise for the shop and have it completely refitted, and a swish showroom for the recently assigned new car dealership would be constructed. But the piece de resistance was to extend the building up above the showroom and the shop, thus adding an entire additional storey to the premises. This new top floor would house the offices, while the remaining area of some two thousand square feet would be fitted out as a high-class restaurant. In the daytime we would serve lunches and snacks and in the evenings customers could enjoy fine dining with cabaret entertainment. Large picture windows at the rear of the restaurant would provide everyone with spectacular views out across the ocean, watching the boating events during the day, and at night the romantic sight of the stately passenger ships gliding slowly across the horizon with their twinkling lights. There would no doubt be many a marriage proposal made and anniversary meals held in this enchanting venue, I felt sure of it. With the idyllic coastal location we could also host wedding receptions, birthdays and many other types of special function. I had discussed it with Patricia and we could see it all so clearly. Further into the future a marina could be built out the back, utilising the slipway of the old lifeboat station. All in all it would be a little piece of paradise. I already had a name for the new restaurant. It was to be called 'The Showboat'.

With the summer holidays coming to an end, extra troops arrived in the province, bringing the army strength to almost twelve thousand. The RUC, including reservists, numbered ten thousand. With the addition of the Ulster Defence Regiment (UDR) which comprised many B-Specials, Northern Ireland was very much an armed camp. Just after 3am on the morning of 9th August 1971, residents of the Catholic areas of Belfast and elsewhere were roused from their slumbers by the rumble of armoured Saracen vehicles. Soldiers ran from house to house, dragging suspected republican activists from their beds and packing them into huge removal vans. If doors were not opened they would be broken down. Shouting and sporadic shots could be heard piercing the night air. All along the houses, from street to street, the dustbin-lids started to bang rhythmically and resoundingly on the pavements. This was the dread signal among the Catholic community that the much-rumoured internment was beginning. Hundreds were rounded up, and despite requests by the British government to the Northern Ireland Prime Minister Brian Faulkner, no Protestants were included in the trawl. The internees were taken to interrogation centres without trial, where, as has been well-documented, they were beaten and tortured over periods of several days. Many were innocent of any crime whatsoever. The list of over four hundred Catholic men to be seized had been drawn up by the RUC's Special Branch.

It was on the 10th August – 'day two' of internment – that I found myself at around ten in the morning, chatting on the sales forecourt to a prospective buyer. The sun was shining and the atmosphere quiet and peaceful. As the customer talked amicably I saw over his shoulder a large car draw up and park on the main road. Inside the car were three men, who appeared to be looking over towards the premises. Perhaps they were interested in one of the vehicles I had for sale, I thought. When my customer left, two men got out of the car and walked up to the forecourt. They wore dark suits and were fairly tall. 'Good morning' said the first man, and asked me to confirm my name. Clearly these were not customers. 'We're with the RUC Special Branch. How do you feel about what's happening in Ulster right now?' I replied: 'I don't agree with violence, I just want a quiet life like most people.' They nodded slowly then the other man said, 'How do you feel about the internments?' I hesitated, knowing this was an attempt to provoke me. 'Well I've a business to run here as you see, and fourteen staff and their families all relying on it for their weekly wage. I have an uncle in the RUC.' I volunteered. 'We know about that' snapped the second man, 'and don't think it'll help you.' The atmosphere was now very strained, and I responded instinctively with a few bitter comments, finding it impossible to conceal my own anger and disgust at what I'd heard about the internments. I also knew this was making my own situation more dangerous. The third man, who by contrast to the other two wore a light blue suit, had now come over, but remained silent and listened to what was being said. After a few minutes the first man said, 'Don't be leaving the premises' and they all three returned to the car and drove off. By twelve noon they were back, and this time the man in the light blue suit did a lot more talking. I was interrogated about my history, going right back to my childhood. They knew all about my time in prison of course, and about my failed attempt to join the RUC. The thought crossed my mind that both these experiences might well predispose me to IRA sympathies in their eyes. 'Maybe', said the man in the blue suit, 'you should come along with us, and we can clear this up.' I said there was nothing to clear up as far as I was concerned. 'I served time in the Crumlin and later was acquitted, that's all in the past. I bear no grudge to any man'. The blue-suited man looked at me. 'That's for us to decide.' Where was all this leading I wondered. If they wanted to take me why didn't they get on with it? Probably they were trying to stir me to anger, to throw a punch maybe, just to get an excuse to brand me a troublemaker and bundle me in that car. The questioning continued for what must have been well over half an hour – about my friends, my family and religion, where I drank, what I thought of the government and the British, my views on the IRA. Finally, with deliberate courtesy, they thanked me for my time and left. Glad of a change of scene, I left the garage and went home for some lunch, not mentioning anything of the morning's events to Patricia. Back at work, I busied myself around the forecourt and tried to forget about what had happened. It must have been about 4pm and I was just about to go in the office and make a cup of tea, when I saw the blue-suited man appear again. My heart sank, thinking they had made some further enquiries, perhaps finding out about my pal in the football team who'd invited me to go shooting with the IRA all that time ago. It would be more than enough for them. This time however, my visitor was very polite, and seemed both relaxed and friendly. We sat down on the low wall bordering the forecourt. 'We know you have sympathy with the Royal Ulster Constabulary...' he began. I made no comment, but felt annoyed. The man's smarmy approach now was suspicious. 'How is your business doing?' the man went on. I made some non-committal replies about the motor trade, and as the conversation moved on, I slipped in the remark that a policeman friend of our family whom we had known in Lisanaskea was now a senior officer in Belfast. If dropping a name would keep me out of the barbed wire of Long Kesh then so be it. Whether this had any effect or not I couldn't tell, but the man finally seemed satisfied with what had passed between us. He got up, thanked me politely once again for sparing him my time, and bid me good day. Back home that evening I told Patricia all that gone on with the RUC men. She agreed it had been 'touch and go' and that they'd been hoping for some pretext to have me interned with all the other poor innocent devils. All I knew was that I had to put this unnerving day behind me and look to the future. My architect had now drawn up the plans for the redevelopment of the business, and I was keen to look over them again after dinner. Northern Ireland might be in turmoil, but one day soon peace would reign, and by that time the famous 'Showboat Restaurant' Donaghadee would be opening its doors to the world.

13

A Visit to Shankill

'Philip can I have a word?'

'What is it?' I replied. It was early evening and I had just got in from the garage to find Patricia sitting at the kitchen table frowning.

'It's the children...'

'What's happened – are they all right?' I asked anxiously.

'No, no they're fine' Patricia reassured me. 'They're playing in the other room now. It was earlier on, coming home from the convent that it happened' Our eldest daughter was now at secondary school in Bangor, but the youngest girl and boy, aged six and five were still at the private school run by the church, and in the evenings would walk home by themselves. 'Apparently they were on the footpath just opposite the petrol station' said Patricia, referring to another garage a little way away, 'when a gang of boys came along and started picking on them, calling names and pushing and shoving them.' I went immediately into the other room and talked to the two little ones. It seemed fairly clear their tormentors had been from the large local comprehensive, and having seen the distinctive convent uniforms had taken it into their heads to attack the two little children wearing them. From what they'd already told Patricia, the owner of the garage had come to their assistance when he saw what was happening, and the gang of youths had fled across the fields to the housing estate. 'They were both very upset when they got home' said Patricia, 'I knew something was wrong. It's terrible that little ones should get treated like that just because of a school uniform.' I felt as aggrieved as Patricia, and decided there and then to telephone the staff at the comprehensive school in an attempt to track down those responsible for this intimidation. The person on the other end said I should talk to Mr McKeag about the matter. This sounded encouraging, since I knew Mr McKeag as a regular customer at the filling station. Mr McKeag however had just gone home. I explained what had happened, and was assured the matter would be looked into. Next morning, still extremely vexed by the incident, I phoned the school again and this time was put through to Mr McKeag, who expressed his regret at what had occurred and told me he was about to conduct enquiries among his pupils. Unable to let the matter rest I called back at lunchtime, but was told the staff had not as yet found out which pupils had been involved. Predictably, none of the boys would own up to such a cowardly assault on two small children. That they were ashamed was right and proper, but it was also in everyone's interests that they came forward. That evening I received a telephone call from Mr McKeag. He had gone through the whole school systematically, questioning the pupils closely about their movements the previous evening and finally succeeded in getting the culprits to own up. The boys had, said Mr McKeig, been left in no doubt about the serious and shameful nature of their actions and appropriately severe punishments had been meted out. I thanked Mr McKeig for his prompt attention to the matter and put down the receiver feeling a little easier in my mind. From then on however I made sure every afternoon to pick the two small ones up from the convent school and bring them straight home. I didn't want to risk a repeat performance. There were no further incidents though, and the children continued to play happily with their friends around the neighbourhood during the evenings and weekends. Hopefully between us the teachers and I had nipped any sectarian feelings among the local school kids in the bud.

In addition to developing the garage site to incorporate the new showroom, shop and restaurant, there was another project I had in the back of my mind. A short distance outside

Donaghadee on the main coast road to Millisle, was a hotel, which had stood empty and up for sale for a long time. Having looked over the place it seemed to me an ideal opportunity to diversify my business interests into the field of tourism. However, with the garage development soon to be underway and requiring funds, I would have to find a source of extra cash to put towards purchasing the hotel. I therefore contacted a large finance company and made an appointment with the manager. Over tea and biscuits in his office I explained about the hotel and how I felt it would complement my garage and proposed restaurant business, each providing custom for the other as it were, especially if the marina idea at Donaghadee also went ahead. The manger seemed suitably impressed and agreed to assist with the finance. As we wrapped up the meeting with some general conversation it transpired he and I were both from County Fermanagh, and he had attended Portora School in Enniskillen. He asked what school I had attended. When I replied with the name of my old school the manager nodded and got up from his desk. As I walked to the door he held out his hand for me to shake. At that moment I had what you might call a gut feeling about what was to happen next. I knew about freemasons and their peculiar handshakes to check who is and is not 'one of them'. The handshake I received from the finance manager that day was definitely unusual, and proffered in a very deliberate manner. As I left the office the manager smiled and said he would be writing to me about our business agreement. Making my way home I pondered on the meeting, which had seemed so positive and then concluded with the enquiry about my school. And the handshake – had it been a mason's, and if so what did it signify that I hadn't returned the appropriate grip? One can never be absolutely certain about these things of course. All I do know is that the man never wrote to me as he said he would, and I never heard another word from him.

However as the saying goes, there are always plenty more fish in the sea, and if it's true in affairs of the heart then it's equally so with money matters. I certainly found this to be the case, for having been given the cold shoulder by one man over the wrong handshake, I soon found another backer, a private individual of means, a Mr Black from Belfast. Mr Black was unconcerned with old school ties, religion or masonry, his chief priority being to invest his cash in an honest well thought out enterprise that seemed likely to give him a good return. Having approved my scheme, Mr Black was more than willing to assist with any finance required. In the meantime I decided to realise some capital of my own, and hold a sale of my existing second-hand car stock at reduced prices, with credit arrangements offered through a small hire purchase company in Belfast. The cars were no use sitting on the premises, and the money raised would be best utilised in developing the business for the future. At keen prices the vehicles soon found eager buyers, many of them from far afield. One buyer, a pub manager, paid me half the money for the vehicle on the day of purchase and, since he had yet to arrange insurance, asked if I would deliver the car and tax book to his workplace in Belfast, when he would pay the balance. I agreed to the arrangement, but when my employees discovered where the pub was, none of them wanted to make this particular delivery with me. And I couldn't blame them, since the premises was located almost opposite Templeton's garage at the top of the Shankill Road, now notorious for some of the worst outbreaks of violence in the city. I therefore asked Tony my younger brother if he would pick me up after I'd driven the car up and handed it over to the customer. It should be safe enough I thought. We were both well known at the garage from buying spare parts for Alfas there, and it wasn't as though we were going to hang around sight-seeing after the drop. I took the vehicle in one Saturday, and after a smooth drive through the city arrived at the pub and parked down a nearby side road. I crossed the street and went in to find the place packed out with afternoon drinkers and very noisy. A TV set above the window facing out towards the Shankill Road was showing the weekend horse racing. At the far end darts were being played and behind the bar six barmen were being kept very busy by the throng of customers. Knowing the pub to be a Loyalist drinking spot I immediately felt uncomfortable, and being clearly not a regular I was already getting some odd looks from one or two people, which added to my anxiety. I looked up and down the bar, trying to see through the crowds and catch a glimpse of the manager to let him know I had arrived. Then I saw him, and he at the same time nodded to me then came over. 'We're a bit busy' he said over the loud hubbub of conversation, 'I'll be with you in a minute or two.' I thanked him, feeling slightly more at ease now it had been seen that the governor of the pub knew me. 'Will you have a drink?' he asked. 'Thanks' I replied, 'just an orange juice.' Leaving me nursing a glass of orange he then disappeared up the other end of the bar. As I'd hoped, now the manager had spoken to me everyone seemed to ignore me. Except that is for one elderly man sat near the television. Catching sight of him from the corner of my eye, he seemed to be studying me closely. Feeling awkward just standing there I deliberately turned my gaze up towards the TV. Then, cutting right through the din of the racing commentary and the animated talk of the crowd, the old man who'd been staring at me rasped out 'Are you a Taig?' I pretended not to have heard and focused my eyes even more intently on the television screen, and fixing such an earnest expression on my face that anyone might think I had a thousand pounds riding on the next race. Meanwhile, apart from the sound on the TV, the bar had suddenly gone very quiet. The clatter of glasses had ceased, the dart players had stopped throwing and every conversation stalled in mid-flow. I sensed several dozen heads turning towards me. Then it came again, loud and clear. 'I said, you down there – are you a Taig?' The silence throughout the bar was palpable, even the TV seemed to have been muffled. At several tables chairs scraped back as their occupants moved around to see what was going on. I'd drained the orange juice and my throat was suddenly dry as sandpaper. I darted my eyes towards the door. If I made a run for it I would surely be pursued, and just as surely caught. God knows what might happen then. Utterly petrified I stood rooted to the spot, my hand gripped tightly round the empty glass. It seemed like an eternity went by, until another voice finally broke the silence. 'Have you the tax book too?' I looked across at the bar. The manager was wiping his hands with a towel and looking enquiringly at me. 'I have' I nodded. He then lifted the bar flap and beckoned me through. As suddenly as it had ceased the pub noise resumed again. The loud conversations took up briskly where they had left off, glasses and bottles chinked and the dart players returned to their game. It was as if for a few moments the whole place had been like a film snagged in mid-reel and the picture frozen in suspended animation. Now, hearing the manager address me in tones of familiarity, the projector could roll again and the characters get back to their drinking and their lives. My identity had been assured and everything could go on as normal. The stranger in their midst was not it seemed a 'Taig' after all. I had been given the benefit of the doubt. The manager led me through to his back office and sorted out the balance that he owed me for the car. As I handed him the tax book and a receipt and we shook hands I realised I now had to go back through the bar to get out. Would the place fall silent again, and, being scrutinised a second time, would the assembled drinkers come to a different conclusion about me? Sensing the concern on my face, the manager suggested I leave by the rear exit, and took me through to a small door which led out onto a side street just around the corner from where I'd parked the car. After a quick check of the vehicle my client waved me off and disappeared back to his duties at the bar. Across the road my brother Tony was waiting anxiously by his car to take me home. 'How was it?' he asked as I climbed thankfully into the passenger seat. 'Not the easiest business trip I've ever made' I replied, and on the way back told him what had happened, whilst looking forward to getting indoors and having a drink of something a little stronger than orange juice. Later on I heard that the bar manager had 'disappeared' shortly after helping me that day.

14

Talk of the Town

The little town of Donaghadee was always full of life. Entertainment for Patricia and I was to be found only a five minute stroll away from our bungalow, at the Moate Inn. This wee pub was convivial and inviting, and the old buildings to the rear of the premises had been converted to house a bar extension and dance-floor. The interior had the quaint old-fashioned look, with fishing nets and other antique tackle suspended from the wooden rafters. The dancing and sing-a-longs at the Moate Inn when everyone joined in were nothing short of electrifying on a good night. Another pub across town was owned by a customer of mine at the garage, a Catholic man, and we would also frequent this establishment. The proprietor's only son Freddie was a fellow pupil of my own lad, now at a private school. Freddie's dad was unlucky however, in that on a few occasions petrol bombs had been thrown at the premises. At first the man tried to ignore the problem and carry on regardless. When the attacks persisted however he decided enough was enough and, for the sake of his family's safety and peace of mind, put the pub up for sale. Lo and behold the business was bought at a rock-bottom price and sold on shortly afterwards making a large profit for someone. Despite the appearance of harmony in the area, such things went on, and one could only guess at who was behind it all. Beneath the day-to-day affability a climate of quiet suspicion had begun to build up. Everyone was anxiously watching their neighbours, yet equally anxious not to betray the fact. One morning, one of my employees took me aside and told me in confidence that my own name often came up at the local Orange Lodge meetings. Being a predominantly Protestant area, the Orange Order naturally held great sway on the council and in local affairs generally. I asked my employee why the Orange Lodge should be interested in me. His reply was that questions were frequently being asked about my business and the plans for developing the site, the restaurant, the hotel and so forth. I thanked him and said I'd be careful, but didn't really think there was much I could do one way or the other. If the local authority voted to reject my plans, I would appeal or reapply, and let the process take its lawful course. I already knew that where the Orange Lodge could have stopped my expansion plans was through financial restraint, yet I'd crossed that bridge after the encounter with the Masonic handshake fellow. I had my own capital accrued from car sales and savings, and my private backer Mr Black from Belfast was right behind me. Furthermore I was not in a vulnerable position regarding overdrafts or loans with my local branch of the Ulster Bank, having only ploughed existing profits back into the business. All in all, the road was clear for me on the money front.

Throughout that year I continued travelling to and from Belfast, trading cars or picking up spare parts. I was a regular customer at the Radiator Repair Centre on the Albertbridge Road, where a friend of mine was a dab hand at refurbishing radiators from crashed vehicles, and would always be pleased to do this work for me and have them ready on time. In the city generally, and particularly in the Albertbridge Road area groups of young men standing around on street corners talking had became more noticeable. What they discussed was hard to know exactly, but it was no doubt of more serious intent than the weather or the price of butter. The mood throughout Belfast remained volatile. After the British Army had embarked on the internments without trial for suspected terrorists, and that terrible wave of violence had been unleashed throughout Belfast, it was difficult to see how the intense atmosphere of conflict could be resolved. In the two days following the internments, when the twenty-one civilians and two soldiers had been left dead, it later emerged that one of the victims had been a young priest who was administering the last rites to a dying man in the street. Nothing it now seemed was sacred and no-one immune from the possibility of violent death. Anxiety had taken a grip on the Loyalist population of Northern Ireland. They now feared more than ever being forced into a 'United Ireland', in which they would lose their way of life and power base. The Nationalist viewpoint on the other hand was that of a long history of injustice towards them, of being treated as second-class citizens in the North, and that the old British strategy of 'divide and rule' had left them the losing side ever since the partition of Ireland. Those with no axe to grind either way could only hope for some kind of compromise. One could certainly find precedents where the sectarian divide had been crossed or simply ignored. It might seem a trivial example, but Scottish and Irish music and dancing have much in common, being similarly 'Celtic' in flavour. And in the south, many Protestants had flourished within a Catholic society, most notably the great scholar and academic Dr Douglas Hyde, who became the first President of Ireland in 1938. Was it too much to expect there to one day be a mirror image of this – in other words a similar acceptance of Catholics in the public life of Ulster? As I say, all we could do was hope and pray.

In the October of 1971 I had the unfortunate occasion to dismiss one of my employees. I now had a total of fourteen members of staff, all of them good workers, save for this particular lad, to whom I had given two verbal warnings, followed by a written one. Finally I had no choice but to sack him. Such things are regrettable but occasionally unavoidable in any workplace, and since I had followed the fair and legal procedure, I thought no more about the incident until the following Monday morning, when the lad's mother appeared at the garage and demanded to know why her son had been sacked. I politely gave her the full story, making it clear he had been given full and proper warnings. The woman remained furious however, and refused to accept the justness or logic of the case. I also became irate at being accused of mistreating an employee. Angry words were exchanged between us, and as the woman left my office she turned and remarked darkly 'It won't be long before you're out of town!' Afterwards I mentioned the incident to my foreman, who of course knew all about the dismissal. He then informed me that the woman was in fact the Grand Mistress of the local Orange Order. As I went back to work I reflected that the Order would now have something else to discuss at their next meeting.

With November the days grew shorter, and the first chill breezes of winter could be felt blowing in from the Irish Sea and across the exposed tip of the Ards Peninsula. Although the nights were turning cold, the dark evenings brought compensations to warm the spirit, not least the passenger ships gliding slowly and silently across the horizon, with their floodlit decks and tiny dots of bright light from the cabin portholes. There is something magnificent and gladdening about ocean-going vessels, even the sturdy and functional container ships that frequently passed us, with their two or three lights signalling cheerily into the vast, black night. Making for Portavogie and the other harbours along the Peninsula, one could also see the little fishing boats picked out by a single bobbing light. Perhaps it is the timeless nature of the sea and its relation to humanity that makes ships so reassuring, the knowledge that man has travelled thus on the great trade routes of the world for centuries and will doubtless continue to do so. Come wars, disasters, technological innovation or what passes for progress, the ships will always put to sea.

Looking to the future, I had now enrolled with Queens University in Belfast to study part-time for a degree that would help me in the business. Meantime I still had my eye on the hotel on the Millisle Road, and was putting together a business plan for the project. I had also received some surprising news via my workshop manager, a long-standing local man, who informed me the RUC were considering choosing my garage for their fuel supply contract for the following year. Police vehicles already called in from time to time to fill up, but I had never expected to have them as account customers. Though predominantly a Loyalist institution, the RUC contained many fair-minded men and women in its ranks, and I thought it was possible they were seeking to award business to a Catholic-owned garage as a sign of good faith and integration. More realistically, I realised the fact that my petrol was the cheapest in town was probably a factor in my favour. The annual fuel contracts were rotated so presumably I was next in line. Whatever the motive, the contract would increase the garage's turnover and the timing for the next year couldn't be better, considering everything else that was now in the pipeline. The architects' plans for the redevelopment of the garage site had been submitted to the local authority, and it was now a case of keeping my fingers crossed while the wheels of bureaucracy turned. I knew these things took time, and that it could be months before full planning permission was granted. I was therefore surprised one morning early that November to purchase the local paper, the Newtownards Spectator and see the following headlines: '£100,000 DEVELOPMENT ON THE COAST ROAD AT DONAGHADEE, BY A THIRTY-TWO YEAR-OLD FERMANAGH MAN, WITH A YOUNG WIFE AND FAMILY – EDUCATED IN NORTHERN IRELAND AND WITH FAITH IN THE FUTURE OF ULSTER' The article then went on: '…his ambitious development is set to include a petrol station, new car showrooms, franchise for a VG supermarket. Above the existing garage building will be a whole additional storey housing a 2,000 square foot cabaret restaurant called 'The Showboat', with French windows leading onto a balcony and a beautiful view of Donaghadee Harbour, the Copeland Islands and Scotland on a bright day…. he also intends building a marina for boats if planning permission is granted…' I read the article over again, not knowing whether to feel thrilled or not. It showed me as a man with grand plans, though I hoped not as some sort of greedy empire builder. Publicity they say is always good, but since the full permission had not yet been granted I was wary of counting any chickens before they'd hatched. Confident, but not overconfident had to be my watchword, as the winter nights drew in and, despite the troubles elsewhere in Ulster, the people of Donaghadee talked more and more about 'the new development up on the coast road…'

107

PART TWO

1

December 8th 1971

'How are you feeling?

It was not an easy question to answer. I turned my gaze from the smouldering building, where men from the RUC were picking their way through the charred rubble and looked at the Fire Chief. I sighed and shook my head a little, unable to give him a proper reply. He understood, and nodded sympathetically. The truth was I felt sleepy, as if I were still dreaming, but that was probably the continuing effects of the sedatives the doctor had given me the night before. If only this was a dream, and that I could wake up and find the garage as it would normally be at this time of the morning – customers queuing for petrol, cars gleaming on the forecourt and the workshop ringing with the sound of drills and spanners. But no, the barely recognisable gaping roof, the steel girders buckled from the intense heat and the blackened walls together with the smell of burnt wood and molten rubber were all too horribly real. So were the expressions on the faces of my employees, some of whom had come along to survey the damage this morning. They too offered their sympathies, but having seen the state of their workplace I also knew they were worried about their own future. The garage clearly could not operate in its present state. The most important thing, as everyone kept saying, was that by the grace of God no-one had been injured. One eighty-three year old lady living nearby had been treated for shock after her house was rocked by the explosion, and a group of people waiting for the bus after bingo had taken cover from falling slates and pieces of wood thrown into the air by the blast, but that was as close as anyone got to being physically hurt. And then there was me of course. I thought back to our troublesome TV which had kept me in the house for those vital few minutes. If some dull programme in which I'd not been interested had been showing I would not have tarried, and would have left immediately for the garage. I never thought I'd be thanking the Good Lord for the gift of a cowboy film. There was something else to be grateful for; the Fire Chief confided to me that his biggest worry last night had been the petrol storage tanks. If they'd blown the damage would have been much worse, leaving just a large crater in the ground and almost certainly casualties in the surrounding area. As it was, at least the site was intact and no residential properties had been touched. Three cars that had been parked on the far side of the sales yard, close to the sea were unscathed, and it was obvious that these would also have been destroyed if the tanks had gone up.

As the Fire Chief rejoined his crew another man came up to me. It was the proprietor of another crash repair garage situated on the other side of Donaghadee. 'You and I are competitors' he said sombrely, 'but it was never meant to be like this now was it. I'm very sorry.' I thanked him for turning up. It was decent of him to show his support, I thought. Back at the bungalow callers had begun looking in with similar kind words and offers of help, particularly our local priest. We had already learned on the news that we weren't the only ones to have been hit the night before, and that a series of bomb attacks, several on petrol stations, had occurred across Northern Ireland. No-one had claimed responsibility, though people were saying they thought it was probably the work of Loyalist gangs from Belfast. Something else we'd been told was that the tanker driver with our petrol delivery had been only a few miles away when the garage went up. When he heard what had happened he'd diverted his vehicle. I wondered – could the bombers have hoped to catch the vehicle in the explosion too? It would have been a nice bonus from their point of view. I pictured the possible scenario if that had happened – a fully laden tanker of petrol, exploding possibly on the move and careering into houses, ours, our neighbours. A quarter of a mile up the road stood our local Cenotaph memorial to the fallen Irishmen of two world wars where, just a few weeks ago, on the eleventh hour of the eleventh day of the eleventh month, we had observed the two-minutes silence and on a clear, cold Remembrance Sunday watched the laying of the wreath. What sacrilege it would have been if that monument in honour of the dead had been destroyed. Perhaps it had in some way safeguarded all our lives last night. Count your blessings they say, count your blessings... But it was hard. After coming close to death in such a fashion I already had the feeling that being grateful to be alive would not be a simple matter. Apart from the shock and disbelief of seeing the business I'd worked so hard to build up smashed and ruined overnight, my own narrow escape was in itself a frightening thing to be perpetually reminded of. I could only hope, in my still tired and stupefied state that time would quickly heal the memory of last night's terrifying flames and that I would be able to get back on my feet, emotionally as well as financially. My suppliers, the Jet petrol company were soon on the phone asking about the incident and seeing what they could do to help in the situation. Meanwhile I had to make some decisions about the staff, and it was with a heavy heart that I informed all of them – save for my workshop manager whom I kept on – that they were now out of work. They understood there was no choice of course, but with Christmas so close it was a tough time. I paid everyone up to the last week of December, together with any holiday money accrued.

At home Patricia and I sat around subdued and anxious, not knowing what to do with ourselves. How could an event such as this have befallen us, we kept asking ourselves – bombs and disasters had always seemed the kind of thing that happened to other people. But looking at the faces of our children, whose only thoughts had been excitement about Santa Claus and the magic of the coming festive season, we knew that for their sake we must be brave, accept our situation and make the best of things. A couple of days later an official from the council called and advised me to contact a solicitor, as I would be able to claim compensation for the criminal damage to the garage. This was a bit of good news, and encouraged us in the hope of getting the business up and running again. Shortly afterwards, the architect who'd drawn up the plans for the redevelopment came round and inspected the damage. His opinion was that the walls on which we'd intended adding the second storey to house the Showboat Restaurant may have been weakened in the blast and that a quantity surveyor should take a look. When the surveyor turned up and gave his verdict it was as had been feared; the building was substantially damaged and now constituted a dangerous structure. Two days later he sent an estimate for restoration of the building to the condition prior to the explosion. Hopefully I thought, this cost could be met in full by compensation as and when I could get it, and after an interview with my solicitor the week before Christmas I had the feeling that at least I was putting the wheels in motion as regards the future. My immediate worry, with the weather on the peninsula liable to be stormy in the winter, was that loose slates and rubble could blow down onto the road and cause accidents, for which I could well be held liable. It was therefore a relief when council workmen arrived one day and boarded up the site. This didn't stop the effects of the driving wind and rain however, which had already begun to wash the mortar from the exposed walls. When I raised the matter with the council's engineer I was told it was not their responsibility. I could therefore attempt either to patch up the garage before it deteriorated further or, as seemed necessary following the surveyor's report, wait and have it completely rebuilt. But this could take some time, and I had been hoping, since the underground petrol storage tanks were intact, to re-open early in the new year for fuel sales, which would provide some income at least. But undertaking crash repairs would require a shelter of some kind from which to operate. One option was to purchase a portable cabin such as are used on construction sites and erect it by the pumps, so I could break off from repair work when customers pulled in for fuel. When I put this to the council they said they'd have no objections whatever. It was therefore decided for safety reasons to demolish what remained of the garage and put a cabin on site as soon as was practicable, which now would be after Christmas.

Knowing now that there was a way of salvaging the business and with the feeling that our friends, neighbours, customers and the local council would be behind us in our endeavours, Patricia and I could in a cautious way at least begin to look to the future. This hope of a renewal made things a little easier to bear than they might otherwise have been that Christmas. Whatever our private anxieties, Patricia and I were determined if possible to create the festive spirit come what may and ensure it was a joyous and pleasant time for the whole family. Fortunately we had been putting some money aside and were able not only to buy presents, but did not skimp on the fine Yuletide food and drinks and all the usual trimmings. Patricia's sister Nora and her husband Christy had already arrived to stay with us over the holiday and their company could not have come at a more welcome time. The kids adored their Uncle and Aunty and having them about the house lifted Patricia and I out of our worries. Christy was handicapped by partial sight, yet was uncomplaining and all for fun, especially when it came to music and a sing-along in the pub. On Christmas morning I arose early and set about cleaning out the open fireplace. It wasn't long before the two little ones appeared with excited faces in the living room, soon followed by their older sister. All three gazed in wonder and enchantment at the tantalising presents wrapped in brightly-coloured Christmas gift paper – snow-covered scenes of robins, sleigh-bells, Santa, snowmen and fairies. Patricia and I had stacked them all beneath the tree the night before and now the house really did look as though Father Christmas had been to see us. 'Go on then' I said with a twinkle in my eye to match the look of eagerness in theirs, 'I know you can't wait – shall we see what Santa Claus has brought?' They didn't need telling a second time and raced with whoops of delight to the tree. Anyone in the house who wasn't by that time up was aroused by the noise and laughter. The floor was rapidly strewn with paper as Patricia and I, Nora and Christy smiled at the unfolding chaos and listened to the children chattering ecstatically about their new toys, whilst helping out here and there with the clockwork or battery-operated ones to get them going. It was the kind of happy scene to be found no doubt in countless homes the length and breadth of the land that Christmas morning. The turkey, stuffed and prepared the night before, was put in the oven to cook whilst breakfast, the traditional Ulster fry, was laid on the kitchen table. With all the excitement the children were slow to sit down and eat. 'Come on now you three' coaxed Patricia, 'we have to be at Mass at eleven.' After the church service we chatted for a while outside the church with others in the small Catholic community of Donaghadee, who expressed their good wishes for us in the New Year. The air was chill, and it was a treat to get back home and light the open fire and enjoy its bright and cheerful warmth. The turkey was almost done, and it was normally the custom in our house that Patricia would take a break from the chores and I would carve and serve up the Christmas meal for everyone. Having been the eldest of eight, I had been used to cooking for several people from a young age, and now with my own family it was something I still loved to do. This year however, with the medication prescribed by my GP since the blast, I got tired very easily, and so it was today for the first time since we were married that Patricia had to help me. Whilst the children amused themselves with their toys we put some carol music on the record player and laid the big oval table for seven including Nora and Christy. The day passed very enjoyably for everyone. Except that is for me. Preparing for the festivities – buying presents, decorating the house and looking forward to the family's excitement – had taken my mind off other things. Now the big day was here thoughts of the business and the consequences of what had happened kept flashing into my mind. Although I kept telling myself we could rebuild, I knew nonetheless the family would suffer. Worries about Patricia and the children – schools, bills, food, the little luxuries we'd grown used to – kept nagging away at my mind as I watched everyone laughing and talking merrily.

A couple of days after Christmas there was a late-night knock at the door. Opening it I was surprised to see my bank manager standing there. 'Won't you come in' I said. He thanked me and said he'd called to offer his sympathies over the explosion at the garage. He condemned what had happened and whoever it was that had carried out such a dreadful act. Patricia and I were sat down in the living room with him when he then said, 'If I were a younger man, I'd not be living in Ireland at all! All my own family are abroad.' I wondered what to make of this remark, but he did not expand on the subject. Before leaving he asked if I would 'kindly call in the bank some time – it's regarding the £80 that is overdrawn on your account.' I felt it understandable the bank should want to clarify how things now stood with my finances, as numerous cheques had been drawn over the past few weeks and no money paid in since the business had been inoperative. Presumably the manager wanted to formalise an overdraft arrangement to tide me through till I had an income stream again. I duly went in the very next day, and paid in £80 there and then to clear the overdrawn amount. I then asked if I could arrange a proper overdraft facility on the account. Since I'd always paid in regular amounts at the branch and had never before gone into the red I had a good credit record. I was therefore shocked when, without a moment's hesitation, the manager politely but firmly declined my request. I left the bank bewildered and angry. Why I kept wondering, had the man called at my home the previous night if he was not prepared to help me? It was not as if I was asking for charity; an overdraft was a perfectly normal business procedure for which I would expect to pay interest. I thought back to what my employee had told me some months previously – that I was under scrutiny by the Orange Lodge. Was my bank manager a member? It was perfectly likely. The Grand Mistress, the woman whose son I had sacked may have carried out her threat and put in a strong word against me long ago. If so the die had already been cast, and now after the explosion they had found their opportunity to try to block me. Taken with the bank manager's veiled comment last night that Ireland was no place for a young man, were they telling me, as indeed she had threatened, to get out? I did not want to jump to conclusions, but this wasn't exactly a difficult one to arrive at.

At the end of the Christmas week Nora and Christy were set to return to their home, and kindly invited Patricia and I to join them and all spend the New Year there together, along with the children too of course. After the incident with the bank manager coming on top of everything else, I was more than ready for a change of scene and so was Patricia. The youngsters naturally begged that we should go to stay at Uncle and Aunties' house. It was therefore unanimous, and having gladly accepted the offer we packed a few bags and set off for Dublin as one big happy family.

2

Holding On

Early in the New Year my architect came down to Warren Road and looked over the ruined garage again. It was clear that the building had become much more dangerous over the Christmas period. Walls were now leaning visibly and some of the steel girders were dangling precipitously from the crumbling brickwork. We agreed a demolition crew should come in immediately to flatten and clear the site. This didn't take long, since the combined effects of the blast and the weeks of bad weather had worn the whole structure loose. Trucks took away the stones, masonry and mangled steelwork, leaving us with an open, though rather rough piece of ground. The portable building I had ordered was a large one made of steel, with sufficient floor space inside to house up to six vehicles and to undertake repairs on them in a sheltered environment. Effectively it would be just like having a garage. The building could be erected in a day or so, and we could then open for business immediately. Before it arrived though, the ground had to be prepared after the demolition and my workshop manager, who was still on the payroll and looking forward to getting back to his old job again, came along to help with the levelling work. With the deposit paid, all we had to wait for now was delivery of the new building, and we could be up and running again, at least as far as doing some crash repairs and trading cars, plus of course the petrol sales. As far as the development was concerned, I told the architect I still had every intention of going ahead, though obviously things would now take longer than originally planned.

There were a few rumours going about the town that the development would be stopped, but I didn't pay too much heed to them. Small towns thrive on gossip, and if there's no interesting stories people will be quick to invent them. Everyone I'd spoken to previously about the plans had been very positive and commented on the general prosperity it would bring to the area.

I was still getting tired easily, and was told this was to be expected with the tranquilisers I was on. Otherwise, I'd been able to function normally, organising things with a view to re-opening the business, as well as the everyday domestic routines such as running the children to and from school. One morning however, the children had just got in the car and were waiting for me to join them, when I suddenly began to feel weak and unable to stand. A few seconds later I passed out and fell limply down in the hallway. I opened my eyes to find Patricia bent over me, her face creased with alarm. 'Philip – what's wrong?' she said, but I could not answer. My brother Tony was present and telephoned my GP Dr. Sargaison. 'He's on his way now' Tony quickly assured us. The children had now run in from the car and were crowded into the hall. With an effort I began to raise myself up from the floor and leaned against the hall table. 'I'm okay' I said. 'I don't know what happened, but I'm okay now.' Patricia looked at me closely. 'You stay where you are. Tony is going to take Aileen to the bus and Phillip and Brenda to St Anne's, so don't worry, you just wait for the doctor.' As Tony left to take the children to school I called after them 'I'll see you this evening.' They called back, 'We'll hurry home tonight Daddy – get better soon...'

In a few hours I was lying in bed in the Newtownards Hospital. Dr Sargaison had said I should come in and see a consultant, who would run some tests. I had been admitted to the coronary care unit, which surprised me as I couldn't believe I'd had a heart attack. Nonetheless here I was, wired up to a monitor and having my blood pressure taken at regular intervals. That evening Tony brought the family in to visit. It was good to see them. Little Brenda ran straight over to my bed and said, 'Are you sick Daddy?' 'I don't feel sick' I replied at once, smiling at her, 'and I shall be coming home very soon.' Looking at Patricia I assured her that this was the truth, I did feel fine. Fainting like that must have just been one of those things. Patricia however wanted to know more and so, leaving Tony and the children at my bedside, went off to find the doctor in charge. Patricia came back to report that my fainting had been the result of kidney failure. It sounded alarming, but Patricia said all the tests they'd run so far had put me in the clear. She added though that the doctor wanted to keep me in overnight, and for a consultant to see me in the morning. This seemed on the whole to be good news, and it was reassuring that they weren't taking any chances with my health by discharging me that night. Everyone was immediately more relaxed, and when visiting time was over, the children, sensing the happier mood of the adults, went off with kisses and waves, knowing I'd be back home with them the next day. Alone in the strange bed that night however, my own frame of mind was not so cheerful. Despite the kindness shown to me by the doctors and nurses, a hospital is always an unwelcome place in which to find oneself and, as one by one the lights of the ward were lowered and the shadows around the bed grew deeper, the sense of anxiety that had never been far away since the night of the bomb began to fill my thoughts again. My last words to Patricia and the children before they'd left the ward had been to make sure to lock all the windows in the bungalow before retiring, and not to open the door to anyone. Though I knew they would follow this advice and take every precaution, I slept only fitfully that night.

It was mid-morning when the consultant and his team arrived at my bedside. 'How do you feel this morning Mr Coogan?' 'I am fine' I replied. It was a phrase I seemed to be using a lot lately. 'I am discharging you back to the care of your own doctor. Your heart is fine, the ECG is clear and your blood pressure as near to normal as can be expected considering your recent ordeal. I'm making no additional prescriptions, but will give you a letter to hand to Dr Sargaison keeping you on the tranquilisers.' I said, 'Why did I have the sudden weakness yesterday?' 'Kidney failure does that, and I'd put it down to nervous exhaustion and trauma – the shock of losing your business in such a devastating way. I understand it's several weeks since it happened, but these things have a way of catching up with us after the event. There's often a delayed reaction before the body goes into crisis. Try not to push yourself too hard now.' The consultant then wished me well and moved on with his entourage to his next patient.

Over a cup of tea back home Patricia told me that some men from the council had been to see me and would call back later. Hopefully, I thought, it would be some good news about the planning application. However it transpired it was the portable building they wanted to discuss, and contrary to what I'd previously been told, they now informed me that formal planning permission was required before it could be erected. I felt very disappointed on hearing this. Why I wondered had they told me one thing, and now the complete opposite – was the local authority turning against me, and if so, why? Perhaps it was a simple misunderstanding of the kind that often occurs with bureaucrats. I decided to pay a visit to the council offices the next day and try to get some definite answers. However all they could tell me was that no decision had yet been taken on the planning and that I would be informed in due course. Exactly what, I wondered, was going on?

A few days after I returned from hospital I had another visit, this time from two detectives. They were investigating the bombing of my premises and one of their questions concerned my staff: Was I aware of my employees' religion? I replied I was not, since when taking anyone on, their faith, creed or colour was in my view irrelevant. The only criterion was whether the man or woman could do the job. The detectives then told me that of the fourteen full and part-time individuals on the garage's payroll plus myself only three of us were Catholics, one of whom was my brother Tony, the other Thomas Owens, a panel-beater from Newtownards. The remainder had all been Protestant. So eleven Protestants – twelve if you counted my workshop manager – had lost their jobs through people presumably claiming to act on their behalf – it was a tragic irony indeed. Whether this had any connection at all with what happened next I could not say. It was in the local paper one morning that I read the following item:

"WARREN ROAD PETITION" – Residents in the vicinity of the demolished premises known as 'Rockview Motors' Warren Road, which was extensively damaged by an explosion last month have submitted a petition to the council. The residents stated that they were very perturbed about recent press reports regarding the building of a supermarket, night-club and restaurant which have been proposed for the site…'

It seemed the rumours I had been hearing were true. I'd also heard that word was out about the possibility of the marina being developed. I knew it was on this stretch of coastline that the Northern Ireland MP Captain Long moored his boat. The fact that he also lived facing the sea close to the planned development and that his wife had been a long-standing member of the local council was not lost on me. Of course there was the possibility Captain and Mrs Long might welcome a marina on their doorstep, but I wouldn't have placed any bets on it. Within days of the petition appearing in the paper I received a letter from the council saying that planning permission had been refused. Upsetting as this was, after reading about the petition it had not been entirely unexpected I suppose, and I had already decided to lodge an appeal and fight on. In the meantime another decision had to be taken. I had already paid the architect and surveyor for the work they had done, also the demolition firm, together with the deposit on the portable building. Now that the future of the business was even more uncertain, and a possible date for restarting much harder to predict, expenditure had to be trimmed, and so reluctantly I told my workshop manager I could no longer afford to keep him on. The one source of bringing in cash remained the petrol pumps, which had survived the fire, together with the small outbuilding which housed the pumps and electrical switches. Being able to turn up myself each day and serve the odd few customers with fuel was a lifeline, both financially and psychologically, and I had been prompt in paying the fee for the renewal of the petrol licence, the current one having been due to expire in a few weeks. On and off, I was taking money, albeit only a few pounds. But money was money, and although manning the roadside pumps on those bitterly cold days, beside the flattened rubble of what a few weeks ago had been a thriving concern, wasn't exactly 'business as usual' I was, nevertheless, still in business.

3

A Drink in Belfast

'Improvements – what kind of improvements?' said Patricia
Our conversation that January morning was about the latest
communication from the council. In response to my application
to renew the petrol licence on the site, they had come back and
asked for certain conditions to be met. 'Well they're talking about
new manhole covers for a start, which we can fix' I replied. 'But
putting up these railings they're asking for is not a good idea
from my point of view. I think they're only going to hamper
sales.' The requests were annoying, but at the same time I
thought, oh well, I've jumped through so many hoops already
another one won't make much difference. Nevertheless, if the
petrol licence wasn't renewed there was still the mortgage and all
the other bills to pay. But there was also a positive way of looking
at this latest hurdle; the time I'd been spending out in the open
waiting for the occasional customer to stop by for fuel might now
be more productively spent. For me, the most obvious alternative
source of cash was to find and trade second-hand cars. I therefore
set to work right away and it wasn't long after this I heard about
an Alfa Romeo for sale, which I figured I could obtain for a good
price. There were two drawbacks however to making this kind of
purchase. Any 'bargain' vehicle usually needed working on in
order to turn a profit, and without proper facilities at present,
repair work was proving difficult. But the more serious
drawback was that the best bargains were now to be found in
the more dangerous parts areas of Belfast. The Alfa in question
was actually for sale at Greenan's garage in Leeson Street, off the

Falls Road. This was a Catholic district, unlike the Shankhill, where the local Loyalists were not kindly disposed to 'taigs', especially those daring to venture into their territory. Even so you never knew what might happen in any volatile area, especially with so many factions now, and it was all too easy for the innocent citizen to get caught up in conflicts. But I had to earn money, and so it was I took my brother Tony along with me to Greenan's to look at the vehicle. Upon inspection it was obvious the car needed some attention, but was basically roadworthy. I therefore agreed a price, settled up and began the return journey behind the wheel of my latest acquisition. I have particular reason to recall this Alfa, for reasons I will now explain. It was some days later that Tony and myself were again in the car, this time heading for Dublin. We were on the motorway, nearing Lisburn when the engine suddenly began to lose power and within a few minutes stalled completely, coming to rest on the hard shoulder. I pulled the bonnet release and got out to take a look. Along the edge of the motorway to our right was a row of newly-planted trees, above which rose a cluster of high-rise flats. I was just about to lift the bonnet when I heard a sharp pinging sound a little way off. 'What was that?' I said to Tony. He didn't seem to have heard it however. 'It sounded like a shot' I said, peering cautiously towards the flats. There was another ping, much closer this time. Tony had heard this one too, and on instinct we both dived down behind the passenger side of the car. A few yards ahead of us, a large and substantial concrete flyover arched across the motorway. 'Come on' said Tony let's push her under there.' With one hand on the wheel and keeping our bodies low, we inched the car forwards, our senses on alert for any further shots. Slowly but surely we steered the car beneath the shelter of the flyover where we were able to open the bonnet and fix the engine in safety and then continue our journey homewards. I figured whoever had decided to take a pot-shot at us must have mistaken the Alfa for an RUC or military surveillance patrol, as they often used the motorway for observation purposes. Who the hidden sniper thought they were targeting was impossible to know for sure, I just kept thinking it was the first time I'd been shot at. It wasn't however to be the last.

In mid-January my solicitor contacted me again. He told me he had now requested a Chief Constable's Certificate stating that the damage to the garage had been a malicious action by an unlawful organisation. Obtaining this certificate would greatly strengthen my claim for compensation. It looked at last as though things might start to move. There was still no word back on my planning appeal though, so whilst waiting, and since trading cars was rather sporadic to say the least, I decided to look round for a part-time job. With the increasing demands of the security situation in Northern Ireland the RUC were now advertising daily for police reservists, and so I decided to apply. These were paid positions, and in addition to the much-needed cash I would feel I was doing something of value in the community right now. I believed very few Catholics had tried to join, and one I did hear of never even received his application form. I was therefore encouraged when my form duly arrived. I submitted it promptly and was sent an acknowledgement by return. So far so good I thought. Next I turned my attention to my finances. After the strange and unhelpful attitude of my bank manager I decided to close the account with the Ulster Bank and approached the Bank of Ireland in Newtownards. Here, armed with a letter from my solicitor about the expected compensation I opened an account. Furthermore, on the understanding all future monies awarded would be paid directly into this account I was given an advance of £2,500. I knew that the compensation when it came would only cover the second-hand market value of my garage equipment, and that replacing everything new could cost three or four times this amount. Still, the new account with the advance felt like a significant step forward. What happened next however felt more like two steps backwards. It was another letter from the council, informing me that 'after some consideration' my appeal against the planning decision on the development had been rejected. Perhaps at a later date I could try again. It seemed the best course of action for now was to apply to simply rebuild the garage to its original state; surely no-one could object to that. Appropriate plans were thus drawn up for this task, and given an estimated rebuilding cost of £13,637.37. Also in respect of compensation, Mr. T.S. Simpson the claims assessor arrived at a figure of £12,978 for replacing equipment and cars, and for loss of income, my accountants Alfred Young and Co. produced balance sheets showing clear profits of £160 per week during 1971. Whilst at the council offices dropping off the plans, I ventured to ask again about the renewal of the petrol licence, advising the clerk that the new manhole covers had been fitted as requested. I was politely told that I would be informed in due course. Assembling all the paperwork and liaising with various officials and departments was beginning to feel exhausting, especially when nothing seemed certain of having a successful outcome. Between all the running around, doing the odd car deal and attending the doctor's surgery for regular check-ups and medication I was becoming a little ragged. Although it was only a few weeks since the bombing of the garage and early days really I was impatient for things to happen, and get the business back on its feet. Despite making my best efforts to do so I was getting nowhere fast and the continual obstacles gave me a sinking feeling that things would never go right again. If only I could see a glimmer of light at the end of the tunnel! There were some brief respites from financial strain, including a cheque from an insurance company for some repair work carried out the previous year. But with still no regular source of income the general worry over money continued to haunt me.

One cold Saturday morning, while the frost lay on the lawn and the roads were still quiet, I arose early and travelled into Belfast to see an old friend. His name was Jack and he was from the Falls Road. In the early afternoon we went to a little pub that was popular with Republicans. It was situated near the city centre at the corner of Chapel Lane. The place was already very busy and we had to wait a while to get a seat at the bar. It was some months since Jack and I had got together and we both had a lot to catch up on. Over a couple of pints Jack asked about my present situation. Hearing of my various difficulties over finance and planning etc, he suggested introducing me to a friend of his, a political veteran by the name of Paddy Devlin, who was a founder member of the SDLP. Paddy had influence, said Jack, and might be able to help. 'If there's anything he can do it would be most welcome' I said. Whilst Jack was away from the bar I heard the pub door slam and looking around recognised another old pal, a man called Edward who had worked for me during our time in Tralee. He had noticed me too and immediately came over. 'Hello boy – how are you!' he said amiably 'Where are you living now?' 'My family and I have been in Donaghadee for some years now' I replied. At this Edward looked puzzled. 'I thought you were in County Armagh' he said. 'No…' I began, and then saw Jack returning. He saw Edward and from his expression I straightaway gathered he knew Edward and that the two of them were not exactly friends. Edward veered off and joined a large group drinking at the far table. 'Stay clear of that company' warned Jack indicating the table. I knew what this meant. The boys on the table maybe Provisionals. Years ago Jack and his friend Paddy Devlin had sympathised with the old Official IRA, but the Provos were a different matter. As Jack and I ordered more drinks, I looked back at Edward, now drinking and laughing with his friends and was reminded of a visit I'd made to another Belfast pub in the late 'sixties. Edward had been there that day too, when a girl, still in her early teens and dressed in her school uniform had come into the bar. She was accompanied by a small boy that she held onto tightly by the hand. The little boy I remember had a slight handicap. Everyone in the bar knew them and called out 'Hi Mary' when they saw her. Edward had been at the bar and was asking for cigarettes. 'Have you a packet of Gallaghers?' The barman replied that they were sold out. At this young Mary said 'I will go and get some from the shop' I was rather shocked to hear a young girl say this, considering the risks from all the shooting and other violence that had been going on in recent days. 'Are you sure?' said Edward uncertainly, and with a glance at the barman. Mary nodded, and Edward handed her the money for the cigarettes. 'Be careful now' he said, which was echoed by several other people in the bar. 'We will' said Mary calmly, and taking the little boy by the hand again went out into the street. 'Who is the child?' I asked Edward. 'The landlord's daughter' he replied, 'that's him helping out behind the bar' And young Mary is doing her bit to help her dad I thought, keeping the customers happy and showing she's not afraid. In a few moments she returned with the Gallaghers and handed them to Edward. 'Keep the change now' he said. But she shook her head and refused to take anything. After much persuasion she finally accepted the coins and handed exactly half to her brother. Its hard to say why exactly, but I was much taken with this scene and the image of the child stayed with me – there was a quality about her – a sort of quiet confidence and dignity which rose above all the gloom and horror of the times. It felt like we were being set an example, one of simple courtesy and courage. Of course none of us knew at the time that the young girl would go on to Queens University and become an outstanding lawyer, later marrying a dentist and renowned GAA footballer called Martin McAleese. Nor that she would one day become the President of Ireland.

Family photo. 1971.

Business bombed. 7/12/1971.

The architects' plan of 1971.

Partly demolished. 1972.

Prt of bombed site. 16/12/2008

4

Bloody Sunday

I hadn't immediately understood why, when seeing me that day in the Chapel Road pub Edward had thought I'd been living in Crossmaglen. It transpired he had confused me with a notorious IRA man of the same name, known at the time to be along that part of the border. Well, that could have been me I suppose, if as a young lad I'd taken up the offer of 'training' with my pals down in Monaghan. That was a time when all Catholics tended to be looked on as 'Officials' of the IRA, meaning of course the old IRA, the 'Provos' did not yet exist. They emerged after the Sinn Fein Ard Feis of January 1970, when, in response to the growing unrest, the party split, forming a new hard-line group committed to the cause of a united Ireland.

A few days later Jack contacted me again. As promised he'd arranged for me to meet Paddy Devlin in Belfast to see if he could help in any way with my difficulties. Jack asked if he and I could meet first on the Falls Road and he would then take me to Paddy's office. Overhearing the phone call, my brother Tony said he would accompany me. On the appointed day we arrived at the Falls Road in the early afternoon and parked the Mercedes near Clonard Monastery. Tony waited in the car while I got out and looked for Jack. I quickly found him, and as we were strolling back towards the car I noticed someone crouched against the passenger door. It was a young lad, who, when he looked up and saw Jack and I approaching, immediately jumped up and took to his heels. Tony had an unusual look on his face. 'What was that boy doing?' I asked Tony. 'Would you believe, he just came up and stuck a revolver in my ribs and asked for the car keys. I told him I didn't have them.' This was true, as I'd taken the keys with me. Apparently the youth was a member of the 'Junior IRA', who, when he recognised Jack with us, had abandoned his plan. We got in the car and Jack directed me to Paddy Devlin's, a small back office, presumably the centre of operations for his political work. Jack introduced me and told Paddy about the problems I was having restarting my business and that no compensation had yet been paid for the bomb damage. I noticed that all the while Paddy kept one hand hidden in the partly-open drawer of his desk. After hearing my story Paddy asked a few questions then wrote me out a letter addressed to a certain solicitor. The letter stressed that I was being obstructed in my livelihood due to my religion and unfairly impeded by people who should by rights be helping me. Paddy then wished me well, and I thanked him for his time and trouble on my behalf. As we were driving back via the Falls Road, Jack came up with another suggestion, a rather unusual one. 'If all else fails' he said, 'you can always go and ask the Reverend Paisley for help'. Well I had to laugh at that. Ian Paisley, the firebrand Protestant preacher forever declaiming against 'Popery'! That he might put himself out for some unknown Catholic with a hard-luck story seemed unlikely. I really did think it was a joke, especially coming from someone living on the Falls Road. But surprisingly Jack seemed serious. I said 'Suppose he refuses to see me?' Jack replied something to the effect there was no harm in asking, to which all I could say was, "I'll think about it.' Back home I told Patricia about Jack's suggestion. She laughed too.

I believe the majority of people, whether north or south of the border, actually wanted little to do with the violence or extremist politics rearing up at that time and were simply striving to make the best living they could and raise a family in peace. Certain elements of course never have respect for 'live and let live', and now especially they were bent on causing trouble. Another undeniable fact was that since the interments had begun the British Army was proving to be the IRA's best recruiting sergeant.

The round-the-clock saturation of small Catholic areas of Belfast and Derry with thousands of troops had quickly ended the so-called honeymoon period, and in place of the friendly cups of tea shared on the doorstep there was only fear, bitterness and anger. There had been many mistakes made by the troops involved in the internment process. Many local families shared common surnames, yet were completely unrelated. Fathers were arrested instead of sons and vice-versa. The often arrogant British officers would not listen when told they were taking the wrong man. (Given Edward's mistake over my own identity in the pub that day I was lucky this had not happened to me – maybe it would yet) Could no-one see the hornets' nest of resentment being stirred up by holding teenage boys and old men at gunpoint? The British were falling right into the trap that the ruthless Provos had laid with their bombing campaign. Many of the innocent victims of internment, being so humiliated and angered by the experience, were to quickly seek retribution and take the road of violence. A new and heroic sense of nationalism was being bred into these young men. Rebel songs old and new, though officially banned, were sung spiritedly in pubs where the RUC seldom ventured. *"She got up and rattled the bin, the Specials were coming in…"* and *"Armoured cars, tanks and guns, came to take away our sons, but every man shall stand behind the men behind the wire"* were frequently heard. The lyrics were sometimes less romantic, and the Loyalists had their own sectarian repertoire too. A particularly chilling song from the heart of the Shankhill ran thus: *"If guns were made for shooting, then skulls were made to crack, and you've never seen a better Taig than with a bullet in his back…"*

Many law-abiding people, including those whose relatives had been wrongly interned, had, especially after hearing reports of beatings and torture, little other option but to take to the streets and demand justice. But peaceful protest did not always end that way. Late on Sunday the 30th January we heard the awful news of what had happened in Derry earlier that day. At a civil rights march which had been declared illegal, tear gas and water cannon had been used to break up the demonstration. Then as the crowd fled, Paratroopers had opened fire. When the dust settled 13 civilians lay dead and another 29 injured. The Army claimed they had been fired upon first and that some of the demonstrators had been carrying nail-bombs. This however was strongly denied by those present on the march.

As a result of what was already being called 'Bloody Sunday' people throughout Northern Ireland began to fear the worst, a massive escalation in violence. Donaghadee was already seeing its fair share of incidents, and many in the community felt action should be taken lest the situation should spiral out of control. To this end a meeting was called in the Town Hall to urgently review the question of law and order. I decided to attend, and went along to find the place almost full. The local RUC sergeant had just opened the proceedings, and as I entered at the back, several faces turned towards me. Some of them did not look pleased. The sergeant was quick to sense the mood. 'Now, now' he said, 'this is a public meeting and all are welcome. We don't want any sectarian trouble or idle rumours here.' After some debate it was decided to set up small night-time vigilante patrols. These unarmed patrols would report any suspicious behaviour or law-breaking directly to the RUC. Two groups were formed, one with myself and four other men, for which I volunteered the use of my large car for making our patrols. We commenced immediately, going out alternate nights and driving slowly around the local schools, the golf club, churches and in and out the side streets, often not returning home till 3 or 4am. As these nightly vigils went on however we found little to report, and concluded that perhaps we were having a deterrent effect. It was some three weeks later, at about 1.30am, as my colleagues and I were making a routine sweep round the grounds of a large hotel situated close the RUC headquarters, that we were suddenly confronted by a blinding light ahead of us. I braked hard bringing the Mercedes to a grinding halt. There was some commotion and slamming of car doors before someone called out 'It's the Vigies!' I recognised the voice of one of our local policemen. When the bright lights were switched off we saw ourselves completely surrounded by about a dozen officers, all armed with sten guns. The senior man then came up to the driver's window, apologised for startling us and proceeded to chat calmly for several minutes before driving off. This midnight encounter with the RUC was the only bit of drama our vigilante group had seen, and as time went on our enthusiasm and numbers dwindled. It was tiring being out half the night, as well as trying to earn a living by day and as the RUC seemed to be on top of things now, we decided to disband our group and leave them to it. I hoped at least, that by this short-lived bit of volunteering those with the unwelcome stares at the Town Hall meeting would be less suspicious of me.

I had delivered Paddy Devlin's letter to the solicitor concerned, but heard nothing back. Meanwhile my own solicitor was still waiting for the Chief Constable's certificate confirming malicious damage, which I urgently needed for the compensation claim. I decided to take the initiative, and put a call through direct to RUC HQ in Belfast. To my surprise I was asked to come along in person the next day, and when I arrived found the staff helpful and courteous. After a short wait a man came out and handed me the requested certificate, just like that. I returned home via Newtownards where I passed the document on to my solicitor, who seemed surprised at the manner of its delivery.

I was pleased at my little success in obtaining the certificate, and thought maybe Paddy Devlin's solicitor had helped by putting a word in someone's ear. The compensation claim would doubtless still take some time, and I needed money badly, or at least some solution that would enable me to earn it. The petrol licence had not yet run out, but neither had it been renewed, and trading cars alone did not provide much income. With a family to provide for, I would have to come up with something else, and soon.

5

The Reverend Paisley

He can only tell me to go home' I said.
'That's true' agreed Patricia.

I had decided to follow up Jack's suggestion and pay a visit to the Reverend Paisley. Having mulled the matter over for some days I finally concluded that 'nothing ventured, meant nothing gained' As I got in the car now beside Tony who was coming with me, and waved goodbye to Patricia I did wonder if I was being a fool to turn up uninvited and buttonhole the man they called 'Big Ian'. Nonetheless as we drove off I felt surprisingly calm about what might lie ahead, reflecting at the same time that perhaps the tranquilisers I was still taking were giving me courage.

The Reverend Dr. Ian Paisley's church was situated on the Ravenhill Road in Belfast. After ringing the bell for the office we stood outside on the steps for several moments awaiting a reply. No-one came. Then, pushing cautiously against the door we discovered it to be unlocked. I entered and found myself at the bottom of a flight of stairs. I peered tentatively up, from where I could hear movement and voices. I went up, followed closely by Tony, till we reached the first floor. There was a door off to the left and a further flight of stairs above us. Which way to go? I decided on the stairs, and began to climb again. We were now both a little nervous at being in this unknown territory, almost that we were trespassing. Then from above came the sound of approaching footsteps. Looking up we were confronted by a broad-shouldered man blocking the stairs. We were face to face with the Reverend Paisley. We stood for a second, speechless with surprise. As the Reverend was smiling jovially, we quickly introduced ourselves. 'A friend suggested asking you for advice with some business difficulties' I said. The Reverend looked at me closely for a moment with his large penetrating eyes. 'I'm busy at present' he said, 'but come on up both of you.' We followed him aloft and through a door. We were now in a surprisingly large office, which was humming with activity. There were a dozen or so staff all busily typing away, filing or on the phone. A busy lady who looked to be in charge of the place I recognised from the newspapers as being the Reverend Paisley's wife Eileen. The Reverend bade us take a seat beside his desk and asked me what the problem was. As I was explaining about the bombing and the troubles I was having with the council and obtaining compensation he nodded, and gave me the impression he was already familiar with the facts. He then asked me if I had a certificate from the Chief Constable. 'Yes, it's already with my solicitor. But I don't know how long any compensation will take to come through.' The Reverend nodded again then asked me if anyone had told me about emergency finance. I asked what was meant by this. He explained that there was now a fund available for businesses in circumstances such as mine, and from what he'd heard of the case I would be entitled to £2,000. I looked at Tony and then back at the Reverend. This was welcome news indeed and could set me back on my feet, though I'd learned long ago not to count any chickens before they were hatched. 'Sit there for a moment' said the Reverend, as he picked up the telephone, dialled a number and asked to be put through to a Mr Kirk. As he began speaking it was apparent he'd been connected to the wrong Mr Kirk, and he quickly asked to be put back to the switchboard. He then bellowed loudly into the receiver, 'I require Mr Kirk in the finance department!' He put the receiver down, waited a moment, then the telephone rang. It was the right Mr. Kirk calling back. The Reverend immediately outlined what had happened in Donaghadee on the night of 7th December the previous year and that the victim was in need of emergency finance. I could not hear Mr Kirk's reply, but whatever he'd said prompted a ferocious response in the Reverend. He banged on the desk and shouted 'To make matters worse, these are Roman Catholics sitting here beside me!' He then said 'Thankyou' and hung up. It immediately occurred to me I had never mentioned my religion. 'Big Ian' seemed at that moment a little bit like God himself – he appeared to know everything and everyone, and he could display great wrath!

Assuring us that Mr Kirk would look into getting the emergency finance, the Reverend said he would walk back down the stairs with us. Passing the door on the first floor he stopped. 'Have you ever seen inside my church?' Tony and I shook our heads. He then opened the unlocked door and ushered us through. One could tell from his demeanour as we gazed around that he was very proud of his church. Indeed it was a sumptuously furnished place of worship; a bright red carpet covering every visible inch of the floor gave a feeling of comforting warmth and welcome. To our right rose a large, handsomely-carved pulpit similar to the one seen in Armagh Cathedral. As we returned out onto the landing the Reverend closed the door behind him with a bang then, with a mischievous twinkle in his eye said 'I hope ye boys have not left a bomb in there!' As we left we thanked the Reverend for his assistance. 'Not at all, I hope you'll soon be back in business.' So did I, and on the way home recalled the Reverend's joke about the bomb. Till that day I would not have imagined the man to have such a sense of humour. Despite the stentorian voice and keen temper, he seemed far from the monster we'd been led to believe. If the emergency finance did come through – and seeing the man in action I somehow had great faith in the Reverend Paisley's powers – it could signal a turnaround for me; the new petrol licence, success with the planning appeal and, who knows, maybe even the development. The Showboat Restaurant could yet rise from the flames and look out on peaceful waters.

'The meeting's nearly over'
The speaker was a heavily-built man standing with several others outside the entrance to the Orange Hall as I approached.

It was a bitterly cold February night and, like the figures I'd observed filing through the door, I was wearing a thick anorak with the hood up. My garments however did not have a paramilitary look about them, unlike many of those who'd entered the hall. I had strolled up to the Vanguard meeting out of curiosity. I knew Catholics would not be welcome, and clearly I had now been recognised by the security staff, hence the warning remark. Vanguard was a new Loyalist movement launched by William Craig, an ex-Northern Ireland minister and former friend of the Reverend Paisley. The movement had attracted the support of rising young Unionists, many already involved with the UDA and other paramilitary groups. At these Vanguard rallies Craig would turn up in presidential fashion, his car flanked by motorcycle outriders. Judging by the vehicles parked outside tonight there was a large gathering in attendance, come to hear Craig's rhetoric of unity. *"If the politicians of the North fail our people then maybe our job is to liquidate the enemy… and when we say power and force, we mean Force! … and to assassinate these enemies as a last desperate attempt to keep our democratic rights and enjoy the higher standard of living by remaining part of the United Kingdom and be free from a united Ireland…"*

Vanguard was already thought to have 50,000 supporters, who were known to be intent on arming themselves. With the RUC freely giving out firearms licences to anyone they decided was not 'a threat to the state' this shouldn't be difficult. There were also rumours of Protestant toolmakers quietly turning out guns in machine shops and small factories across the province. There was believed to be one such place right here on the Ards Peninsula. *Our job is to liquidate the enemy…*Cheers could be heard coming from the Orange Hall as I walked on past. I did not look back, knowing the security men would probably still be watching me. I thought of Patricia back at the bungalow. She would now probably be getting the children ready for bed. Pulling my hood tighter against the falling sleet, I hurried on home.

One morning while I was manning the petrol pumps, a plain-clothes officer stopped by and asked if Tony and I could come along to the RUC HQ the following evening. They wanted us to give a statement regarding the evening of the bombing and, in their words 'have a chat'. Arriving there the atmosphere did seem almost convivial. We were taken through the security door and shown into a cosy room where a large turf fire was burning merrily. The officer who I'd seen the day before came in but did not introduce himself and I wondered, was he Special Branch, perhaps MI5? Tony and I were offered two armchairs by the fire. 'Would you prefer coffee or tea?' We both said not to go to any trouble, but the man seemed quite insistent, so we assented to some tea. He disappeared and returned a few moments later bearing a tray with two cups of tea, sugar bowl, milk jug and a plate of biscuits. A few words were exchanged before the officer promptly left us alone again. We helped ourselves to the tea, expecting someone to come along any minute and take our statements. As the minutes ticked by Tony and I began to exchange somewhat puzzled looks. What was going on? Eventually the same officer reappeared and asked us was 'everything alright? He then put some more turf on the fire and departed yet again. Finally a different officer entered the room. He nodded, then carefully picked up the tea-tray and took it from the room. He came back, sat down and began talking about the night of the explosion. I had expected to see him taking notes but there were none. Everything he mentioned had been gone over several times before. Barely five minutes had elapsed when he rose decisively, thanked us for coming and ushered us out through the security door. We'd been in the police station half an hour and done little more than drink tea and warm ourselves by the fire. 'What was all that about?' said Tony. I shook my head. I couldn't work it out either, though thinking later about the way the tea-tray had been deftly removed it seemed obvious. Maybe they'd already tried to obtain my fingerprints from the Crumlin Road Gaol, where they'd been taken seventeen years earlier. If not it might have saved them the trouble of a pot of tea. Also I suppose, they wanted Tony's prints too. What did they suspect us of? With Catholics you never knew; all Taigs were likely rebels. There was also a little bit of family history we had been careful to keep quiet about during our time in the North. Namely, that Patricia's father had been a serving member and quartermaster of the old IRA, and a personal bodyguard to Eamon De'Valera himself no less. I now wondered who else knew about this.

6

The Waiting Game

The Reverend Paisley was as good as his word; an emergency finance cheque from the Stormont Government had arrived in the post. The £2,000 was to be deducted without interest from the malicious claim payment when settled. I telephoned the Reverend and thanked him. He had been the only one to help financially. Now with this money in hand I felt motivated to approach the North Down Council again about rebuilding the original garage premises. This time however I was met with a blank refusal, being told no plans whatsoever would be considered. Enquiring at the same time about the petrol licence, now due to expire the following month, I was politely informed that 'no decision had yet been taken'. I decided there was now only one option, which was to bypass the council and go to a higher authority. I would make an appeal directly to the Ministry of Development, under the Planning Acts. This government department was headed by Roy Bradford MP, who resided, as chance would have it, in Warren Road Donaghadee. Given the petition against the development the chance of success might have seemed slim, but I could only hope the man had a sense of disinterested duty. I was given a date for an oral hearing on 18th May that year.

A few days later I was pleased to see that another wheel I'd set in motion was at least moving in a positive direction, as one morning I received the following letter: "With reference to your application for appointment as a part-time Constable in the Royal Ulster Constabulary, please attend at Bangor RUC Station at 7pm on Friday 10/3/72 for the purpose of: a) Being tested educationally, b) Having height and measurements taken. Candidates competing at the Educational Examination must bring their own pen". So far, so good, I thought.

On February 2nd that year the British Embassy in Dublin had been burned out in protest against what was happening in the North, particularly the killings of Bloody Sunday. The rapid growth of William Craig's Vanguard paramilitaries was now regarded as a threat upon the lives of all Catholics, and it was felt the British Army and RUC were in collusion. In Belfast the streets were far from safe, and many people predicted things would get worse. At home we'd recently been getting the odd nuisance phone call; being Nationalists in a Loyalist area this was now par for the course I suppose, though it made us very uneasy none the less. As far as business was concerned, with a lot of people reluctant to travel it was easy enough to pick up vehicles, though of course these were slow to sell on, which some days made me very despondent. I kept busy though, using some welding equipment salvaged from the garage to carry out repairs. I could park up to six cars in our driveway, and split my time between mechanical work on these and sales. I liked to keep the personal element when doing business and would often meet other motor dealers in Belfast, sometimes in the Chapel Lane pub or at a cafe. Most frequently I'd use the Abercorn Bar and Restaurant. Located in the city centre, the Abercorn was always a friendly, lively place, ideal for a chat and for shaking hands on a sale over a friendly drink or a cup of coffee. It was on the evening of Saturday 4th of March that Patricia and I were settled in the living room watching TV when the news came on. We sat rigid with horror as it was announced that the Abercorn Restaurant had been bombed, seriously injuring up to eighty people. As the full story unfolded over the next few hours, tragic details emerged. As usual for a Saturday, the restaurant had been crammed with young people meeting up before going for an evening out on the town. One young girl present when the bomb went off had been due to marry a man from over the border. She lost both of her legs, an arm and one eye. Numerous others lost their limbs and their sight. Many of the parents of these young people had to be sedated on hearing the news such was the severity of their injuries. Two other young Catholic girls in their early twenties were killed outright in the blast. The coroner later described the incident as "...pathological murder of the most depraved kind...." Perpetrated by the provisional IRA, the Abercorn bombing was one of the most horrific attacks carried out since the so-called Troubles had begun. I had been sitting in the restaurant only a few days earlier.

What with the harassment calls to our home and the steadily mounting atmosphere of violence, I was now seriously starting to fear for my own safety and that of the family. My brother Tony and his wife had discussed the idea of leaving the country altogether and seeking a new life for themselves overseas. Perhaps it was the sensible thing to do. Aside from the chilling menace of the Vanguard and UDA killers now known to be seeking out and killing Catholics, law and order was rapidly breaking down, chiefly in the city centres, but elsewhere too, with sporadic shootings, looting and arson. You never knew when or where it might happen. Hijacking of trucks and vans was becoming commonplace, with gangsters and racketeers from both sides of the sectarian divide carving up the spoils.

Perhaps, if the RUC application was successful, I would be doing my bit for law and order in the country, if I still had the stomach for it. The date of the exam at Bangor Police Station arrived, and on the night I found myself able to complete the paper comfortably with five minutes to spare. A number of people had advised me against applying for the RUC in view of the added dangers now, and no doubt they were right. However having started the ball rolling, I felt I had to see the process through, and when a letter arrived telling me I'd passed the exam and to await a final decision, it looked as if my life may perhaps soon take a new path. If I was offered a place it would certainly be none too soon in terms of helping the family finances. We could no longer afford the fees for our eldest daughter Aileen at the private boarding school in Holywood and she had now started as a day pupil at the state Grammar in Bangor, travelling the six miles from Donaghadee by bus each morning. The next blow to our fortunes was the refusal by the council to renew the petrol licence. Maybe now this was just as well. The 'premises' looked like the bomb-site that indeed it was, and what customers there had been were slowly dwindling in number. What could I now pin my hopes on – the planning appeal to the Minister, the payment of compensation, and possibly the RUC application. Meanwhile the hand-to-mouth existence was becoming increasingly pressurised, as indeed was the situation in the country. Sometimes it seemed a matter of conjecture which would collapse first – me or the whole province of Northern Ireland.

And how could there remain any faith or fear of God left in people when witnessing brutality and injustice within their midst day after day? Faith is perhaps all one has left in times of injustice, and becomes more important than ever. On the Loyalist side, many were putting their faith not in God but in the likes of the Ulster Defence Association and William Craig's Vanguard, which had partly banded together for the 'defence' of Ulster from the Catholic population. Together they could now muster a terrifying estimated force of 100,000 men onto the streets. Answering questions about a possible backlash Craig claimed that "…it may not go as far as killings, but Ulster would be in the same position and resembling the situation in 1920…" Of course it was already going further even than killing now that the horrifying reports of the Shankill Road Butchers were circulating.

Craig's euphemistic words implied that Roman Catholics identified as Republicans against the Northern State could find themselves unwelcome in their place of work and inevitably under pressure to leave their homes. Whether this was made to sound like reassurance or was a warning, his ambitions seemed clear enough to some. A breakaway Ulster declaring its independence from the United Kingdom was much talked about, as were rumours of the Government's extraordinary plans to redraw the boundaries of the six counties, thus effectively forcing Catholics out of Protestant areas and largely into southern

Ireland. The Irish Prime Minister Jack Lynch spoke angrily to the British leader Ted Heath, telling him internment had been a fatal mistake. Meanwhile the Chairman of the UDA Charles Harding Smith and four others had been arrested in London attempting to illegally purchase arms. One of the other four was a member of the RUC, adding further fuel to the allegations of collusion. In certain parts of Derry and Belfast the residents were in a near civil war, and the fear now was that this would spread to all-out war throughout the province. The monster created by Craig with the tacit blessing of the British Army and the RUC was running out of control, with many of the gunmen under the Vanguard and UDA banner actively out looking for Catholics to shoot. On the 24th of March the British Government, alarmed at the scale of the conflict, took decisive action, terminating Stormont and imposing immediate direct rule. After fifty years as a province, Ulster was now under the full command of Westminster. No-one could say with certainty what the outcome of this was likely to be. On the morning of the 24th every soldier in Northern Ireland must have been on duty. Driving along the Bangor coast road I was stopped by a British patrol, a rare sight in that area. After some routine questions the young officer asked what I thought of Direct Rule. I said I welcomed it for now. It seemed likely at least to put a stop to William Craig's power bid, and keep us all a bit safer.

It was not until late April that I received the long-awaited letter from the RUC HQ. It read as follows:

"Dear Mr Coogan, I have been asked by the Chief Constable to refer to your application for appointment as a part-time Constable in the RUC Reserve, and to say that your case has been considered carefully and sympathetically. I regret to inform you that you have not been selected and therefore no appointment can be offered.

Yours faithfully..."

Naturally no reason had been given, but one could imagine

the fears in some quarters. For a Catholic to take the RUC Oath of Allegiance would be seen as meaningless. A Catholic officer hearing of possible collusion between elements of the police and the Loyalist paramilitaries, would be sure to blow the whistle, may indeed be an IRA man attempting to penetrate the force and gather information. The Loyalists were rumoured to have caches of home-made machine guns, sealed in lead to escape detection and buried across the Ards Peninsula. An RUC man could find out the location of these weapons. I remembered again the advice of my late Uncle Owen Coogan, who had joined the force when it was the old Royal Irish Constabulary. He made it to Inspector but had been blocked from achieving the higher ranks. He'd told me not to apply to the RUC, and had I suppose been right. Despite discrimination he must have been a well respected officer though, since his funeral had been attended by one of the largest gatherings seen in Northern Ireland at the time. Ah well, I had tried.

Now it was only a few weeks till my planning appeal hearing. All things come to those who wait, we are told, and, sometimes, things come along unexpectedly to help us. The Jet petrol firm had been in regular contact with me about re-starting the business, and knew all about the planning problems and delays. One day they telephoned to ask if I would be interested in another opportunity. I was told that Jet had another filling station, with a substantial forecourt and large garages. I was assured the premises was in good condition and that up to ten vehicles could be securely stocked. It sounded ideal for running a similar business to Warren Road, perhaps as a temporary measure till my own land could be rebuilt on. I immediately asked for the location. 'It's called Brookspeed Motors' said the Jet representative on the phone, 'and the address is 1010, Crumlin Road, Belfast.'

7

The Lion's Den

Crumlin Road had of course a deep significance from earlier in my life. However it wasn't just the poignant memory of being in prison there which made me pause on the telephone. On one side of the Crumlin Road lay the small Catholic stronghold of Ardoyne. The other side borders the Shankill-Woodvale area, home of the Woodvale Defence Association (WDA), a large and growing Loyalist paramilitary group. I would effectively be trying to run a business in the middle of two vehemently hostile factions. The Ardoyne was notorious for its sporadic gunfights with the British Army, while the WDA were known to be responsible for numerous atrocities including a bomb that had killed fifteen people in McGurks Bar North Queen Street on the 4th of December the previous year, three days before my own business had been hit. For all I knew WDA members had been involved in that too. Could I now seriously consider setting up shop in such an area? With Direct Rule now in force despite much opposition, one could only hope things would stabilise. 'Brookspeed Motors' was in fact situated on high ground overlooking the city and opposite 'Ballysillan', a largely Loyalist estate. It would undoubtedly be taking a risk. Then again one took a risk on every drive into Belfast. I thanked the company for the offer and said I would need to think about it, and that I'd come back with an answer as soon as possible. The planning appeal on the 18th May wasn't too far off, but even if successful it would surely take months before Warren Road could be rebuilt and operating again. I thought long and hard;

money for the mortgage and other bills would have to come from somewhere. After much soul searching I phoned back and told Jet I was interested in taking over the Brookspeed site providing the terms were satisfactory, and made an appointment with them for the following day.

By the end of April the death toll from sectarian violence for that month was twenty-two. This was twenty-two too many but in January it had been twenty-six, February thirty and March twenty-nine. It looked as though the conflict might be on the turn thank God. I signed the lease with Jet and on May 5th took over the running of Brookspeed Motors in Crumlin Road. Lorries arrived to replenish the petrol storage tanks and bunting was hung across the forecourt of the newly painted property. A handful of cars were put on show, with price tickets and terms displayed. After five months of scratching around I was finally running a proper-looking business again, it wasn't my own business as Warren Road had been, but it was something. The first few days saw a steady but unexciting trade in petrol. No-one however even looked at the cars on the forecourt. When travelling to and from the business I would alternate my route, one day using the Crumlin Road itself, the next going via the Shankill and Woodvale Roads. On Sundays I would first call in and attend morning mass in the market area of Belfast then drive along the Grosvenor Road, crossing the Falls Road and up Springfield Road by the RUC station, turning onto Woodvale Road further up. One particular Sunday after leaving mass I was driving past the RUC station at about 9.15am when a few hundred yards in front there appeared two Saracen armoured cars. Many of the side-streets off Springfield Road were now derelict from the civil unrest, and as the armoured cars moved slowly past these streets the sound of gunfire could now be heard rattling out. It seemed to be coming from one of the turnings that led to the Falls Road. The noise was loud, and I thought was most likely the Provos with their trademark WW1 Thompson machine-guns. In response to the gunfire the Saracen nearest me began to swing across the road. At the same moment the firing ceased and was replaced by the silence of early Sunday morning.

It did not seem a peaceful silence though but a feeling of eerie calm that might be shattered at any moment. When that moment came, I realised I might quickly find myself in the middle of something appalling. I had two choices – either to stop the car immediately or drive straight on. Although the armoured cars were now partially blocking the road, I quickly decided that remaining in the vicinity was likely to be far more dangerous. I therefore changed down a gear, took the Mercedes up onto the footpath and steered a narrow course past the first of the Saracens. Mercifully the lull in the firing continued and I eased swiftly past the other vehicle. Glancing in the rear-view mirror I saw both the armoured cars with their gun barrels fixed ominously on one of the side streets. When I got to the Woodvale Road I stopped the car and took my hands off the wheel. Although early morning the weather was already warm, yet as I sat there I began to feel very cold and my body was trembling. I waited for several minutes till I felt a little steadier, then started the car again and made my way to the filling station as usual.

The 18th of May, the day of the planning appeal, had arrived. Those present were informed that 'This appeal arises out of the decision of the Donaghadee Urban District Council against the application of Philip Coogan for permission to replace a petrol filling station and workshop at Rockview Motors, Warren Road'. The hearing began at 11am and did not take long. At the close it was announced that a decision would be given in six to eight weeks. Further waiting and uncertainty was not good news, either for my health or peace of mind. The sense of being conspired against by an unseen hand visited me again with renewed force, draining my spirits and drawing a dark cloud of foreboding around me.

All I could do for the present was try to optimise the earnings from the Brookspeed business. My brother Tony was helping me, and in addition to petrol sales we were concentrating on building up the revenue from selling accessories. The cars on the forecourt were still not selling and there was probably a very good reason for this. The decline in sectarian violence of April had been reversed, with the number of killings in May reaching forty-one.

Few people relished strolling round an open forecourt in full view of the Loyalist flats on the Ballysillan estate, especially with preparations for the 12th of July Unionist celebrations already underway. Union colours were already adorning the area, with flags flying and the kerbstones being painted red, white and blue. Gable walls on the ends of houses were having their murals freshened up. This insignia of the Loyalists was clearly visible from the Brookspeed premises. A friend of mine in the trade, on hearing precisely where I was now working, had recently counselled me earnestly to get out of the area as soon as possible. Events were soon to prove his advice sound. The first incident occurred during one of the school holidays. Children the world over get bored when they have nothing much to do, and we all know who makes work for idle hands. The devil had clearly got into the large group of youths Tony and I observed one morning making their way towards us from the Ballysillan flats. There were about twenty of them in all, chanting and shouting abusive slogans. Several were waving union jack flags. In no time they were blocking the Crumlin Road. One by one, in a display of bravado, they began to move onto the forecourt. Tony and I decided to remain calm and sit it out. A few youngsters had climbed up onto the roof of the filling station, shouting and waving their flags. The ones on the forecourt were now playing around with the petrol hoses. I watched anxiously as one or two of them eyed the switches on the pumps. I then noticed a lady who lived near the premises drive by. She slowed down as she passed and seemed to be taking in what was happening. Some time later an RUC Land Rover with armed officers arrived on the scene accompanied by two army jeeps. The senior officer asked us if any damage had been done and if we wanted to press charges. We replied that we just wanted to be left in peace. If the youths could be moved off the premises we'd have no complaints. The RUC then ordered everyone to leave, nudging them as diplomatically as possibly back across the road. They were told to behave themselves and return to their homes. Slowly and quietly the group departed towards the high flats and we saw no more of them. Our refusal to take the bait of provocation seemed to have paid off; we had not provided the sport they were looking for. What we did know for certain was that if we'd had anyone arrested we would have been burned out of the station within hours.

The next few days passed by peacefully enough until one afternoon we decided it might be a good idea to switch the cars around on the forecourt in order to perhaps liven up the display of stock. In doing so I noticed one vehicle had a partially deflated tyre, and asked Tony to man the office while I moved the car the few yards to the air-line which was by a grass embankment. As I knelt down by the wheel and began to inflate the tyre I heard a sharp pinging sound, quickly followed by another. At the same time I felt a splatter of wet mud hit my face. The realisation that someone was shooting at me sent me diving for cover behind the car. I waited there breathlessly for a moment, then, keeping low, made a dash for the office. Tony and I remained out of sight there for a while before locking up early and heading off home. On the drive back to Donaghadee the seriousness of what had occurred sank in. I told Tony I would close up the business for a few days, and suggested he remain at home as much as possible, as his wife Pat was expecting their first child in a few months time. Today had not been about a few young lads shouting their mouths off. It had been attempted murder.

8

The 12th of July 1972

Over the next few days I caught up with some work in the garden. We were proud of our flowerbeds and lawns, and liked everything to look nice. Now, with the summer in full swing the plants and foliage back and front of the bungalow were in joyful profusion and the grass high. I took out the mower and the shears and took my time, enjoying the fresh air, stopping and sitting with Patricia for a cup of tea and a chat whenever we felt like it. We also took the children for long walks down by the sea, breathing in all the calming sights and sounds and smells of nature. As we watched the children playing in the sand the sun moved in and out behind white clouds, illuminating the sky and warming us with its radiance. Looking out across the deep waters of the Irish Sea I recalled that it was scarcely twelve months ago that the speed boats had been racing across this same bay, and customers flocking to my business. Today this same stretch of coast was silent as a millpond, with just a few gentle waves breaking on the shoreline as the tide slowly ebbed. I thought about my current dilemma and came to the conclusion that abandoning the Crumlin Road filling station would be the best course of action. Under the terms of the monthly lease I could be out by July. Mortgage payments were important, but not enough to risk life and limb for. I would sort things out one way or another. As we walked home from the beach the children reminded me of the ice-creams and sweets they used to enjoy from the garage shop and asked me, as they often did, when the shop would be open again. I smiled and reassured them it wouldn't be long now, as we were hoping for good news about the planning permission very soon. I told Tony of my decision to quit and we began taking the more valuable of the sale cars off the forecourt and driving them back to Donaghadee, where we parked as many as would fit in the driveway of the bungalow. Two vehicles remained – an Alfa and a Morris Minor – and these I took up to the Warren Road site.

It was towards the end of June at about seven-thirty in the evening that the doorbell rang. Patricia looked through the window and came quietly through to the dining room where I was sitting with the children. She reported that there was a large grey Vauxhall car parked on the road. The vehicle she said had ladders strapped to its roof, and waiting at our front door were three men. We looked at each other with a mutual sense of caution. There were still the unpleasant phone calls to the house now and again, and these unexpected visitors did not sound like anyone I knew. The doorbell rang again. I motioned Patricia to look to the children, then fetched down my Browning shotgun, loaded it and went quietly out the back door. I padded softly round the side of the bungalow, and when I reached the corner put the shotgun down resting against the gable wall. As I came round to the front I could see the three men still waiting by the door with their backs to me. 'Yes, can I help you?' I said. They turned and looked at me over the line of cars in the driveway, which being parked bumper to bumper formed a solid barrier between us. Judging the distance between myself and the concealed shotgun I watched and waited for their reply. One man took a few steps towards me and said 'Would you be able to have a look at some machinery that needs attention for us?' 'Where is it?' I asked. 'In a quarry – not far, we can drive you there. We'll pay you for your trouble of course.' This sounded a very strange request and the man's stilted politeness did not inspire trust. 'I'm sorry I can't' I said simply and without explanation. This point-blank refusal to co-operate seemed to annoy them, which only served to strengthen my suspicions. I then noticed that one of them was wearing a Vanguard lapel badge, which I knew could only be obtained by sworn-in members of that organisation. The three of them then started talking about the civil unrest, making various assertions about politics and the killings. I listened attentively, giving only a non-committal nod of the head here and there. Before leaving, the party informed me in hostile tones that their 'day was coming soon' when they would 'get their own back'. The mask of politeness had been dropped, revealing a face of naked and uncompromising hatred. I watched them get into the Vauxhall and drive off before picking up my shotgun and returning to the house via the back door. I took the warning about revenge to be personal. Whether or not they thought I was in some sort of collusion or sympathy with the provisional IRA was probably of little importance. They knew me for a Taig, and worse a Taig with a big Mercedes and ideas above my station. If I'd got in the car with them I doubted whether my family would have seen me again. Once indoors I did my best not to show how frightened I was by this incident. I didn't want the children upset, especially after all the trials of the past few months.

Next day I called into the police station to report the harassment and attempted abduction. I also mentioned the Vanguard badge, but the officers said anyone could pick them up and didn't think it was significant. They didn't seem much interested in my story at all. Given it was a busy station and no-one had been killed perhaps this was to be expected. The alternative which crossed my mind was that they themselves knew more about last night than they were letting on. While I was at work that day a neighbour of ours called Betty told Patricia she had witnessed the three men on our doorstep, got a grasp of the situation and reported it all herself to the RUC. I arrived home in the evening to find a female police officer and the RUC inspector from Bangor at the bungalow talking to Patricia. They took the description of the men's car and told us never to open the door to strangers after 6pm and to take care during these dangerous times. This was advice we were well enough aware of. However both officers were kind and diligent in carrying out their duty and wished us well as they said goodnight. It was good to meet two such decent people in authority and know they were concerned for our welfare.

With the date to leave set for the end of July I was only opening the filling station part-time now, and using the remainder of the time to try selling the cars. One day I had someone interested in buying the Morris Minor which I'd parked up at Warren Road. However when I drove the man up there I was angered to find the car had vanished. I reported the particulars to the police and left it at that. With so much else to deal with, a stolen second-hand car wasn't going to be top priority. Moving around and talking to other car dealers I tended to hear a lot of news on the grapevine, including stories of thefts, lootings and other crimes in and around Belfast over the past few months. Such incidences were becoming so frequent they were almost losing the power to shock. This was not so when I heard the news about Gerald McCrea and James Howell. Partners in a car dealing business and both Catholic, the two men had been snatched off the street one night, hooded and then shot dead. Gerald was twenty-seven years old and married with five children, James was thirty-one. Apparently the shootings had been carried out by the UDA at Forthriver Road, close to Woodvale Road and a stone's throw from the Brookspeed Motors filling station. Like me, Gerald and James had driven a Mercedes.

Word had gone around that the UDA were now stopping vehicles across all the Loyalist areas of the city. In order to avoid the Shankill and Woodvale area, where these checkpoints were sure to be in force I took a different route along the Oldpark Road. As I turned off onto Ballysillan however I saw a group of men blocking the road. I knew if I turned back I would be under immediate suspicion, and these groups had walkie-talkie radios and were highly organised. My retreat would almost certainly be cut off. What might happen then didn't bear thinking about. Perhaps I wouldn't be stopped I thought, and continued on at the same speed. As I approached the group however one of them stepped out and raised his arm. Fighting with myself to stay calm I drew up, wound down the window and said 'Good morning'. I saw now that it was a young man, who answered me very politely. Maybe I had been taken for a Loyalist, since many of them drove Mercedes. I said courteously 'Is there a way through to the Crumlin Road from here, to take me up by the petrol station?' The young man paused. I glanced at the rest of the group. They were a tough, hard-faced bunch. They had stopped talking amongst themselves and were now peering curiously towards the car. I had a sudden flashback of driving through a Loyalist area recently and seeing the slogan 'K.A.T.' daubed in huge letters on the side of several houses. It stood for 'Kill All Taigs'. I could feel my palms sweating on the steering wheel and prayed to God my trembling arms were not noticeable. After a moment the young man lowered his head towards the driver's window. He began giving me directions towards a narrow alleyway, and a few seconds later I was steering my way to safety.

With the 12th of July now only a few days off and the effect of the marching bands likely to stir up Loyalist sentiment to highly volatile levels in some quarters, I decided to close the filling station right up until the 15th. As a result I was at home when the postman delivered a by-now familiar type of envelope. It was from the Ministry of Planning. The contents of the envelope contained, I hoped, the one chance I now had of rebuilding the business in Donaghadee. I opened it and read the letter in the presence of Patricia and the children. Scanning the contents I took in the following 'During the short number of years Mr Coogan, who lives in Donaghadee, had built up a considerable business. He had a manager and fourteen full and part-time employees this time last year. It was his intention to provide a high-class restaurant and night-club, supermarket and car showroom on three levels, and in the future a marina beside the old lifeboat slipway…the plans…were acceptable…there had been objections…

> …and in refusing this application the council had in mind a policy whereby it seeks to develop this great potential at present not fully realised in Donaghadee. I have decided that this appeal be dismissed'

I noticed that the letter was signed 12th July 1972, a day on which all government departments had been closed for the Unionist holidays.

9

Death of an Innocent

The full significance of the council's letter took a little while to sink in. Through no fault of my own my business had been destroyed, and I now owned a piece of land I could not build on, a derelict, useless site from which I could generate no income. The finality of it all was devastating news for the whole family, and I realised how much I'd been counting on the appeal being successful. Things had been difficult up to now, but the hope of restarting the business had been keeping me going. What on earth was I to do now? Some form of compensation would presumably arrive eventually, but it was anyone's guess when. And would I then be able to find, let alone afford alternative premises? Warren Road had been perfect, both as an existing business and for the wonderful potential of the shop, the Showboat Restaurant and eventually the marina. Trying to start up somewhere else would be a dispiriting experience after all the struggles. The dream seemed well and truly shattered now. And all on the whims and prejudices and probably vested interests, among the powers that be in the local community. It was a bitter pill to swallow. I had heard word already that the site might possibly be 'taken over' by Donaghadee Urban District Council to extend the adjoining park along the seafront, which of course just happened to be opposite MP Roy Bradford's home. Well I thought, the land was still my lawful property, and if anyone wanted it they'd have to pay me for it.

The possibility of selling the land was no help in the immediate term though, and not something I wanted to think about at present. Besides I still had to look after the Crumlin Road filling station till the notice on the lease expired. With a heavy heart I said goodbye to Patricia and children, who were all looking equally subdued, and made my way into Belfast. On opening up the garage I found the forecourt littered with empty beer cans and paper debris, and fetched a stiff broom in order to tidy the place up. When I'd finished sweeping and everything was looking clean again I went to turn on the illuminated signs. However when I threw the switches nothing happened, and it appeared there was a power failure of some kind. On examining the transformer for the premises I saw that some thick cables that been thrown across it, which had presumably blown out the circuits. I made a phone call to Jet, who said they'd send someone to have a look. About an hour later a man arrived with a special handle and showed me how I could use it to operate the petrol pumps manually. Apparently it was going to be some days before the electricity board would be able to fix things and restore the power. It occurred to me that maybe the same thing had happened before and Jet had decided not to tell me about it when I took on the lease. No sooner had the Jet man left the premises than the sound of heavy gunfire was heard coming from the Ligoniel area on the far side of the road opposite Ballysillan. I later found out the Provos had attacked the Royal Marines post at Mountain Mill. What with the sabotage on the electricity and now more shooting I wondered once again where or when it was all going to end.

It was on the 21st of July, around two-thirty pm, whilst sitting in the office of the filling station that I heard an explosion some way off. Looking out from the high vantage point of the forecourt I could see smoke drifting across the city, then came more explosions, followed by further plumes of smoke. This went on for about an hour, with the sound of ambulances and fire engines continuing into the late afternoon. That evening as a precaution I put as much of my own accessory stock from the garage as I could into the boot of the car and began the drive home. The atmosphere throughout the city was tense, with groups of teenagers and men out on the streets in both Loyalist and

Nationalist areas. In all nine people had died in the bombs that day and over a hundred and thirty injured. There had been twenty-three car bombs set off, with the Provos claiming responsibility for all of them, saying they had given thirty minutes to an hour's warning before each explosion.

For the next twenty-four hours I stayed out of Belfast, but by the following day the city had quietened down, and I told Patricia I would take the opportunity to go in and check over the Crumlin Road premises before finally handing over the keys in a few days. My young son Philip, hearing my intentions, was keen to go for a ride. We'd not been out a lot lately and, being a normal lively six-year-old lad he always loved an excursion in the car. I therefore decided to take him along while things were peaceful, and so with a nod from his father he jumped proudly into the passenger seat of the Mercedes and off we set. When we arrived Philip was eager to run around the forecourt and play, but this being far too risky I insisted he came straight into the office and remained there with me. Having collected the post and paperwork and checked nothing else had been interfered with. I took Philip back to the car and began the return journey via Shankill Road. I was just taking the bend at Ligoniel when I felt a sudden bolt of fear go through my body. The car which had swung out in front of us was the same Vauxhall in which the Vanguard members had come to my home the night they threatened me. It even had the ladders still strapped to the roof, and straining my eyes ahead I could clearly see two of the same men within. Turning into Woodvale I slowed up and let a bus overtake us, praying the occupants of the Vauxhall had not observed me. As I turned onto the Shankill the bus stopped beside the Malcolm Templeton garage, the main Alfa dealer. The Vauxhall was again directly in front, travelling slowly. By this time I didn't think I had been noticed, and on a curious impulse I followed on into Berlin Street. The narrow maze of roads had now become very deserted and quiet. I saw one old lady open her door a fraction. She watched as we drove by then shut the door again. In a flash I realised what was happening – I was being drawn into a trap. I looked down at young Philip sitting beside me and made a quick decision. As the Vauxhall turned off into another side-street I braked hard and reversed the car back up the road at high speed. I then got quickly back on the Shankill Road, where there were at least some people about, and feeling a lot safer, headed directly homewards. For days afterwards though the thought of what had happened, and how the detour through the backstreets might have ended, at the hands of the UVF, sent shivers up my spine.

Early on the morning of the 23rd of July I met up with Joe again in Belfast. 'Have you heard the news about Francis Arthurs?' he said. Francis was a mutual friend of ours who worked in the car radiator repair centre on the Newtownards Road. He was also a customer, having bought a car off me the previous November. 'What about him?' I asked Joe. Listening to what Joe told me next, I started to feel suddenly faint. Francis was Catholic and like Joe, from the Falls Road area. Yesterday evening said Joe, Francis had been for a night out at the Belfast Engineers Club with his girlfriend, who lived in the mixed area of Ardoyne. Afterwards they'd got a taxi home with some friends, and were travelling along the Crumlin Road when they were stopped by men wearing UDA combat jackets. Everyone in the taxi was asked their identity and where they were going. Francis worked in a Loyalist area and everyone knew he would never be mixed up in any trouble. But coming from the Falls Road he now feared for his life. When asked who he was he therefore gave the UDA men a false name. On doing so they had immediately dragged him out of the taxi, taken his wallet and examined his driver's licence. The thugs now had all they needed. The rest of the group were told to go and Francis was led away. The taxi driver had driven directly to the RUC station at Tennent Street where he and Francis's girlfriend had reported the kidnapping. After being pulled from the taxi Francis had apparently been taken to the Loyalist 'Lawnbrook Club' where a UVF unit including one of the notorious Shankill Road Butchers had beaten him to a pulp before shooting him. His body was later found dumped in a stolen car. It was later confirmed by a detective at Tennent Street station that there had been a concerted hunt for Catholics in the area that particular night, with five including Francis having been assassinated. Talking to Joe I told him about my experience with the men in the Vauxhall, both on the night they came to the bungalow, and the night before down the Crumlin side streets. It seemed highly likely they had been setting me up for a rendezvous with the same gang that killed Francis. I felt cold when I thought about it. The Shankill Road Butchers didn't get their name for nothing, and were known to use guns, knives and axes, stabbing and mutilating their victims to a slow and tortuous death. At Francis's inquest his distraught girlfriend was heard to declare, 'I don't know why they had to kill him, he was such a harmless fellow.' As I drove home I kept thinking, will they soon be saying the same about me?

10

Gift to a Young Soldier

The car bombings of the 21st of July had sparked a wave of tit-tit-for-tat killings, and July ended with ninety such deaths across the six counties. Fifty-eight of these occurred in Belfast, of which twenty were Protestant and thirty-eight Catholic. An eye for an eye, a tooth for a tooth as it says in the Bible. The Ten Commandments also decree that thou shall love thy neighbour as thyself and that thou shall not kill. But men pick out the parts of the good book that suit their own intentions, whatever God himself intended. The intentions of the British Government however now became more resolute. On the 31st of July the Army sent bulldozers and thousands of troops into the Catholic 'no-go' areas of Derry and Belfast, determined they should be no-go no longer. Two civilians died but the IRA showed little resistance, most of their leaders being thought to have now crossed the border into southern Ireland. Extra British soldiers arrived from the mainland, together with more Centurion, Saracen and Saladin tanks, jeeps and helicopters. There were now a total of twenty-one thousand British troops in the Republican areas of Belfast and Derry. Army command posts were erected in West Belfast, one in the Gaelic football ground of Casement Park and another massive and much talked-about corrugated-iron structure appeared on the Crossmaglen ground in Armagh, a very tough Provo stronghold. The message from the British seemed clear – the sectarian killings must stop and law and order now prevail.

The abusive anti-Catholic phone calls which we had been

163

plagued with at home during the marching season had now largely ceased. Leaving Brookspeed Motors was one worry off my shoulders at least. When I'd handed the keys over I decided to put the ever-pressing anxieties over money and the future onto the back burner for a few days, and try to unwind a bit. Though rebuilding the original business looked to be finally out of the question, at least on the old site, there would be other opportunities – there had to be. This is what I had to tell myself. Meantime I could still earn some money repairing cars. I had the tools of my trade at home, including some gas bottles for welding that I'd salvaged from the garage after the night of the bomb. We wouldn't starve, not as long as I had the will and the strength to work. For now though I was going to try to recoup some of that strength by giving myself a breathing space. There was always plenty to do in the garden, and busying myself with some pleasant jobs around the home would help take my mind off things. It was while I was out mowing the lawn one evening that a police car drew up outside the bungalow. An officer got out of the vehicle and walked briskly towards me. I was now increasingly nervous in situations like this, and felt my heart beat faster as he approached. 'We've located your car' he said, 'The Morris Minor?' My pulse was still thumping as I took this information in. The sense of relief stemmed from the realisation I was not about to be arrested, interned or called in for questioning. They had found the car I'd reported stolen from Warren Road some weeks ago. Well, the car was not all that valuable, but the news was something to be glad about for once. I was given the address of an army camp close to Crumlin where I could collect the vehicle. I thanked the officer and told him I'd call there as soon as I could. A couple of days later my brother Tony was free, and I took him along with me to the camp so he could then drive the Morris back. At the main gate we were detained for some time for security checks on both our drivers' licences. The engineers' depot was called up on the phone and numerous questions asked, till the sentry was finally satisfied the car we were talking about really existed and we were allowed in. Arriving at a large hangar I saw the little Morris parked inside, overshadowed by tanks and armoured cars. The bonnet was up and a young soldier was bent over doing some work on her. When we got closer I saw that the engine had been taken out and was being overhauled. I introduced myself as the owner and asked the soldier how the car had come to be in their hands. 'It was found on the roadside somewhere' he said, 'They just brought it in here for safekeeping'. He then said he was interested in mechanics and enjoyed working on cars. Being a born mechanic myself I could easily accept this explanation, a love of cars was more than enough reason to take the time and trouble of repairing and restoring one. We got talking and he told me he'd only been married a few months and that he'd had to leave his wife behind in Germany when he was posted out to Northern Ireland. It seemed hard on a young fellow only in his mid-twenties by the look of him. 'It's difficult, because everyone looks the same to us' he confided. 'We don't know who the enemy is, or why they're fighting each other. That seems depressing too.' He meant of course that Protestants and Catholics are to all intents and purposes indistinguishable from one another. All he could see was fellow-countrymen bent on slaying one another and couldn't understand why. 'I've got two more months here and then I go back to Germany and the wife. All I want is to get through this tour in one piece.' After a quick word in private with Tony I made a decision. I was so taken with the way the young soldier was nursing the Morris back to health, and with his frankness about the situation he found himself in that I felt I wanted to make a gesture. I told him I wanted him to have the car. After all I said, he'd spent not only time, but also bought spare parts from the look of the engine. He was delighted and couldn't thank us enough. On the way back Tony and I mused on how the Morris may have got from the coast road at Donaghadee to the army base in Belfast. Perhaps it had been stolen by the army themselves for some undercover work; it was not uncommon for the Military Reconnaissance Force to gather information in this way, by posing as civilians and infiltrating the Republican and other factions. The young soldier lovingly repairing the car probably knew no more than we ourselves.

165

Despite attempts to think positively about the future, circumstances were now weighing very heavily on my mind. The general climate of fear all around us was taking its toll, especially since the horrific murder of Francis. In Belfast and elsewhere, many who had lost friends and loved ones in the violence were already dependent on drugs to keep sane. In some cases whole families were put on medication, and I was now being prescribed regular tranquilisers by Dr Sargaison. I was lucky in the sense that I and my family were still in one piece so far. But supposing the men in the Vauxhall still had me on their list? I was already convinced my car registration had been noted. At home I had now fixed up alarms and monitors, with intercom speakers which picked up and allowed me to hear any movement outside the bungalow. This was switched on from six in the evening through till the next morning. Thus the first thing to wake me would be the hooves of the milkman's horse and his master's cheerful whistling, emanating loud and clear through the speakers in the hall just after 5am. This was followed by the almost deafening crash of milk crates and the chink of the bottles on the step. Although the worry still overshadowed me, at least I had some productive work and a daily routine to occupy me. It was also a comfort for all of us that I was now doing this work mostly at home, repairing engines and bodywork of the odd car and turning a small profit to put towards the household expenses. One day however, just as I was in the middle of some welding, a man in a truck called at the bungalow. He was from the BOC, the gas company, and stated that he was here to collect the two gas cylinders I was using. I told him I had an agreement with the company and had just had the cylinders refilled. He maintained however that I did not have proper garage facilities for undertaking gas welding and if I refused to hand over the cylinders he would report me to the RUC. I immediately gave him my answer that I would not surrender them, whereupon he disappeared and returned a short time later with an RUC constable, one who was in fact known to me. Both men were insistent that the BOC cylinders be taken, and with the authority of the law now behind it I had no choice but to comply. 'Here is a receipt for the gas.' said the BOC man, 'you'll be sent a refund.' Without gas I could do no more welding, which drastically cut down the amount of repair work I could undertake. It felt like a noose was tightening around my neck. I wondered who it was in Donaghadee that had informed BOC I was doing welding at home.

Amidst the gloom, there was, apart from the loving spirit of Patricia and the children, a reason for hopefulness. This hope came in the form of a communication from my solicitor, telling me the compensation claim for damage to the business was due before the courts at Newtownards on 21st November, almost one year on from the night of the bomb. The total amount claimed, and verified by professional people, amounted to £38, 915.37p, which included my own wages at £100 for each of forty-eight weeks. This fell short of what it would cost to replace everything, especially the garage equipment, but at least it should be enough to get some kind of new business up and running. The 21st of November was now only about twelve weeks away, and with something to look forward to I felt inspired to look around for a job. It was not easy to obtain employment, especially as I dared not risk going into Belfast for fear of the Loyalist death squads. After much persuading on my part I was taken on for a week's trial by the firm of 'M&T Motors' in Bangor. On my second day I was asked to replace the front wing of a VW using filler. Looking at it I told the manager that filler wasn't required, and a perfect job could be done in half the time. He took my word and I got to work panel-beating the wing and then spray painted it. The two owners of the garage were more than pleased with the finished result and told me I could have the job. Back home that night the family were delighted to hear this, even though the pay was only £30 a week, a big climb-down from running my own show. However this was a going rate and despite being back in overalls I was grateful to be earning both a wage and my self-respect. It was a six mile drive into Bangor and the army presence on the roads was very noticeable, which I found reassuring. The army could still be frightening though, especially when vehicles were stopped and searched for arms or explosives. One time I saw a soldier removing the door panel of a car as the driver looked on in shock. A woman stood with him on the roadside, her young children crying hysterically as she tried to comfort them. They all looked innocent enough, then as I drove past by I saw an RUC patrol arriving to pick them up.

The new job was giving me some of my old confidence back, though taking medication and doing hard physical work meant that I tired easily, and would return home with limbs aching and weak from the constant hammering. I was careful to keep a good record though, including my time-keeping, and always ensured any medical appointments were made outside of working hours. One morning however I was laid very low, and phoned the manager to tell him I would be unable to come in. Next morning I returned to work, handing in the sick note Dr Sargaison had given me. All went well till mid-afternoon, when one the partners in the firm came to speak to me.

'I know you are a Catholic' he began, 'and what I'm going to say has nothing to do with that.' I looked at him with a now-familiar feeling of bad tidings. 'Your work is also of a very high standard, but business has got quiet lately and I'm sorry to say we have to let you go.' This was the first time in my life I'd been sacked, having worked mainly for either my father or myself. An awful sense of rejection hit me like a kick in the ribs. I felt angry and utterly betrayed. The man had been polite and apologetic but I couldn't help wondering if he had he been telling the truth, or whether someone had put a spanner in the works when they found out I was successfully holding down a job. Depressed and close to tears I went home and told Patricia the news. Naturally she was upset, and so were the children, though I put on a brave face for them and said I'd soon find another job. At this the youngsters' smiles returned and they resumed their games around the living room floor. Patricia looked thoughtful for a few minutes and then made a suggestion. 'Why don't we think about leaving?' she said. This was the first time she'd aired such an idea since our troubles had begun, though I was sure she must have thought of it often enough, and after all that had happened I of course understood her reasoning well enough. I reminded her however that the compensation claim was due to be heard in November. When the money was finally received we could pay off our mortgage arrears – we had fallen behind in the last few months – and start a new business somewhere else in Donaghadee. Obstacles had been deliberately and maliciously placed in our path, and threats had been made, but so far we had survived and kept a roof over our heads. There was also a stubborn streak in me, and frightened as I had been by the attempts on my life I was determined not to be driven away by that fear. While the children amused themselves Patricia and I quietly talked the matter over. In spite of everything we both liked the place we'd chosen to make our home, and had numerous friends in the area. Also our standard of living could once again be good when we got back on our feet. For now I would have to be a wheeler-dealer again. The 21st of November was not far off.

11

The Meek Shall Be Murdered

On the 7th of September I went to the Falls Road to meet Jack again. Over a cup of tea I told him how worried I was about the mortgage payments on the bungalow. Earlier in the day I'd been wheeling and dealing, trying to buy and sell cars among the Belfast traders, the old insecurities haunting me again. We were being pressurised about the mortgage arrears, and the possibility that the bungalow might be repossessed was becoming all too real. Such an event would be unbearable and I didn't want to contemplate it. But Jack, ever practical, said if it came to the crunch he may be able to arrange with the Catholic Housing Association to provide a house for us in Andersonstown. This was one of the safe areas of the city for Catholics where many provos lived, and was largely controlled by the IRA. 'You'll easily get a job there in your trade' 'Thanks for the offer' I said, 'but I've the compensation claim due in November. I'll wait for the outcome of that first.' Jack then confided that if I wanted to make a bit of money I could buy a truck and do some haulage, bringing wheat across the border and claiming back the VAT. Apart from my poor health and the fact this was an illegal racket, the idea was tempting, but where would I have found the money for a truck?

The nights were now beginning to draw in, and under cover of darkness the gunmen were returning to the streets. Even in the daytime there would be Loyalist units on the streets looking for any Catholics straying into their territory. After leaving Jack I avoided the Shankill on the way home, but still noticed several groups in combat jackets, with dark glasses and scarves over their faces. That evening things came to a head when UDA men attacked two 1st Parachute Regiment Land Rovers that had driven into Berlin Street. Reinforcements were called in, and their commanding officer Lieutenant-Colonel Derek Wilford, who had been in charge in Derry on Bloody Sunday, ordered a raid on the UDA HQ in Wilton Street, where stocks of bomb-making equipment and paramilitary kit were found. The fighting spread, with more UDA men arriving to take on the Paras, and it was when a BMW with headlights full on drove into nearby Matchett Street, that yet another tragedy of the innocents was to take place. The Paras claimed they shouted at the BMW driver to extinguish his lights. When this order was ignored the car was fired upon indiscriminately, shattering the windscreen and killing Robert McKinney at the wheel. A Protestant father of five, Robert had heard about the rioting in the area and driven quickly over to collect his wife from her place of work in Wimbledon Street. Concern for his good lady's safety cost the man his own life. Later the same night another Robert, Robert Johnston, known as the 'harmless Shankill Road drunk' also became a victim. After a heavy day on the booze he was out near Berlin Street shouting 'The meek shall inherit the earth.' A witness stated he saw a soldier take aim and fire down the street, whereupon Johnston fell dead onto the pavement. Crowds on both sides now became very hostile, with insults traded across the street, the Paras shouting to the UDA, 'Take in your Union flags you bastards, you are not fit to live under them!' These crowds rapidly swelled in number, including many angry women. As they pushed towards Tennent Street RUC station, windows were broken by flying stones. In the violent skirmishes twelve policemen were injured as the troops joined in hand-to-hand fighting. William Whitelaw, now Secretary of State for Ulster told the Protestants they were playing the IRA game, 'This un-British behaviour was completely unwarranted in view of the action that has been taken against the IRA. Worse, it comes from those who profess with forcefulness that they are and wish to remain British.'. For their part the UDA called for the removal of the Parachute Regiment.

The Belfast Orange Hall statement read 'Never has Ulster witnessed such unlicensed sadists and such blatant liars as the 1st Paras. These gun-happy louts must be removed from the streets.'

The UDA not being banned or outlawed meant they could operate their patrols and checkpoints freely. This made driving around dangerous and difficult for anyone trying to earn a living on the road. My mind, rather like the situation on the streets of Northern Ireland, was becoming increasingly muddled. My once-busy way of life was now quite altered. I was pottering around, trying to make a few pounds here and there, but without any real sense of direction. The things I had strived for had disappeared in the explosion of almost a year ago. Those hopes I had since clung onto as stepping stones back to the old life had one by one been removed; the planning application, the application to the RUC, the petrol licence, the appeal against the planning department, even the taking of the gas cylinders. And then, an opportunity to earn my living as an employee had been offered, only to be quickly snatched away again. The drugs I was taking, though calming my nerves, were not really helping my clarity of thought. I still got tired easily and found it difficult to concentrate for long. Finally, the thing Patricia and I had been dreading happened. The summons for repossession of the bungalow arrived just as we were having breakfast one morning. Having the threat of losing our home made official was not the happiest of starts to a family's day. Amidst the sense of gloom everything now seemed to hinge on the compensation. The weather was now turning colder as the mild autumn breezes gave way to winter. With the leaves deserting the trees and the daylight diminishing each day the outlook seemed more miserable than ever. Looking back over the last eleven months gave me the very opposite of any sense of achievement. Rather it seemed I had been on a slow but relentlessly downward spiral, leaving me feeling increasingly wretched, worthless and unhappy. Meanwhile my solicitor in Belfast had written and asked to see me again about the compensation. The letter was not encouraging. It seemed the loss adjusters for the state were disputing the amount of the claim. Instead of the £38,915.37p they were offering the paltry sum of £6,000. Patricia was as horrified and concerned about this as I was. I could only hope this was some form of negotiating procedure to see how little I would accept. My solicitor had already given an undertaking to the Bank of Ireland for £10,000, which covered the outstanding separate mortgage on the business. The bank held the deeds of the business, against which they were to pay my outstanding invoices. I made an appointment to go in and see my solicitor the following week. The possibility of losing the bungalow was becoming ever more tangible. I could feel a sense of panic start to take hold of me and began to have visions of Patricia, the children and myself walking the streets with our possessions on a handcart. I decided to contact the Northern Ireland Housing Trust over in Newtownards and tell them of our uncertain situation. The lady I spoke to informed me there was a waiting list, but having a young family might make me an urgent case. She gave me a telephone number to call the next afternoon. Back home Patricia again brought up the subject of us leaving Northern Ireland. My brother Tony, his wife and young baby had by now already decided to do just this. 'Maybe', said Patricia, 'we could go to Canada or New Zealand and start a new life for ourselves' Maybe we could I thought, maybe we could.

Next day I 'phoned the Housing Trust again and was told bluntly that the waiting list for needy families was so long they could barely cope, let alone allocate us a house immediately. I didn't understand the comment, since I'd not asked for any such thing, only enquired about what might be available. We had something of an argument, at the end of which I was told I could leave my name on the list but it might be twelve months before we could be re-housed. Demand was high partly because many of the refugees who'd fled the ethnic cleansing and gone to the field camps in the south were now returning to new accommodation in the safer Catholic districts. It was upsetting to learn that reprisals were now taking place along the border against members of the Protestant community, many of whom had absolutely nothing to do with the sectarian violence that had been meted out elsewhere. It was heart-breaking to hear of families I'd known in Fermanagh, many of them farmers who'd been there all their lives, being forced to uproot themselves for fear of assassination from one side or the other. Patricia increasingly mentioned the idea of moving. The continuing struggle of everyday life, worrying about me and the children as well as our financial plight, was a growing strain on her. A number of her friends however, those who had been supportive since the bombing of the business, whilst appreciating her desire to leave, had warned that to do so might give the authorities an excuse to avoid paying us any compensation. Those who had opposed the planning application, and the Grand Mistress of the Orange Lodge who had vowed to drive me out of town, would no doubt derive satisfaction from this.

On the day I was to see the solicitor I first drove Brenda and Philip to St Anne's Convent, then went to collect my brother Tony who was coming with me. The meeting was not what I had hoped for from a Catholic firm. The agenda seemed dominated purely by what the Council's loss adjusters were offering me, which had now been raised to £8,000. Against the fair and accurate figure of over £38,915, as agreed by both my own and the state's accountants though, this made little difference. £8,000 would barely cover the business's debts, and wouldn't keep us in our home. I said I could not accept the offer. After talking the matter over for an hour we were no nearer a conclusion, and agreed that on the day of the hearing we would meet at the court an hour before proceedings commenced. As Tony and I left the building a bomb exploded up near the Shankill. On the return journey I kept my head till we had driven well out of the city then felt the perspiration rolling off my forehead. Feeling weak I slowed down and thought about Patricia's words: 'We could start a new life somewhere...' I wondered, should I cut my losses and take the £8,000? Would I not be a wiser man to let my enemies win?

12

The Stranger

The optimist it is said sees the glass not half-empty but half-full. Before that meeting with the solicitor I had nothing, now I had the offer of £8,000. From an empty glass to one brimming over, a true optimist might say. But naturally I could not help looking a little further back in time, to before December 7th 1971, to assess how well off I was. Perhaps, by wanting more than £8,000 I was a greater optimist than I realised. My mood however on the entering the courtroom on the morning of November 23rd was not one of hope. £8,000 was too little too late. It would not be enough to save our home. Once again Tony was with me, as was my former garage manager Sam, come to give his support and any evidence that might be required. The loss adjusters for the state, who had examined the wrecked garage back in the spring, were in conversation with my solicitor when we arrived. The hearing opened, and quickly took on the nature of a tennis match, with my man against the loss adjusters, batting the ball to and fro over the amount that should rightly be paid. Our family's future hung on the outcome, and watching the proceedings I felt like a gambler whose whole fortune has been wagered on a single game, the only difference being I had not placed the bet willingly. Despite being on strong medication, I began to feel unwell, and at one point left the courtroom for some fresh air and to try to calm my nerves. I'd also noticed that my stammer, pronounced again after being incarcerated in the Crumlin jail, and then melted away by my happy courtship, marriage and Patricia's loving care, had recently returned. I found this extremely embarrassing, especially during such a vital public occasion as today when I might be required to speak. During the break I met with my solicitor in the corridor. 'They've increased the offer' he said. 'By how much' I asked. '£2,000' He looked at me for a response. £10,000 seemed neither here nor there, it wouldn't save the bungalow. The barrister joined us. 'It would be advisable to accept' he said. 'I don't know...' I said, feeling the tremor in my voice again. 'If we reject it there's the risk you'll end up with much less' said the solicitor. £10,000 was the exact amount of the Letter of Undertaking he had extended to the Bank of Ireland on my account, so this would cover him; I could not blame him he'd been decent to help; in any case £2,000 would be earmarked for return to Dr Paisley's emergency finance fund. 'Take this amount now' said the solicitor, 'and later on you will have a much larger claim to come.' Ought I to go for the bird in the hand? It was an agonising choice. I consulted with Tony. Accepting the £10,000 would pay off all my business debts. It would also mean everything my wife and I had worked for – the business itself and our home – would be lost. Tony and I agreed I should hold out and go before the Justices again for the full and fair amount of the claim, and told the solicitor and barrister as much. However they were equally adamant I should accept what was on offer for now, and so finally, with painful reluctance, I conceded. The bird would be in the hand (or at least my debtors' hands!). Maybe the two in the bush would yet be mine.

As we left the courtroom my solicitor tried to console me, repeating that the claim for personal injuries would be a much larger amount. The question of when it might arrive however was anyone's guess, and on the way back to Donaghadee I remained disappointed and depressed. I told Tony how lucky he was to be leaving his home in Millisle for overseas, the departure date now just a week away and how Patricia and I had discussed emigrating. I arrived home mentally exhausted. Patricia had already collected Brenda and Philip and Aileen was back from the grammar school in Bangor. Over a quiet tea I told them what had happened at the hearing and afterwards Patricia and I talked through our position. The people at the housing trust seemed unable to help us, and the only other option seemed to be to ask Jack to get us into a house in Andersontown. But the idea of living in Belfast right now with our young children was not inviting. And staying on in Donaghadee, or anywhere I was known, carried with it the cold fear of men in Vauxhall cars, hidden snipers and the late-night knock on the door, not to mention devices left on doorsteps. I could never be free of such anxieties in Northern Ireland. Tony's imminent departure for foreign shores sprang to both our minds, and now that it seemed clear we were to lose our home, the idea of starting a completely new life in another part of the world seemed to beckon even more strongly. Patricia had cousins in New Zealand, in both the North and South Island, and the images of sunshine, fresh air and wide open spaces, suggested this would be a wonderful place to set our sights on. Such a move would require time and planning, and we decided to write immediately to Patricia's aunt and uncle, who lived in Hamilton, near Rotura City in the North Island, and ask their advice.

To give us a breathing space I applied to have the repossession hearing put back till after Christmas. Meantime we put the bungalow on the market at a keen price to attract a quick sale in the New Year. We'd need a 'half-way house' before we were able to go to New Zealand, and decided to look over the border for a cheap place to rent. I began making weekly trips to 'Eason's' newsagents in Belfast, and picking up copies of the various southern Irish county papers. We would then scan the classified columns in the back pages, phoning for further details of any likely sounding properties advertised for rent. We received a reply from Patricia's relatives, including lots of information about New Zealand. Rotorua was famous for its health-giving thermal waters and the Rainbow Springs. Mokia Island in the centre of Lake Rotorua had once been a stronghold of the Maori people. Patricia's aunt and uncle assured us New Zealand was a lovely country in which to bring up a family, with plenty of work for those with a skilled trade. Patricia's cousin ran his own motor business, and could no doubt guide me and help me find my feet in the local job market.

Around mid-December we phoned a number from one of the newspaper property adverts and spoke to a lady in the west of Ireland. She had a cottage for rent which sounded ideal, and we duly arranged to go down and look the place over. Our first impressions were somewhat disappointing. The brick dwelling was nestled between tall trees and resembled more of a barn or granary than a home, lying in a remote spot just off the main road. It looked decidedly bleak compared to the luxury of our modern bungalow, and there was no central heating, a comfort we had grown very accustomed to during the long cold winters. Nevertheless the rent of £1.50 per week was affordable, the area safe and the landlady, who lived nearby seemed a decent old type, besides which our sojourn there would not be long. I therefore paid the landlady a few months rent in advance and said we would move in sometime in early January. Apart from a few army checkpoints along the Fermanagh border our journey back to the North was smooth. It was late evening by the time we arrived at the bungalow, and after securing the doors and windows we all retired for the night, secure in the knowledge that now we would at least we have a roof over our heads. Some time in the small hours we were disturbed by a noise coming over the monitors in the hallway. I jumped quickly out of bed, put on my gown and slippers and picked up my gun. The sound seemed to be emanating from the back of the bungalow. Stealthily and without putting on the lights I made my way out the front door. The street lamps shone dimly but showed up nothing unusual. Again I heard noise from the rear, and cautiously went around the side. Straining my eyes into the gloom I noticed saw some slight movement along the shrubbery, going along as far as next door's hedge. Betty our neighbour was already at her back door. 'Philip' she called over, 'I saw someone going out through our back garden'. Being on her own she was clearly frightened and asked if I would check her house and garden to make sure everything was alright. For her peace of mind and my own I made a careful sweep of both our properties but could see nothing out of place. I slept fitfully for the remainder of that night, thinking someone may have attempted to leave a device in the hedge. Next day Betty called the security services who made a thorough search. As I watched the uniformed officers grimly poking around the shrubs and manhole covers the prospect of New Zealand's peaceful sunshine seemed more beguiling than ever.

As Christmas approached everyone was on alert. The year having seen so many sudden violent deaths already meant that vigilance was a common state of mind in the community. Christmas was Christmas however, and being not entirely immune from the festive spirit, I called one December evening for a drink at one of the seafront hotels in Donaghadee. I knew a few of the people there, and was sitting talking quietly at the bar when a man who I remembered had entered the premises just after me, came up and joined our group. How exactly he did this I still cannot recall, perhaps he knew some of the others. He was certainly unknown to me. The stranger seemed very friendly, especially towards me, and at one point bought me a drink as he conversed with all and sundry. After a half hour or so the man leaned over and suggested to me that we both go for a trip to nearby Portaferry, seeing, as he put it, that I had 'such a good car'. To this day I do not know why, but I assented to the suggestion. Finishing our drinks, the stranger and I left the hotel and got into the Mercedes. As we set off my passenger suggested a particular route he said was best for Portaferry. I declined, saying I knew the road I was taking and preferred to keep to it, which he accepted and said no more. The fishing town of Portaferry was a largely Catholic place in which I felt safe enough. Nevertheless as we arrived there I began to feel annoyed by the stranger's company and regretted my easy-going compliance back at the hotel. Because the man was on his own didn't mean it was a good idea to give him a lift. As we drove along the seafront he pointed out an establishment saying it was a good place for a drink and a meal. I didn't like the look of this place, and fortunately it looked to be closed. The stranger suggested we go up and ring the bell, just in case, at which I demurred. I was now suspicious of the man, but couldn't be sure if he was looking for a free meal or had some darker motive. The stranger then mentioned an alternative location, to which I replied that I'd better be getting home now. We had travelled but a little distance when the man asked if I might stop while he made a telephone call. It seemed a reasonable enough request and seeing a nearby phone box I pulled up. The man made his call, got back in and we resumed our journey. A few miles from home, driving carefully along the narrow road there was sudden bang and the car lurched abruptly to one side. Struggling desperately to retain hold of the wheel I just about managed to keep us on the road. I must have had a blow-out, which surprised me since I always kept the car well-maintained, especially checking the tyres for wear and tear. The stranger advised me to stop the car, but I told him firmly that it was better to press on. At this point the man's tone of voice and general demeanour became noticeably altered. After a few curt comments he sat silently as we bumped along with one wheel on the rim for the remainder of the journey. Reaching Donaghadee I asked him to get out of the car at the seafront and then made my way home. Patricia was waiting up worried that something had happened to me. I never told her the full details, just that I'd gone for a late drink. Next morning I examined the Mercedes. I was expecting to find that a shot had been fired at the tyre but there was no particular evidence as such, apart from the tyre having been in good condition beforehand. I changed the wheel and repaired the wing and bumper which had sustained some damage. Later on I went over to the hotel to enquire about the stranger. Nobody it seemed knew who he was or had even seen him before the previous evening. The thoughts were now tumbling about in my head. To whom had the stranger made the phone call and why? The tyre blowing so soon after could not have been a coincidence, and the man's attitude – so over-familiar at first, then sullenly hostile as I refused to co-operate. If it had been another attempt on my life was it Loyalists or, being staged in the Catholic area of Portaferry perhaps there was collusion with the intelligence services to pin a murder on the IRA. I fixed the memory of the stranger's face in my mind, in case I should see him again. I hoped I would not.

It was now nearly Christmas and I wanted it to be as peaceful and happy a time for the children as possible. A buyer had now been found for the bungalow, so the last and most significant detail of our flight was in place. I had begun selling off my remaining vehicles to raise a little cash to tide us over. The festivities came and went quietly for us, and I made sure to stay around the house as much as possible. All I wanted now was to see my family and myself safe in the little cottage in the south. I felt sure that despite my often poor health and lack of energy I would be able to earn a living doing repairs down there. After that would be the welcoming shores of New Zealand. Meantime I would continue my fight for compensation for the livelihood that had been destroyed. Tony and his wife and child had now departed for foreign shores, with barely a penny in their pockets, but glad for the most part to be going. He and I would be on opposite sides of the globe, vast oceans and continents between us, but close in spirit; each of us poor yet rich in the love of our families, and embarking on a whole new chapter in our lives.

PART THREE

1

Exiles

It was a cold, miserable day as we drove away from our home for the last time. Patricia and I barely exchanged a word as we took one final look at the bungalow. There was no point pretending to ourselves. We felt sad, bewildered and bitter at having to leave the place in which we'd invested so much of our lifeblood. We would arrive in our new place as complete strangers, though being fifty miles south of the border we would at least feel safe. Aileen, Brenda and Philip were disconsolate at saying goodbye to their familiar surroundings and the many friends they had played so happily with, though their youthful spirits were balanced by a sense of adventure for what lay ahead. In the car (an ageing Datsun now, since I had cashed in my prized Mercedes)were all our worldly goods, such as they amounted to, together with a puppy that had been given to us by a kind neighbour. The children were enchanted with this bounding, four-legged new member of the family, whom we had named Rover. As we motored on the weather remained cold, with icy patches on the narrow roads. All was quiet and peaceful in the countryside, and looking out at the tangled and unmanaged hedgerows flanking our path, our thoughts must each have dwelled on what life would be like for us now. Passing through little towns we were struck by the carefree air with which shoppers went about their business unhindered by security checks or barriers. There was not a soldier in sight, law and order being left to the Garda.

It was late afternoon when we pulled up outside the old

single-storey cottage. The January sky was already darkening behind the tall trees and the scene which greeted us looked bleak, a forlorn pile of stones in a frozen landscape. The children lost no time in tumbling out of the car, with Rover's bark echoing through the chill air. Patricia and I both shivered as we opened the front door and went into the kitchen. The old iron range didn't look as though it had been used for years, but it was vital that a fire be lit straightaway or we'd all catch pneumonia. Exploring the shed Aileen discovered some bags of turf which seemed dry and solid and lit up easily enough. We soon had a good fire burning, though there was quite a lot of smoke at first which obliged us to open the kitchen window for ventilation. It soon settled down though and gave a better draw allowing us to close the window. The chimney breast warmed up, taking some of the dampness out of the air. Rover had at first been shivering like the rest of us, and the children had put some spare clothes over him to keep him warm. He now settled himself down by the range and looked more content, wagging his tail as everyone made a fuss of him. Luckily the electricity was working, but apart from that the services in the cottage were very antiquated. The landlady had explained that for bathing and washing clothes rainwater off the roof was collected in an outside tank. Water suitable for drinking and cooking however had to be drawn from a pump about a mile away in the village. I found a small container in one of the cupboards and headed off to fill it up. On my return the kitchen had warmed up nicely. I plugged in the electric kettle and made a pot of tea, while Patricia and the children organised the cooking. Apart from fruit and a few sweets during the journey we hadn't eaten since leaving Donaghadee and were more than ready for a hot meal. Rover was fed too, his tail swaying with gratitude. My next task was to assemble the beds we had brought with us. Since there were only two small bedrooms in the cottage Aileen, Brenda and Philip had to share, and had only enough space to walk up one side and get into bed. Patricia and I told them we might buy new bunk-beds, which would give them more room. The children knew money was short, and jumped for joy at this prospect.

Next morning the weather was bitterly cold again. With my fingernail I scraped the frost from the inside of the tiny bedroom window and checked on my old Datsun parked across the road. I got dressed and went into the kitchen, where I made some tea and then set about cleaning the range. I went outside where a bitter easterly wind was blowing, and fetched some more turf in from the shed. I got a good fire going and checked on our supplies. There was very little food and the drinking water I'd collected last night was nearly all gone. I decided that when the frost lifted we would drive to the nearest town for some shopping and try to buy some larger water canisters, together with a few bags of coal. Glancing out of the kitchen window I noticed there was another car parked opposite. It was a police vehicle, and a Garda officer appeared to be examining the Datsun. A moment or two later he crossed the road and came towards the cottage. I opened the door. 'Good morning' I said. The officer said abruptly 'Are you the owner of that vehicle?' I confirmed that I was. He then asked why I was living in 'this old building'. Being on medication I was often short of patience, and I found myself offended by this questioning. I replied that we were the lawful paying tenants of the property, and furthermore that although in poor condition it was now our home and all we could afford. I then told the officer what had happened to us in Donaghadee and thus how we came to be here, after which he went away. Meantime Patricia had got up, and having heard the exchange on the doorstep was as upset as I was. Such a suspicious intrusion on the first day in our new abode seemed as though the problems that had beset us in the north were pursuing us even here. I now felt quite unwell, and unable to go into town. Patricia was very understanding and told the children, who were straining eagerly at the leash, that we would all go into the village later on. I had some breakfast and after a couple of hours I began to regain my composure when the Garda officer returned. This time he was very polite and sympathetic, and apologised for disturbing us earlier on. He wished us well he said, and hoped we would settle down in the area alright. Perhaps he had been doing some checking up on us.

Nevertheless we thanked him for calling back and for the goodwill. My mood now improved we set out for the ten-mile journey into the town. The outing was a tonic for us all. We bought two big water containers, plentiful groceries, some sweet treats for the children and ordered bunk beds, returning to the little cottage with the sense we had made a start in improving our new life. Within a few days the bunk beds arrived, much to the children's delight. Our electric cooker which we'd brought from the bungalow, I wired up to the mains, which made Patricia's life easier in the kitchen. Next Patricia and I went to register with the local doctor, and explained our circumstances. The doctor was a very pleasant man and asked about the children's health as well as our own. He gave me the medicine I required but refused to accept any payment, commenting that he did not wish to add to our burdens at present.

Being mid-January every day was icily cold, with softly falling snow muffling the cottage in deep folds of white, much to the children's pleasure. To keep the chill and damp at bay we added some coal to the turf fire in the range, which pumped up the heat and kept the kitchen warm as toast. We were concerned to re-establish some sort of normality in the children's lives, and to this end Patricia visited the local school and met the headmaster, who said our three would be very welcome. The Irish language was taught in the south but he said being young they'd pick it up and the school would help them along. Another visit I had to make was to the local Garda station. I had brought my Browning shotgun across the border, together with a letter from the Justice Minister Des O'Malley T.D. granting me permission to import it. This letter I left with the Garda pending the arrival of a firearms licence, which I applied and paid for immediately. The gun would be handy if there was a chance of wildfowling for food, and also gave me a sense of security. After a week or so we were beginning to get a feel for the quiet life of the country-side. The place seemed very isolated after what we'd been used to, but the tranquillity was also soothing. What was more difficult was the absence of 'creature comforts'. After our spacious, centrally heated bungalow daily life in the cottage seemed primitive. The children especially missed having running hot water whenever they wanted it. There was a bath fitted into a small extended area, but every bit of warm water we wanted had to be heated up on the old range or boiled in the kettle, making it a laborious process. And though there was an indoor toilet, it was not working properly and meant we had to face the cold and go to the original outdoor facility. Life in the outside world was different too. One day the local Garda sergeant called round to deliver my shotgun licence, and Patricia took the opportunity to find out more about the local shops and services. Previously we'd had our own telephone line at home, but couldn't afford it here, and wanted to know the nearest call box so we could phone relatives, and also to keep in touch with my solicitor about the garage site and injury claim. The sergeant gave Patricia the location of the post office where letters and parcels could be sent and said that calls could be made from there. This was not however a modern payphone such as were common in the North, but an old-fashioned machine, manually operated by the postmistress turning a handle. The quaintness of this system served as a picturesque reminder of the very different ways of life north and south of the border. Here time had to a large extent stood still, which wasn't a bad thing in itself, though it seemed peculiar to us.

The main concern now was money for the basic essentials of rent, food and fuel to keep us warm. Our meagre reserve of cash was all but gone and I had not found a job yet. Trying to do car repairs from home would be very difficult with no workshop or vehicle access and impossible during such inclement weather. One day a man called at the cottage and introduced himself as Mr Green, the 'social welfare officer'. He had heard of our enforced exile from the North presumably from the local doctor, and wanted to see how we were faring. Sitting down over a cup of tea, Mr Green looked around at the damp, peeling walls and creaking, draughty windows. He could clearly see the conditions we were living under and that the place was not ideal for raising a family. 'How are you planning to earn a living here Mr Coogan?' he asked. 'I'm a skilled motor repair tradesman and am looking around in the newspapers, but have yet to see any vacancies' I replied. Mr Green nodded and put his briefcase on the table. He then took out a long form and began filling it in. 'I'm going to arrange Home Assistance money for you from the Western Health Board' he said. 'It'll help pay for food, rent and some coal for the range.' This was good news, even though it didn't help one's pride to take money that had not been worked for. Mr Green then produced another long form. 'Both yourselves and your three children are entitled to free medical treatment from the Board.' Having established that we had no income, property or land he completed all the paperwork then handed us a small advance of money to see us through the next few days. 'Thank you so much Mr Green' I said, feeling genuine gratitude towards the man. 'I don't know what we'd have done' joined in Patricia with great relief. 'You are entitled to it' said Mr Green. 'I only wish it could have been more. You can call at my office in the town each week for your allowance. Good day now.' Of course I did own some land, and had told Mr Green so – the site on which the business had stood was still legally mine, though I could realise none of its value at the present time. The future was another matter.

2

The Granary and the Path

Slowly we began to make friends in the area. Some mornings when the weather was very bad, I would scrape the snow and frost from the car and ferry the children the mile into the village and drop them at school, returning to collect them at home time. Sometimes Patricia would come along, and we would get chatting to other families at the school gates. We did hear there was a rumour going around that I was an IRA man, and another one that I was a Protestant, due mainly it seemed to some people not seeing me at mass. But such gossip was not unusual in rural parts. At the cottage I had now managed to get our washing machine wired up and plumbed in, and fixed the indoor toilet up to the tank so that it flushed. A coal delivery arrived paid for by some of the welfare money and we were able to keep the range stoked up against the bitter northerly winds that buffeted day and night. Our thoughts now turned to the future, in particular New Zealand and how we were to raise the money for the fares. Patricia's aunt Nora had been keeping in touch from Rotorura, assuring us that her son Percy would provide information about employment in the local motor trade. Alternatively her other son Victor was in a position to secure me a job at the airport in Christchurch. There seemed no shortage of opportunity in New Zealand; the problem was how to get there. Sitting over a pot of tea with Patricia one grey afternoon and gazing out of the back window of the cottage, my eye travelled across the walled yard to the old granary shed where we had found the turf and now stored the coal. The shed was dry and sound with a solid gravel and cement floor. Though large enough inside to house a car, the shed had only a three-foot wide door. Besides which how would I bring a vehicle in from the main road, the surrounding area being very littered and overgrown? I had noticed however that beneath the accumulated rubbish and tall weeds at the back of the shed, there were some solid stones showing through underfoot in places. However I would really need a flat surface the whole way, leading right round to the iron gates at the front of the cottage and out onto the road. Having such access might make the old granary shed very suitable as a workshop. It would take a lot of hard work to clear and level the ground before a vehicle could get through and to lay even a rudimentary road surface was really a civil engineering job. Perhaps I could get away with a dirt track. But then there was the matter of access into the shed itself with just its single narrow door. The first task would be to investigate the state of the ground, but with all the snow and ice this was difficult at the moment. In the meantime I decided to go and have a look at the doorway. I finished my cup of tea, put on my overcoat and scarf and went across the yard, Patricia looking curiously at me through the window. I examined the doorway and the surrounding walls of the shed. The brickwork was solid and strong. To create an entrance wide enough for a car would first require a steel joist to be inserted overhead, after which the walls on either side could be pared back. I could certainly do the job, if I paced myself, however the crucial aspect was obtaining the landlady's permission. If, when the weather allowed I could also clear the access, the finished job would be an improvement to her property. I went back indoors, since it was nearly time to fetch the children from school. 'I have an idea' I announced to Patricia, 'for earning the money for our fares to New Zealand' Patricia's face became animated. 'I thought you were up to something out there in the cold all that time' she said with a smile. 'But tell me all about it later. I don't want the children to start walking home and getting their feet wet. The snow's still awful deep Philip, so off you go to school! They'll be cold and hungry so I'll get some dinner on.'

192

After dinner that evening, while the children did their homework and Patricia and I washed the dishes, I discussed my plans for turning the granary shed into a workshop. Patricia was delighted. 'Philip that's the best news I've heard in a year!' The children, overhearing the conversation, were overjoyed, and began to jump up and down shouting 'Daddy, daddy – will we have lots of money again?!' I explained that yes, I hoped to begin earning some money when the work was completed, if God gave me some help. At this they all promised to say extra prayers that night and little Brenda ran over to cuddle Rover in his basket and tell him the good news. 'You'd better go and see Mrs Law as soon as possible' said Patricia. This was true; Mrs Law was the landlady, and without her consent the scheme was a non-runner. 'I'll wait till the snow has thawed a little' I said. It struck me the landlady might not know or recall the full history of the outbuilding and the land leading off it. When the snow and ice was gone we could both establish whether there was indeed a pathway, and get a better idea of the feasibility of the plan.

Over the next few weeks the temperature began to rise a little each day. When the snow had dwindled to patches and as the ice slowly liquefied and drained away, I took a spade and for several days began to probe the terrain around the shed. The ground was still hard as iron, or so I thought. For digging under the clay and grass, I discovered my spade was actually striking stone. Peeling back small areas of this surface covering revealed ancient cobblestones, which must have lain buried for many long years. Was there really a cobbled pathway, stretching from the granary shed out to the road? It was too good to be true! I made further excavations in different parts of the field and found to my excitement this must be the case. The cobbled lane seemed uneven, but more importantly it was solid, and when uncovered and swept clean would undoubtedly make a respectable driveway for bringing in client's cars for repair. Not that I had any clients yet, but that would come. I told Patricia of my discovery and brought her out to have a look. She could see the evidence of the buried pathway, but had reservations about the work involved. 'You'll never be able to dig and lift all that undergrowth and soil away by yourself' she demurred. This wasn't a lack of faith in me; the area of the lane measured about seven feet across and stretched a good three hundred feet from the granary shed out to the road, all of it buried under at least six inches of matted grass and clay. Patricia knew how physically vulnerable I often was nowadays, and was worried about the consequences of over-exerting myself. But I was well aware of the need to pace myself. Time was one asset I had in abundance, and I now had the opportunity to use it wisely and profitably. 'I'll be alright' I assured my wife. 'With a barrow and spade and the weather improving I can take it steady, a little bit every day will get us there.' Having answered Patricia's concerns she looked much more positive. 'Well that's good. And you have all your tools you brought with you for when the workshop is ready' I nodded. 'And operating from home I'll have no overheads to pay, and no time or expense travelling' Patricia beamed. 'I think it's a wonderful idea Philip. But there's still one thing you've got to sort out first – Mrs Law.' This was true. I mustn't count my chickens before they hatched. 'I'll call on her tomorrow' I said.

Next day after dropping the children at school, I went around to Mrs Law's nearby home. 'Ah hello Philip, won't you come in' she said and ushered me into her cosy parlour. 'How are you all settling in? I've heard you've done some work on the cottage. I must call up one day when the weather gets better.' I told her she'd be very welcome of course, then immediately broached the reason for my visit. 'I wanted to ask you about some further improvements to your property Mrs Law, things I can carry out myself and without any expense to you.' The old lady looked at me steadily. 'What kind of improvements?' she asked. 'Well, I want to install a larger door to the granary, sufficient to accommodate a motor car.' She said 'What do you want to do that for?' I thought, I had better give her the full story. 'I'd like to convert the granary into a workshop. I'm a skilled motor repair man as I told you, and have been looking for work in the area but without success. Having this facility would give me the chance to work for myself. I need to work, and the family needs an income…'

I tailed off, watching the old lady's expression. I prayed she would not refuse me. After a moment she got up from her chair, opened a cupboard and took down two glasses and a whiskey bottle. 'The granary is very old' she said. The walls may not stand it; supposing they crack? It might bring the whole place down.' I explained to her my plan to do the job correctly, using a steel girder of sufficient dimensions and to re-point the mortar around the stone walls to strengthen them. Mrs Law listened, inclining her head as her finger traced the neck of the whiskey bottle. 'And furthermore' I said sitting up 'did you know there was a cobbled lane leading from the granary and buried beneath the grass? I could clear it and restore the vehicle access to the property, which would greatly enhance the place...' Mrs Law remained standing, meditatively caressing the rim of one of the glasses, which glimmered as it caught shafts of mid-morning sunlight which had just begun to peep across the parlour windowsill. 'Well now' she began carefully, 'I will say this. A man has a right to earn his living, and if the use of the granary will assist you then you have my permission to carry out any necessary alterations, provided they do not damage the building.' I didn't know what to say, apart from to thank her and give my assurance that every possible care would be taken. 'And now Philip will you take a glass of whiskey with me' said Mrs Law pouring out two generous measures and handing me one. 'Thankyou Mrs Law, I'm most grateful.' As the whiskey warmed my throat my own spirits began to expand in a way they had not done for some time. I felt quite convivial sitting drinking with Mrs Law, almost as if she were family. 'I'll also cut back and prune the overgrown bushes at the front of the cottage if you wish' I said. 'And I was thinking the plot to the side could be cultivated for a vegetable garden. It would be good to put the soil to use. You would be welcome to a share of whatever we can grow there...' Mrs Law sipped her whiskey and smiled, nodding kindly as she listened to my plans.

3

A Place to Work

You've got a smile on your face!'
'I was given a whiskey!'
'I can see you've had something.'

Patricia was standing by the front door of the cottage as I arrived back from Mrs Law's. We went in and warmed ourselves by the range while I told her the good news that our landlady had given permission for me to convert the old granary and restore the cobbled lane out to the main road.

'I told her I'd do up the flower beds at the front too and generally smarten the place up a bit.'

'And will she be paying you, or taking something off the rent for all this work?' asked Patricia.

'Getting her consent was more important, and having a workshop that's rent-free is worth all the work.'

'I suppose so' agreed Patricia 'but are you sure you can cope with the work?

'The lifting of the steel beam might be tricky, but I'll deal with that when the time comes.'

'I can help with that' volunteered Patricia.

'No, no, thanks, but it'll be too much for you.'

Patricia looked concerned again.

'Don't worry' I said, 'The work will give me something to do.'

'When will you start?'

'Tomorrow, I shall start tomorrow.'

Next day I began digging up the earth from the lane just inside the main gate. My plan was to first bring my own car in and park it on our side of the road, closer to the cottage. Once this was accomplished I continued digging back, lifting and scraping the earth up from the old cobbles and gradually inching towards the granary which would soon be my workshop. When the weather was wet I took shelter inside the granary, clearing out rubbish and repairing the walls. Tiredness and pains came and went, and I continued taking the tranquilisers originally prescribed by Dr. Sargaison. One morning a particularly acute bout of toothache forced me to take the day off and go into town for an extraction. Every now and then the family came out to inspect progress, the children laughing and jumping around the newly created space inside the granary. It was a few days after my visit to the dentist that, whilst taking a mid-afternoon break and a cup of tea by the range, I began to feel peculiar. It was the same strange sensation I'd had just before taking the children to school that day in Donaghadee after which I had fainted in the hall way of the bungalow. This time however I remained upright, though my whole body began to tremble slightly. It lasted only a few seconds, but Patricia who was with me in the kitchen noticed immediately. 'Philip, are you alright' she said, with alarm in her voice. The children had just returned from school and also looked at me anxiously. 'It's that feeling I got last year, but it's passing, I'm fine now' I said. Patricia rose from the table. 'I'm going round to the neighbours' she said decisively, 'I'll get them to call the doctor.'

When the doctor arrived Patricia apologised for calling him out. 'I was worried doctor. I wonder if you' take a look at him. He just started shaking all of a sudden.'

'How are you now?' the doctor asked me.

'Fine' I said, 'the same thing happened a while back in our old home and I was alright afterwards.'

The doctor and Patricia left the kitchen and I could hear them in conversation, though couldn't make out what was being said.

'I'd like you to see a consultant as soon as possible' said the doctor on his return. 'Over at the hospital. Will you go if I make an appointment?' Presumably he'd had people not turn up before.

'I will doctor, if you think it necessary' I said.

'It's nothing to get frightened about, but I think there's a chance you could have developed epilepsy, and it's best to get a specialist opinion in these cases.'

'What's epilepsy?' I asked, having no knowledge of the condition.

'It's a disorder of the nervous system and can be caused by a number of things, a serious car accident for example. Or in your case suffering a trauma from a violent act, such as the bombing of your premises, can bring it on. Epilepsy is not harmful in itself and can be treated.'

On this note of reassurance the doctor concluded his visit and left us alone to take in the implications of the news. However as yet we knew so little. Epilepsy – what did it mean?

'It'll be for our peace of mind to see the consultant' said Patricia, to which I could only nod in agreement.

At the hospital, the consultant looked down at my medical notes and then back at me. 'I see that you have never suffered from epilepsy before…' Did this mean I definitely had it now then? I wondered. '…apart from probable symptoms shortly after your property was bombed fourteen months ago. And you have always had an active life without major illness apart from the TB at an early age and mumps after your youngest was born'

'That's correct' I said. The consultant continued, 'I'm going to put you on some tablets called Epanutin for the epilepsy and I want you to come and see me again in three months time' He handed me an appointment card with a time and date. 'You can carry on with the work you've been doing around the cottage'

Patricia and I thanked him. It didn't seem too bad, and the main thing was he hadn't stopped me from working, which would have been a real blow now the plan for the repair business was looking promising. Later that same day however, I received some less encouraging news. After the evening meal I went off to see my GP and give him the consultant's letter regarding my prescription. 'I've already had a call from your consultant' he said. 'What did he say?' I asked, worried there may be further complications. 'Oh, nothing he hasn't already told you. Of course you'll have to be careful when handling machinery and also when you're driving.' On hearing this, a sudden shadow of depression appeared on my horizon. 'Now don't be too downhearted' said the doctor, 'You'll be fine.' After leaving the surgery I went straight to the chemist and collected the tablets. Back home I took out the bottle and examined the label. It read: "Do not drive or go near machinery". The black cloud on the horizon intensified. This was a far stricter prohibition than the consultant or my GP had suggested. Did taking the prescribed medication mean that I was forbidden from doing the two things on which my whole livelihood depended? Was all the work of restoring the lane to be fruitless? I felt an intensity of anger, as if a door was being shut in my face. 'Look at these instructions!' I said to Patricia, handing her the tablets.

She read the label, and trying to hide her concern said 'All you can do is to be as careful as you can.' I sat at the table and calmed myself a moment. I said 'How can the consultant be sure I have epilepsy when no tests have been done?' Patricia nodded. 'That's true' she agreed. I then said quietly 'I shall keep on working just as I have been ever since the bombing. The granary is almost complete, and only requires the raising of the steel beam into position. With all this rain nothing can be done outside on the lane, so tomorrow I will raise the beam.'

The following morning I drove the children to school and returned home to commence work immediately on the most important task for the creation of the workshop. There was a strong wind blowing along with the rain, which made the ground outside slippery, but I had all the equipment I needed ready on the inside of the granary, which remained dry. I had already hollowed out an eighteen inch aperture in the brickwork on either side of the existing door, ready to accommodate the beam, and to lift it to the required height I had assembled a large trolley-jack, stout wooden props, some planks and two lengths of rope. Having laid the beam onto the jack I began cranking it up to its full height. From here, using the ropes, I lifted each end at a time a little further up, bracing against the wall with the planks and props. Eventually the whole beam was lying level with the top of the door and I was able to slide it carefully bit by bit into the apertures. With the beam safely inserted I stood back and allowed myself a brief moment of satisfaction. The most difficult part was done. I secured the two wooden props under the beam then mixed up some mortar and cemented around the apertures, leaving some parts till when the material had hardened and set in a day or so. That night I retired to bed with a pleasing sense of achievement, and over the coming days, despite the continuing dreadful weather I was now sufficiently inspired to press on with clearing the lane. When in a few days I had made the ground level and firm enough I drove my car along it and into the rear yard of the cottage for the first time. Though only a few hundred feet, freeing up the lane also felt like a considerable achievement. If I cleared out the rest of the weeds and rubble from the yard I reckoned five or six cars could easily be parked on the premises, more if the small field either side of the lane were to be used. Word had got round about my activities, with John our next door neighbour looking in and offering high praise on the transformation. Mrs Law soon heard glowing reports, and when calling on her to pay the rent, she smiled at me and said, 'I hear you are still working terribly hard.' Everyone seemed very encouraging.

By the first week of March spring was well and truly on the way, with songbirds singing their clear notes in the hedgerows around the cottage. Having only ever known our new habitat in the winter, we now had the pleasing expectation of seeing the place in a whole new light. My health remained much the same and I only felt really well when working hard and fully absorbed on whatever was the job in hand, the repetitive movement of the spade or the trowel lulling my spirit to a more harmonious plane, lost and at peace in the natural rhythms of toil. However with the days getting longer, the weather warmer and the workshop almost ready, there was also a growing sense of possibility in the air. There was now only one thing left to do to complete the conversion of the granary into a workshop, and that was demolish the walls on either side of the old narrow doorway. The cementing around the beam and the general strengthening of the brickwork that would remain had now had plenty of time to settle. Taking a club hammer and crowbar I began chipping away between the stones. The ancient soft clay wall soon crumbled and fell away. Having pared back the wall on both sides I then took a shovel and cleared up the pile of brick debris which had fallen onto the concrete floor. When everything was tidy I stood back and surveyed the wide entrance space, which seemed vast, and had the effect of making the interior of the granary itself appear larger. Apart from a little bit of making good where the walls had been demolished, the conversion was all but finished. I'd need to run an electric cable in for light and power tools, but that wouldn't be difficult. When they arrived home from school the children got quite a surprise seeing half the granary wall missing. They ran in and out across the threshold, with Rover chasing wildly alongside. 'Daddy, daddy, it's so big – we can put the car in.' Since they were so delighted by this idea I said I'd park our Datsun in there just for that night. Before I had chance though a thunderstorm blew in and we all ran into the cottage to escape the sudden downpour. Eating dinner in the kitchen we watched the rain falling in great sheets, while the noise as it lashed the tin roof was deafening. The storm was still raging at bedtime, with thunder and lightning making the children excited and Rover skittish. We could also hear that the outside water tank, which collected the rainwater from the roof, was overflowing onto the yard. This opening of the heavens might almost have been a dramatic salute to mark the completion of the workshop. So long as it didn't last forty days and forty nights, as I hoped to open for business before then.

4

Just One Cortina

The small compressor for spray painting and the electric lights were now installed, and I began looking around for business. This was a case of talking to as many people as I could in and around the village, and letting them know I was ready and available for all types of mechanical and car bodywork repairs. Since we had no telephone, customers would have to call at the cottage in person. When touting my services I made particular mention of the fact that my rates would be below the average, since overheads were low and I was eager to take on work. Everyone was pleasant and said they'd bear me in mind and put the word around. However as the weeks went by I had still not secured a single customer. I tried to fathom the reason for this. There were repair shops over in the nearest town and doubtless other mechanics locally, but on the other hand I also saw plenty of cars on the roads. I realised that in many respects we were still outsiders here and I could not expect to set myself up overnight. I also began to realise how much hope I had pinned on getting the granary converted. The objective of creating a workshop had driven me on; now it was done but with no jobs coming in, I was no further forward than before. Though Patricia never complained about our situation, she was not her old self, and I knew that she felt the loss of our comfortable way of life. Gone was the dishwasher and the central heating, together with all the other comforts of the bungalow. Though we'd made the best of the available space in the cottage it simply wasn't big enough for our growing family, and the cramped conditions were depressing, as was the incessant battle against the damp. The children were cheerful enough and had already made new friends, but I couldn't help feeling sad when they talked of the 'goodies' they used to buy in Donaghadee and the great times they had there. With the prospect of earning money looking uncertain again and with it the chance of going to a new life in New Zealand, a mood of quiet despondency settled on our once joyful and resilient family. Here in the south the fear of the gun may have gone, yet it felt like we were merely existing rather than living. When I had little to occupy my mind, anxiety tended to plague me more, and the strength of my medication was therefore increased. I had also started drinking, admittedly only Guiness, but I'd gone from having just one pint to two. I found now that my memory was often dimmed, perhaps due to the combination of the tablets and the drink, but this in itself did not worry me unduly. Perhaps slowly I was ceasing to care. The sedative effect helped me cope, and served to blot out the outside world.

To keep busy I worked on the vegetable plot at the side of the cottage, often from early morning till late at night, sowing potatoes and other produce for the coming year. Our neighbour John would call round for a chat, and we would sometimes discuss the troubles in the North and news from the TV or the papers. 'It's terrible the things that go on up there' he would say, 'but I suppose it's only those who live there who know the full story.' I would then tell him these were 'the truest words ever spoken' and he'd nod gravely. One evening, as I was knelt down pulling out some weeds he said to me 'Have you any promise of work yet?' His question seemed one of genuine concern. 'No, it's been very disappointing' I said. 'That fine workshop and so well equipped' he sympathised 'I shall speak to a few people who may be able to help.' Then changing the subject completely he asked me 'Do you like fishing? That river a few fields away has some good sized trout in the deep holes.' I told him I'd thought perhaps there were fish there, but hadn't had time to investigate. However John's comment had reminded me that at the moment, with the workshop finished, there was nothing to stop me doing a spot of fishing. Maybe it would be a good idea. 'I'll buy a fishing rod later on and try my luck' I said. 'I've caught some nice trout there' said John 'and I can lend you a rod' I thanked him but said I'd prefer to get my own. 'I'd be worried about damaging your rod.' This was how cautious I'd grown over money.

Life went on in this uneventful way for several weeks, till one Friday morning, chatting to a young tractor driver called Patsy in the village, the talk got round to bodywork. He mentioned he had a Cortina and had smashed the front wing. 'Would you be able to repair it and do a re-spray' he said. 'Certainly!' I replied enthusiastically and without hesitation, even though I'd not even seen the job. On inspecting the vehicle I gave him a price and told him I'd have it done in time for the weekend. Patsy readily agreed the terms and the car was brought round to the cottage. That same morning Patricia had received a letter from her aunt in New Zealand, containing a vast amount of information about the place, together with local newspaper clippings. As she was reading I steered the Cortina into the workshop and began removing the damaged bumper and broken headlight. By early evening I was a good way through the job. That night Patricia and I pored over the letter and newspaper items from her aunt. 'Property seems very reasonable out there' I said, glancing at the houses for rent or sale. 'And there are plenty of skilled jobs advertised here. Perhaps I ought to write to the New Zealand High Commission in London and find out about entry.' I already knew Patricia was all for the move, and since I would soon have earnings from my first repair job under my belt, it seemed a good time to begin planning. 'Hopefully there'll be more work where this came from, and we can start putting a bit away for the fares' Furthermore I'd received replies from my solicitor that the injury claim and sale of the business premises in Donaghadee was being looked after. If monies from either of these came through we should be able to afford tickets to New Zealand there and then, so it would be as well to prepare the ground. 'Write whenever you get the time Philip' said Patricia, 'The weather will be warmer and as we've always said it'll be a bright new start for us and the children.'

I finished off the Cortina on the Saturday, and when young Patsy called in the evening he was more than pleased to see his pride and joy restored to her former glory in time for the weekend. I'd had to use our social welfare money to go out and buy some materials, so it was reassuring when he paid the agreed bill in cash. 'I'll tell my friends where to call in future for any repairs' said Patsy. When he'd left, Patricia, seeing the money in my hand, gave a sigh of relief, 'Thank god, now we can get out and buy some groceries.' The cupboard was indeed bare, and Patsy's payment was none too soon. A trip to the shops usually meant sweets, and as soon as our departure for town was announced the three children and Rover were the first ones into the car. Next day I wrote to the New Zealand High Commission in London requesting details about emigration and jobs, also asking for the address of the NZ motor trade union.

Meanwhile we received another letter with some press clippings. This one was from my father in Dublin. We had of course heard all about the car bomb that had gone off there back in February, and my father had now sent the reports from the Dublin paper. The explosion had taken place on a Saturday evening in the same location as a previous atrocity, Sackville Street, a turning off O'Connell Street next to Cleary's department store. The bomb had been placed in a red Vauxhall stolen the same morning from up in the Shankill. The UVF were known to be responsible, with speculation about the SAS also being complicit. The newspaper recorded that Thomas Douglas, a twenty-five year-old bus driver died in the blast. He had arrived in Dublin just a few months ago from Sterling in Scotland, and had been due to marry. It was rumoured that by bringing the bombing campaign across the border the UVF hoped to lay blame for the troubles in the North on the Dublin government. But the vast majority of Nationalists in the North would always know the truth; that it was the violence and injustice against Catholics which had sparked off the conflict and still lay much at the heart of the matter.

With the workshop once again empty I began spending my

days pacing around it, sweeping the floor, rearranging and tidying my tools, anything to give me the sense of industry I craved. Another week went by and I began to wonder if the Cortina job had been a flash in the pan, yet another false dawn. 'I wonder if we'll ever get enough customers, this being a country area' I lamented to Patricia. 'Calm down Philip, you only had your first customer a week ago.' Her patient attitude was, as so often, the right one, for a couple of evenings later a man came to the door. 'I've seen you around the village' I said peering out into the darkening night. 'My name's Frankie, how are you' he said. 'I'm Philip' I said 'Welcome to this part of the country Philip. I hear you do crash repairs – would you come and take a look at a car of mine? I've been told it's a write-off.' I fetched a flash-lamp and followed Frankie out.

5

First Christmas in Roscommon

'Well, what do you think? said Frankie.
It had taken me some time to look the car over, and
Frankie was now driving me home.

'It can be repaired' I said, 'it all depends on how much you
want to spend.'

'That's good news. Obviously I want the price as reasonable
as possible.'

'Call round tomorrow' I said, 'and I'll have two prices for
you – one with all new parts and another for some repairs on the
panels and a replacement second-hand section taking in most of
the damaged area. Either way you'll have my guarantee the
vehicle will be roadworthy' Frankie opted for the second-hand
treatment, saving himself a lot of money, but leaving my charges
for the work more or less the same. I went to a breaker's yard
and found some good matches for the bodywork. Frankie came
by the workshop several times over the course of the week to see
how things were progressing. When he could see that his car was
well on the mend he handed me some money on account. A day
later someone else called with a repair job, leaving their vehicle
with me in the yard. It seemed that word of mouth had at last
started to work in my favour. Frankie, pleased that his car was
now anything but the write-off he'd feared, paid the balance of
his bill and drove off a happy man. From here on the trickle of
business quickly became a steady stream, and my skills in engine
repairs, panel beating and spray painting were all put to use. I
was soon working every day, and many times the yard had

vehicles awaiting attention parked bumper to bumper. With the summer weather I was able to double up on jobs by spray painting in the workshop, and while the layers dried go out and fix engines in the yard. The prices I was charging were a lot lower than in Donaghadee but by working long hours I could get through a high volume of work. With minimal overheads I could still make a reasonable living, and was soon putting a little money by each week. Patricia and I now went together to see Mr Green, the man who had arranged our social welfare money, and informed him that we no longer were in need of the payments. 'You are both very honest' he said, which was a nice thing to be told. 'If ever you're in need again' said Mr Green, 'call and let me know.' We hoped we wouldn't be, but the thought was reassuring.

Feeling more on top of things, I purchased a fishing rod and one Sunday took the day off and went out to the river with our neighbour John. Despite not catching a thing, the time was pleasantly spent, and John showed me all the large holes where the trout usually appeared. There would be other fine days for fishing, and plenty of them. John also invited me to join the local gun club of which he was a stalwart, and was kind enough to make me a gift of two young gun dogs. The little Cocker puppies were immediately taken under the wing of the delighted children, who named them Patch and Scampy and took them to romp the fields and meadows with Rover our Labrador, who had now grown large and was known as 'the dog from the North'.

When the summer of that year ended, Aileen, Philip and Brenda returned to their daily studies at the village National School. They had settled in well and took an active part in many of the extra-curricular pursuits, plays and sports. They were also making good progress with the Irish language. Information had arrived from New Zealand House about emigration procedures and job prospects. We were now well on our way to having the air fares saved and extra money to set us up there, yet with that felt less of the need to escape. The situation of a few short months ago had altered and over the summer we seemed to have turned a bit of a corner. My health was still not good, including my stammer, and I remained under the care of the GP and hospital, yet I had plenty of work which put food on the table and more of a spring in all our steps. One thing that hadn't altered was the lack of space in the home, and with the children still growing something had to be done about our cramped living conditions. As winter arrived, crows and pigeons nestling in the tall trees could be seen swooping down on any crumb of food that was left out in the snow for the robins and songbirds, and we were reminded it would soon be a year since we had moved in. One evening Patricia made a suggestion. 'Now that we're undecided about New Zealand, would it be possible to find some land around here and build our own home and a proper garage for you Philip?' I thought about this for a moment. Not only had we an income now, but we had begun to fit in to the area. People had accepted us and even bestowed gifts on us, such as John with the puppies. Another kind neighbour had given us a dozen chickens which supplied us with plentiful fresh eggs. I had erected a six-foot wire fence to protect the birds from prowling foxes, and some of my customers, knowing we were from the North had jokingly dubbed the chicken-run "Little Long-Kesh". With so much goodwill, and the children doing well in school, should we not think again before uprooting ourselves? Building our own place would mean designing it the way we wanted, with all the space we needed, and it could easily be as comfortable as our old home in Donaghadee. All we needed was some land. 'I tell you what' I said 'Next time John from next door calls I'll have a word with him and see if he knows anyone with a small plot who might be willing to sell. But let's keep our options open on New Zealand' John called round a few days after and enquired again about my becoming a member of the gun club. I agreed to join and said I hoped to make time to visit the Lough after Christmas. 'The duck shooting there is good when there's a flood' said John. 'Yes' I said 'I saw the wild geese flying over today. They're very hard to get a shot at'. I decided now was as good as any time to ask about building land. I told him how difficult it was in the cottage with the children growing up. 'Leave it to me' said John, 'I'll ask around for you.' Thanks John, I'll not forget you.'

We now had several things to look forward to. For myself there was the pleasant prospect of a bit of convivial shooting in the New Year, together with the chance of John coming up with a piece of land for a new family home. And as far as conviviality went you couldn't want for better company than Patricia's sister and brother-in-law, whom we had invited to join us in Roscommon for the Christmas festivities. Sharing the holidays with these much-loved relations under our roof we could forget how damp and narrow were the walls, and the house would be a real home, full of yuletide warmth and laughter. A fortnight before Christmas John came round to find me in the workshop. 'I think I may have a site for you' he announced. 'It needs to be confirmed with others in the family that own the land. They'll decide over Christmas.' Excitedly I asked John where the land was situated. 'Why just across the road from you' he replied. 'That's great news!' I cried 'We'll start drawing up some plans. Will you come in for a drink or a cup of tea John?' 'Thanks Philip, but I have a few things to do before darkness falls, I'll call again.' I went straight into the kitchen and found Patricia. 'I saw you with John' she said 'What were you two discussing?' I took her arm and led her through to the front door of the cottage. 'Come and look now while there's some light left in that overcast sky' I said. I opened the door and pointed across the road. 'What am I looking at Philip?' 'Listen' I said, 'you see that lovely dry field with its unbroken view, the one we see when driving to Mayo or down to Dublin? Would it not be a great place for a bungalow?' I explained about John's news, and with my own thoughts already racing ahead, I added 'and how about a filling station and a shop, a whole business, just like we had in Donaghadee?' Patricia, though thrilled with the idea of creating a business as well as a new home said 'Where will you get the money to build?' I said that a petrol company would probably assist if they thought the location was a good one.

The week before Christmas I went down to Dublin to collect Nora and Christy. I had sold the Datsun and was now driving a Mercedes again, a year-old model that I'd bought badly damaged at a bargain price and had repaired. The car was now worth a good deal of money. After tea and sandwiches at Nora and Christy's we loaded their cases into the boot of the car, along with an abundance of enticingly wrapped presents. During the journey Christy remarked on how comfortable the Mercedes was, which gave me back some of that old sense of well-being. Arriving at the cottage Nora and Christy were as excited as the children themselves, who gave them a great welcome, and the sisters Nora and Patricia were always pleased to be in others company again. Christy, ever one for a joke, spun the children a yarn that Santa wouldn't be coming this year because he'd 'heard on the wireless that Santa had been kidnapped by the bad men in the North of Ireland!' This proved to be no joking matter however, and Brenda our youngest was the first to shout 'No, no, it's not true, you're telling your lies again Uncle Christy!' Christy persisted for a while, but seeing the children genuinely distressed, he quickly revised his story. The news on the wireless was wrong he said, it was all a big mistake and he would make sure Santa came with presents for everyone. This brought smiles all round and peace reigned once more in the kitchen. Although the cottage was small, we managed to accommodate our visitors in reasonable comfort and began to enjoy Christmas. On the morning of the 25th Santa left the promised gifts as requested by the children's letter written a few weeks earlier. On St Stephen's evening the whole family went to the village pub, where we were entertained by the music of 'The Wren Boys' dressed in their colourful costumes with tall straw hats. Patricia and I were not yet that well known in the pub, but as we sat with Nora and Christy a customer came up and cried 'How are you Christy! Give us a bar of a song.' It was clear the two were old Dublin acquaintances as Christy replied genially 'Hello Percy, what are you doing in Roscommon?' It turned out Percy, who worked behind the bar in one of Christy's Dublin haunts was staying over Christmas with his parents who lived in the next town. Christy asked what he should sing. 'Give us "Father Murphy"' said Percy. Christy was well-known in the Dublin pubs for his singing, and as his strong voice rang out everyone fell silent, a few people even coming in off the street having heard the strains carrying through the night air. Christy's song was well received with loud applause, the landlord sending over free drinks for all in his company and the laughter and singing continuing till closing time. Christy and I revisited the homely little pub every evening after that, enjoying folk songs, rock and roll from the Elvis era and rousing rebel ballads. These nights of song and friendship put me much in mind of when Christy and I had shared similar good times out in Donaghadee. One occasion during 12th of July week, when the business was still thriving, we had gone along together to the "Moat Inn" early in the afternoon. What started out as a quiet drink was to turn into a lively session of music and quaffing in the small back room where an open fire blazed merrily. There were more than a dozen in the drinking party, all of us well known to one another, and after introducing my brother-in-law, the sing-song soon took off. As the drink flowed we must have covered every style, with modern ballads from the hit parade, the Northern favourites and the old songs. When it was finally time for home Christy announced 'I'll play you one last tune on the mouth-organ.' He put the instrument to his lips and the notes of "God Save the Queen" began to emanate forth. There was a hush in the bar right to the end, when a round of applause was given by all those in our party. One young man called Sam then jumped to his feet and declared 'None shall leave till I give the last tune!' I replied for him to go ahead, whereupon he asked Christy for the loan of his mouth organ. Christy said certainly and handed it over. The tune that Sam played us was called "Kevin Barry" an old Irish rebel song from 1916. Again there was complete silence till the last note. Sam handed Christy back his instrument. 'That's a good mouth organ you've got there boy' he said. After more spirited applause and back-slapping we all drank up, made fond farewells and handshakes and left for our homes the best of friends. As we all knew, Christy and I were not of the same religion as the others present on that wonderful afternoon, but it mattered not a bit to anyone. We had been united by music, good ale and the sheer warm-hearted enjoyment of each others company. It was an experience of pure fellowship, not a holy communion perhaps, but a genuinely true, human and happy one.

6

The Perfect Plot of Land

The Christmas holiday period was over, and Nora and Christy had to return to their jobs in Dublin. After taking them back down, I had a quick cup of tea and set off for home. I had jobs of my own waiting and wanted to make an early start the next morning. That night the frost fell with a vengeance, making the roads treacherous for motorists, and over the next few days their mishaps on the ice added to my workload. I had now purchased a breakdown vehicle, and was kept busy recovering cars that had skidded and crashed. I was obliged to put customers on a waiting list as I dealt with the growing backlog in the yard. A heavy snowfall slowed things further while I found tarpaulins and covers for the vehicles and in this weather all the repairs had to be carried out inside the workshop. I was working longer hours than ever now, but being so busy, and seeing the money coming in, I had no chance to dwell on the past.

It was mid-January when John from next-door called in one cold morning with a purposeful look about him. 'It's a frosty one John!' I said. 'Cold for your work, but I have news for you.' he said cheerfully. 'I hope it's good' I replied. 'Tim, the owner of that land wants to meet you tomorrow afternoon. Can you see him?' 'I sure can.' This was certainly good news. Discussing it with Patricia that evening her words were 'I hope and pray Tim will sell, and that the asking price will be reasonable' Amen to that I thought.

The next morning the postman arrived with several newspapers from New Zealand and a letter from the national parliament in Wellington no less. 'Look at all these!' exclaimed Patricia. 'Yes great' I said, draining my teacup and putting on my coat 'but I can't stop now, I'll read them tonight. You have a glance through in the meantime.' I had a stack of work to do and my mind was also much preoccupied with the meeting later that day about the land. 'Go on about your business then!' chided Patricia good-naturedly as she cleared the breakfast things away. Over lunch I asked Patricia if she thought I should take some money with me when I went to see Tim, by way of a deposit. 'I think so' she said. 'Then could you fetch me £500 from the savings in our room.' Armed with the cash I presented myself at Tim's house. 'Please come in' he said, 'I understand you wish to purchase some land from me. I never intended to sell such a large block you understand, but I know of your circumstances and I would like to help.' I expressed my appreciation and Tim straightaway named his price, which being under a thousand pounds indeed seemed reasonable. 'Thanks very much' I said again. 'Not at all, I only want to help.' I then said 'How about accepting a deposit now – and who will mark off the site?' Tim said 'Everything's okay. John has told me what you want the site for and I've arranged for him to mark off part of the field with his own surveyor's chains.' I took the envelope of cash from my pocket. 'Here's five hundred pounds' I said. 'That's over half your asking price.' Tim waved his hand. 'I'm not in a hurry for payment. Go and obtain your planning first and then you can pay me' he said in a kindly voice. 'Are you sure?' 'Yes I'm sure.'

Back home I returned the £500 to Patricia for safe-keeping and told her everything that Tim had said, and about paying for the land when we had the planning consent. 'That was very kind of him' she said. 'Yes, I thought so' I agreed. I then went next-door to see John, who was busy with his plane on some wood. 'Did Tim tell you he's asked me to mark off the site?' he said. 'Yes, but he'd not take a deposit' 'That's alright' assured John 'he'll be true to his word.' I told John how pleased I was to have secured the land, and that it was all thanks to him.

If the future was now looking brighter for us, matters from the past showed far less sign of hope or resolution. I had intended to cut my losses on the bombed out Donaghadee site and sell off the land, which was ideally situated for residential building. I was therefore enraged one morning to receive a letter from the North Down Council informing me a 'Compulsory Vesting Order' had been made against 23, Warren Road. Such a move was as I understood it, an attempt to seize the land at far below its market value. I immediately contacted my solicitor, who wrote by return with assurance he would fight the case for me. This development had a marked effect on my equilibrium, and after a further visit to Roscommon Hospital I was diagnosed as suffering from post-traumatic neurosis, and given increased medication. Patricia came to my aid by dealing with all my paperwork. Invoices and receipts were now prepared and ready for customers when they came to collect their cars, and by agreeing cash payment terms we had no outstanding accounts to worry about. I began to feel increasingly under pressure with the workload I was taking on. But knowing the importance of maintaining a good reputation each repair job was carried out conscientiously, ensuring the customer went away satisfied. One day however a man stopped by the workshop and claimed that since getting his car back it was pulling to one side. 'The chassis must be bent' he said. As I accompanied him out to the roadside to have a look I said 'Have you been doing a lot of driving?' At this point another man got out of the waiting car and said in a pugnacious tone 'Yes he has, and the car is in a dangerous condition since you had it. Drive it yourself if you don't believe me!' 'I don't disbelieve you' I replied. The customer then said 'This is my brother, and by the way, he's a mechanic.'

'Well' said the brother, 'what are you going to do about it – do we get our money back or what?'

'No' I replied. 'I'm not going to give you your money back.'

I felt sure there was an explanation for the car pulling, though seeing the two men bristling for an argument, I hoped I was right.

'I can see you've had to change a wheel' I said pointing to the front nearside tyre. 'We got a puncture' came back the blank reply, as if to say 'so what'.

'The replacement tyre is almost bald, look' I said, indicating the wire threads showing through at the edges. 'If you've the punctured tyre I'll repair it for you now.'

'I've already mended it' said the mechanic brother.

'Can we put it back on and then have another drive around?'

The two men shrugged and without a word the wheel was replaced with the original one. They then got in the car and drove off up the Dublin Road. Fifteen minutes later the car came back round the bend at high speed and pulled up sharply. My customer wound down his window.

'How is it now?' I asked, 'still pulling?'

'We've both driven, and it's fine now.'

I noticed that the brother in the passenger seat was looking embarrassed. I bid them both good day and returned to work.

By early April we had completed drawing up the plans for the new bungalow and business premises, and on the 23rd of that month received acknowledgement of our application for planning consent from Roscommon County Council. A further letter arrived from my solicitor in Belfast, with assurance that my written instructions to oppose the council's vesting order would be implemented. 'Well that takes care of that for the time being' I said to Patricia as I passed her the letter. 'What do you mean 'takes care' she said sceptically. 'You'll not get anywhere, not with the corruption and now these strikes they're threatening.' I looked at my wife's face which was stern, and with a deep sadness in her eyes. 'You are right' I said quietly. 'The North has shown us no justice so far.' Patricia then said 'Worse still Philip, though you are a Catholic from the North, you were born in Manchester.' I was dumbfounded by this simple observation. It was true that though I'd been raised in Ireland since a very early age, my birthplace had been Manchester, my parents having lived there at that time. Those Loyalists waving their Union Jacks who'd been determined to see me ruined and on the run might be shocked to learn I could claim to be more British than them. Whether it would have changed their attitude to me is doubtful. All they'd seen was another 'Taig' in their midst, and what was worse, a successful one. 'Nevertheless' I said to Patricia, as she handed me back the letter from the solicitor, 'I shall continue to fight.'

The strikes in the North which Patricia mentioned had been

rumoured for some time, and in May of that year 1974, they began to take effect. By fear or favour, the UDA and the UVF began to tighten its grip on the infrastructure, suborning workers and taking control of many of the key positions on which the economy depended, power and petrol stations among them. Road blocks went up throughout the six counties, manned by uniformed and masked paramilitaries armed with pickaxe handles. To obtain petrol motorists were forced to obtain passes issued by these new forces of 'law and order' as transport slowed to a crawl and the RUC and Army stood idly by. Occasionally British soldiers would take photographs or laugh and joke with the paramilitaries. Power cuts were frequent, and as the Northern Ireland Assembly let control slip further from their grasp each day, the country virtually ground to a halt. There were now whispers of a war between the North and the Republic, and certain elements attempting to engineer it. During the second week of May I told Patricia that I would be going into Dublin at the weekend to pick up some spares from Duffy's breakers yard in Smithfield and also had a call to make in the city centre. 'There's going to be lot of extra traffic this weekend because of the bus strike' said Patricia. 'I had forgotten about that' I said 'I'll leave it till the Monday in that case. On Saturday the 17th of May, the day I had originally planned to be in Dublin, the city was rocked by a series of car bombings, in Parnell Street, Talbot Street and South Leinster Street near to the Irish Parliament building. The deadly work was carried out courtesy of the UVF and the sophistication of the devices indicated the use of professional military expertise, with British Intelligence the likeliest candidate. The carnage on the streets of Dublin that afternoon shall never be forgotten by those that saw it. They spoke of a battlefield with blood flowing down the streets. Twenty-five lay dead or dying and over a hundred and forty were injured in the first three explosions. A photographer taking pictures vomited after seeing the river of blood coursing along the gutter. No warnings were given. When asked 'Why?' Sammy Smith, a UDA spokesman said 'I am happy about the bombings in Dublin. There is a war on with the Free State and we are now laughing at them.' When Patricia and I heard the news our first thought was thank God for the bus strike. Thank God too for her advice. A bomb had also been detonated that day at Monaghan, close to the border, killing six people. The new Taoiseach Liam Cosgrave had promptly despatched extra Garda to seal off every possible inch of the border from further intrusion.

When summer arrived again I was able to catch up on the jobs that had accumulated during the icy and difficult weather. Eventually the small field beyond the yard which I'd used for the overspill of vehicles was clear. With an easier workload I now had time for fishing, and in the warm evenings would walk down to the Carricknabraher River, often coming home with a few nice trout. Our two faithful gun dogs Patch and Scampy would accompany me on these trips, bounding and frolicking on the way. Yet they were always obedient when required, and would sit quietly by my side as I fished, listening like me to the ripples of the fast running water, and watching as the trout leapt elegantly for flies. The dogs were the same in the workshop, resting close by while I was busy, but always on the alert, with a wag of the tail for anyone they knew or a warning bark for those they did not.

On the 26th of June the postman brought our regular newspapers from New Zealand, together with two letters. The first was from Nora and Christy accepting our invitation to come and stay at the end of July. 'They'll be here for the festival and the swing-boats!' exclaimed the children delightedly. There was to be a local carnival in July, with dancing in a marquee. 'Yes, and they'll enjoy the bands' I said, 'we must all go along.' The other letter had an official looking envelope and turned out to be from Roscommon Council. 'Is it about our new home? Oh read it out to us please Daddy!' pleaded Aileen. 'Yes Philip, read it out' joined in Patricia. I began to read:

'Dear Sir,
In pursuance of the powers conferred upon them by the above-mentioned act, the Roscommon County Council...have by order dated 25th June 1974 decided to refuse to grant permission....'

7

Christy's 'Blue Suede Shoes'

'Have you been to the little pub lately?' Christy asked me as we were driving up from Dublin.

'I have indeed, we usually go on Sunday after second mass, and they've been asking after you! We could look in tonight if you like.'

Christy chuckled and smacked his lips at the prospect of a drink and a few songs.

'I shall be thirsty for one of them good pints of porter!'

We would soon be back in Roscommon with Nora and Christy staying for two whole weeks. Just knowing they would be coming had helped cheer me up over the last month. I'd had further health problems, including anxiety and asthma attacks. Recently I had also been experiencing frightening flashbacks of the burning garage and of the other occasions when my life was threatened, including the Vanguard thugs coming to the door, the shots fired at the car and the mysterious stranger who'd lured me out to Portaferry. My stammer could now be so severe as to cause embarrassment, though the asthma I'd managed to conceal from Patricia by carrying an inhaler. The refusal of the planning hadn't helped matters, but in this as with other worries, I now tried increasingly to carry on as normal and not show my feelings. However the anticipation of seeing these two dear relations in the car with me now had helped my spirits a good deal, and the children were so fired up they had come down to Dublin with me to pick Auntie and Uncle up. As a treat Patricia had dressed them in their Sunday best to see the sights of the city on the way. She too was glad I would be having the diversion of Christy's company.

'Christy and I were very disappointed for you when we heard your planning application was turned down' said Nora as she handed round some sweets she'd bought for us on the way.

'And you need a new home, for the health of all of you' added Christy.

'It was a terrible setback for us' I said. 'The council said it would create a traffic hazard. But revised plans are ready, and I'm going to talk with the architects before we resubmit.'

'When will that be?' asked Christy.

'Monday morning. Come with me for the drive if you like.'

'I shall. But Philip, does that rooster of yours still crow cock-a-doodle every morning?'

'He does.'

'Then I'll not oversleep!'

'You've done great work out the back' said Nora when she'd seen the converted granary and the lane.

'It feels lovely and smooth underfoot' said Christy, whose sense of touch grew keener with his failing eyesight.

'Yes, he's put a whole lorry-load of chippings down' said Patricia.

As I took their cases through I heard Nora say quietly to Patricia: 'And how are you keeping since we last met?'

'Well, we could be better – but we're glad to see you and Christy...'

Patricia's voice was low and broken with emotion. She did not know I was listening, and I realised with a shock that I was witnessing her mask of outward strength momentarily lowered, and her feelings of despondency about our reduced circumstances were plain to hear. This intimate exchange between the sisters confirmed my worst fears about the effects on all of us of the trauma and what we had lost, and I was suddenly filled with guilt and despair that as a husband and father I could not provide better for my family. I now felt more keenly than ever the need to improve our lot, and resolved I would secure us that new home come what may. That night in the pub though, any regrets about the past and worries of what might be in the future were put to one side, as Christy led the singing and the sparkling glasses were filled. It was a grand session, as we all finished the evening in holiday mood, promising ourselves lots more nights like this. And on Monday Christy, true to his word rose with the cockerel, and came with me to the architect's and then the council offices where I deposited the new set of plans. A new home being more important, we had abandoned the proposal for a filling station on the land. Instead, my father and mother, with a view to retiring close to us and their grandchildren, had asked if they could build a bungalow adjacent to our own, a suggestion which Patricia and I both readily agreed to. My final call that day was in County Leitrim, to a meeting with Patrick J. Reynolds TD, a government deputy and good friend of my mother, who promised to make representations to Roscommon Council on our behalf.

Christy, Nora, Patricia and I spent many happy hours together over the rest of the holiday, going often to the pub and to several of the dances in the big marquee in the village. On one occasion the band leader announced 'Could Christy, the singer from Dublin, come up on stage please.' All heads turned as Christy stepped forward and made his way to the front. My brother-in-law's fame had spread far and wide! After his first song he was asked for another, whereupon Christy said, 'Okay – I shall sing "Blue Suede Shoes".' And off he went 'one for the money, two for the show' and away as the drums thundered, rocking and rolling and whooping it up to the great delight of all, and with the band joining in the chorus the dancers went wild with joy. Further encores were insisted on, till Christy was finally allowed off the stage and rejoined us, his face flushed and perspiring. 'You look warm' said Nora. 'You've never lost your touch Christy' I said 'would you care for another pint?' Catching his breath he replied 'No, no I'm full.' His performance and the riotous response of the audience had been intoxicating enough no doubt.

At the end of the holiday I left Patricia and the children at home and drove, Nora and Christy back to Dublin. On the way the conversation got round to the recent bombings in Dublin.

'We were lucky' said Nora, 'we would have been in the area that day too but for the bus strike.' '

'We knew some of the people who were killed and injured' said Christy.

Nora and Christy were regulars at the bingo and the singing pubs close to where the explosions occurred.

'We're still getting over the shock, and it makes us realise what you all went through in the North. But at least everyone is still alive.'

I gripped the steering wheel of the Mercedes a little tighter as Nora spoke these last words.

'We were blessed.' I said quietly.

8

The Best Laid Plans

With summer over and the days growing short, I was back to spending long hours inside the workshop. I had joined the gun club now, and was looking forward to going up to the lough when time permitted. In full flood this small lough could greatly enlarge, providing the wild fowl with good feeding on the rich, green, marshy grass. Sometimes, working late on a clear calm night I would hear the far off widgeon, or see a skein of wild geese flying low under the moonlight, heading for the lough where they gathered in huge flocks.

On the 4th October the postman brought a registered letter from Roscommon Council stating that our planning application for the two bungalows in a 'blue ribbon' area' had been refused. 'It's worse than the North!' I stormed, throwing the envelope down on the kitchen table in disgust. 'There's no justice here either, even if you work hard and are honest!' 'Now, now it's no use getting upset' said Patricia calmly. 'We shall think of something'. That night, after the children had gone to bed I put some more turf and coal on the range and came to a decision. I said to Patricia 'I shall write a letter to Mr Tully TD, the housing and planning minister in Dublin, and I'll take it to his office and hand it in personally!' 'I'll make a pot of tea before you go to bed' said Patricia, 'and you can take your tablets' 'That sounds good' I yawned. 'I do feel tired. Must be from being out in the wet all day.'

Mr Tully was unavailable when I called at the Custom House in Dublin. This was understandable, since I had not made an appointment and the minister was a busy man. When I explained the position to his secretary however, she was both kind and helpful, saying that Mr Tully would write to me with a decision about the matter within two weeks. True to her word, in a fortnight's time an official looking envelope arrived bearing a Dublin postmark. I tore it open hurriedly my heart and mind now in a great state of anticipation, steeling myself for yet another disappointment. Next moment however I cried out 'I think we have the planning!' Patricia gave a little gasp. 'You think?' she said. 'Read it again to make certain.' It did seem too good to be true, and I looked again, scrutinising every word of the letter. 'There is one condition' I said. 'What's that?' asked Patricia anxiously. 'There must only be one entrance off the N5 road for both bungalows – well that's not a problem.' Mr Tully had signed the letter himself. We had our planning permission to build two brand new bungalows on the dry field opposite the old, leaky, cramped cottage in which we now sat. Patricia could soon have a modern kitchen the children would get rooms of their own and no more mould and water running down the walls. We could even have central heating again. Heavens be praised! 'It's the first good news we've had since leaving the North' said Patricia. 'Now we can pay for the land and confirm with the bank we'll need the loan they promised for the building work' I said. 'I'll go and see the owners tomorrow.' After finishing breakfast I went straight round to tell John the good news, and thank him again for his help in finding a site for our new home.

The following day, calling at Mr McCabe's home in order to settle up for the land, the door was opened by his mother, who informed me her son was away working and would not be back until the weekend. The following Saturday morning Patricia handed me an envelope containing the cash we had put away to pay for the site. 'It's all counted out' she said. Going again to McCabe's home I this time found him in, and suggested we sit in my car if he wished to conduct our business in private. 'Certainly' replied McCabe as he followed me out to the Mercedes 'though there is a problem…' 'What problem?' I asked as McCabe got into the passenger seat beside me. 'I've been given the planning permission, and I have the sum we agreed here in cash for you.' McCabe said slowly 'I've been up to my field today, and looking at the size of the site that's marked off I would not be prepared to sell for that amount of money.' I stared at the man in disbelief. 'But what am I to do now?' was all I could say in reply. 'I don't think I would like to sell any of my land' continued McCabe. 'My brother James would not be in favour of it either.' I was almost bursting with rage and incredulity that someone could so completely reverse their position and renege on an agreement without warning. 'What about my going to all the trouble of obtaining the planning, and John marking off the site for us?' I fumed. 'I never thought you would be successful with the planning' said McCabe. This really did beggar belief. How could he calmly sit there and say such a thing? Tense with anger and distress I said, 'That isn't a good enough nor a very kind answer, after telling me you would sell and us having a gentleman's agreement' At this point McCabe got out of the car, and having nothing more to say walked back to his house. Much upset I drove home, calling in first to see John, who was amazed at this extraordinary turn of events. 'I'll have a word with McCabe' he said 'and see if I can get him to change his mind'.

The following day my parents arrived from Dublin. They had received a copy of the planning consent for their own proposed bungalow, and were naturally eager to see us. When I told them about McCabe's sudden about-turn, they both looked crestfallen. My father shook his head and said 'That's the worst news I've heard, especially after all the trouble you've gone to. Is it a question of more money – or did the owner want you to get the planning permission so he could build later on?' I said 'I don't think the money is important, the family has plenty.' But if my father's other suspicion was correct, then we had been so deceived by McCabe that it didn't bear thinking about. 'If it is the money then we'll pay it, if a reasonable sum' said my father. Later that morning, John came to tell us he had seen McCabe in the village, and had broached the matter of the land. The only reply he'd received was that there had been a 'misunderstanding' and he would need to discuss it with his brother, who was now he said, against selling the plot. 'Well' said my father philosophically, 'if the man has gone back on his gentleman's agreement and won't honour his promise, nothing can be done. Something may yet turn up.' With a feeling of resignation I replied 'We may decide to go to New Zealand. I have the address of a firm in Dunedin in the South Island who are looking for a general manager for their crash repair workshop.' 'Dunedin is a long way away' said my father, 'the family would miss you both and the children a great deal. Do nothing in a hurry.'

My father was right of course to advise not rushing into anything. But our decision to emigrate had been long in the making, and only put aside when we thought we had the chance of building a proper fit home for our growing family. With the land now unavailable there seemed nothing to stop us leaving Ireland for pastures new. We owed it to ourselves and the children to have a good life, and New Zealand, with its job opportunities, better living standards, warm climate and completely fresh environment finally seemed the right place for us. I also knew in my heart that my continuing resentment and fight for compensation from the North was draining the life out of all of us. Furthermore, and it seemed ironic, the rumour persisted here in the South that I might be an IRA man, probably due to the confusion with the man Coogan active along the border and known for his many disguises. The Gardai would sometimes drive at high speed and without warning into the backyard, have a look round and screech off again. Having nothing to hide they were welcome to inspect the premises anytime as far I was concerned, but at the same time it gave me the sense I'd been persecuted as both a sheep and a lamb. In October of that year 1974, I sent my application for the Dunedin post, at the same time informing the Chief Migration Officer in New Zealand House London of my intentions. All the family now hoped and prayed my letter would prove successful.

Late one afternoon of that same month a violent storm broke over the cottage, setting the tin roof rattling as the wind and rain lashed down in buckets. I had been working late to finish a repair for a customer and after locking up despite dashing quickly across the yard, I was soaked before I reached the kitchen door. 'Change into some dry clothes' urged Patricia, seeing my dripping form. 'It's after ten so finish your work for tonight and come and sit by the range.' I soon felt very tired, and said goodnight to Patricia who was sitting up with a book. Despite being fatigued I spent a restless night, tossing and turning as the storm raged on outside. On waking the next morning the weather was much calmer and I could see through the little bedroom window that the rain had ceased and it would be a good day for working. The only problem was I could not get out of bed.

9

A Time for Prayer

'I don't wish to alarm you Mrs Coogan, and it's only my opinion, but I suspect your husband may have polio.' Lying in the hospital bed I thought back to the look on my dear wife's face when the doctor uttered these words. He had not hesitated to send for an ambulance. Patricia had tried hard to contain her feelings but how could she be other than distraught at this latest blow. As images of paralysis and leg-irons flashed through my mind, I too made a show of carelessness. The look on the children's faces at seeing their dad unable to walk was something I'd not witnessed since that dark night the garage had gone up in flames, and their upset was for me the worst sorrow. 'Don't you all worry now' I'd smiled as they lifted me on the stretcher, 'I'll be home in a few days.'

'Only my opinion' the doctor had said. It seemed unfortunate to have to pray for a man to be mistaken, but pray I did that night. The isolation ward I'd been placed in felt every bit as lonely as the name suggested, and during the long silent hours of darkness I realised it had been a long time since I had spoken to God in earnest. Working in Belfast during the height of the troubles I had always found time to call in for mass even while bombs were going off around the corner, and continued Sunday attendances after moving to the South. Had this been mere habit? My experience of the dark tunnel during the time of my TB and the appearance of Our Lady in the field at Arboe had filled me with a passion to serve God. However after my early ambitions for the priesthood had been abandoned I knew I had not felt strongly religious. Working, surviving and making plans had taken up almost all my thoughts. Yet I still believed that my guardian angels and Our Lady had remained in watch over me, or I would surely not have survived thus far. Would they continue now to do so? I prayed to them that night for a cure, and that I would soon return home to Patricia and the children.

There followed several days of blood tests and repeated examination of the rash and swelling which had appeared on my body. I was allowed no visitors and my only view of the outside world was now from the ground floor window onto a small grassed area of the hospital grounds, though only the occasional person passed by. One afternoon I heard a gentle tapping on the window and looking up saw Patricia smiling in at me. With her was our landlady Mrs Law and her daughter May. We spent some time mouthing conversation through the glass as best we could till the doctors came in to inspect me, then waved and blew kisses goodbye. I made gestures of thanks to Mrs Law, who must have driven Patricia all the way into Galway.

When the consultant did deliver a medical verdict it was that I had suffered a severe rheumatic fever. 'Were the tests for polio clear Professor?' I said 'Yes – you've nothing to worry about. But you'll have to avoid all strenuous exercise, possibly for some months, or even longer.' Polio ruled out was a relief, but I was already worried at this advice. 'What brought on the fever?' I asked. 'Damp, poor housing, overcrowding – many possible reasons.' 'And would my experiences in the North have had anything to do with it?' 'Put it this way' said the consultant, 'it certainly wouldn't have helped your situation.' After this I was moved from the isolation ward and allowed to mix with other patients. It felt good to have some company, and even watching the television seemed like a big treat. Next day I was allowed out of bed and walked about a bit, chatting with other people on the ward. By the time I was discharged it was late autumn and the nights were noticeably drawing in. Gerry, a local taxi driver from Roscommon, who'd sent my first client with the Cortina my way in fact, came to pick me up. 'I couldn't leave a neighbour stranded in Galway' he said cheerfully as we set off along the dark winding roads towards Roscommon. Back at the cottage I thanked Gerry for his kindness and went in to a great welcome from Patricia and the children. Although I'd only been in hospital a fortnight, it struck me that they all seemed to have aged. Perhaps it was just my tiredness. I felt suddenly alarmed and upset, but said nothing, not wanting to upset them. 'Are you warm enough?' asked Patricia, as we sat by the range. 'Yes, it's nice and cosy here. I feel so good now I'm home' I replied, noticing the chimney pipe glowing red and that everyone seemed concerned I should not be cold. The children were all delighted to see their dad and during dinner talked excitedly, Philip about his school sports, Aileen and Brenda about how they'd helped their mother look after the dogs, who had jumped up when they'd heard my voice and begged to be let in the kitchen. 'How were you able to get drinking water while I was away?' I asked, since Patricia did not drive. 'The neighbours brought some but mostly we had to boil rainwater from the outside tank' said Patricia. 'How did it taste?' I said. 'You're drinking it now!' I looked down into my teacup. I had no reply. My only thought was that the family had been reduced to an abject existence, and that somehow I was responsible. I blamed myself and felt a sense of shame for the utter state of ruin in which my once proud and happy wife was now forced to live. 'Don't worry' I said. 'What do you mean don't worry' replied Patricia heatedly, 'sure we have nothing – look at us! Ah, but what can we do.' 'If I secure that job in New Zealand we are going' I said. 'I only wish we were there now, and away from here' Patricia replied wistfully. Changing the subject she then went on 'Nora and Christy wrote to say they were upset to hear you were in hospital, but they'll still come up for Christmas. They said they'll get the train to Boyle, to save you driving all down to Dublin' 'That's thoughtful of them but I'll be well enough to drive' I said. 'No you won't' insisted Patricia emphatically, 'the doctors told me you wouldn't be up to it for a while.'

'I won't argue with you' I said.

'No, you won't. We've had enough quarrels ever since the

bombing. It's late and the fire is almost out. I'm sure you're as tired as I am'

'Yes. It's time we were all in bed.'

Early in December a letter came from New Zealand House with details about the immigration procedure. When Patricia saw the part about medical examinations she looked very concerned. 'Will we pass?' she said. 'Of course we shall. Our application must be accepted' I replied. 'You've not heard about the job yet.' 'No – but the firm may have been in touch with immigration, hence this letter' Patricia agreed this was possible adding that she hoped it was true. A week before Christmas a second letter arrived from immigration. It contained a medical form which my consultant was required to complete and sign. Reading through, one word jumped off the page at me – epilepsy. I stuffed the form hurriedly into my pocket, but not before Patricia had noticed the look on my face. 'What's that form for?' she asked. 'Just something for my doctor' I said casually, 'nothing to worry about. Now let's get on with those Christmas decorations...'

Nora and Christy's usual good cheer was felt as soon as they set foot in the cottage. 'Come on inside out of the cold Uncle Christy' called Aileen as soon as I had parked the Mercedes in the yard. 'I'm coming' he replied, 'Where's Philip and Brenda?' 'Philip's helping daddy' said Aileen. Then Brenda stepped forward and caught hold of her Uncle. 'Oh it's you Brenda' he cried, recognising the grip and feel of her hand. 'How are you? Is Santa stopping at this house' 'He is' replied Brenda, 'and don't you tell me lies!' Aileen quickly reassured her little sister, just in case Uncle Christy should begin his usual teasing. 'Yes' went on Brenda 'and Daddy met Santa in his shop in Galway and he promised my daddy he would be coming to see us with presents' Christy said, 'Well then he is coming!' There were broad smiles all round.

Come the big day I cooked the turkey and ham for Christmas dinner and when we'd all eaten our fill the talk got around to New Zealand. Nora and Christy were not in favour of our move. 'We're going to miss you, you know' said Nora. 'We've had such great times together' agreed Christy. 'Well it all depends on whether I get the job.' I said. 'Yes, we shall all have to wait and see' added Patricia. It was just after Boxing Day, while Nora and Christy had taken the children out for a walk, that I decided to tell Patricia about the form asking about various ailments, one being epilepsy. 'Oh goodness!' she exclaimed, 'what will you do?' 'Well I never had it fully investigated. After the holidays I'll get my consultant to arrange a proper ECG test.'

The same week I saw my consultant to arrange the ECG we had a bit of good news. 'Listen to this' I said to Patricia, reading a letter from the chief migration officer, 'we are entitled to a subsidy scheme for assisted passage to New Zealand. The whole family can go for £10.' Patricia beamed. 'That means we can keep our savings to get us settled in Dunedin' she said. 'They just need confirmation from my sponsoring firm, and the medical form.' At this we both went quiet. Now that everything was slotting into place so well, it would be a cruel twist of fate if the ECG was to let us down. In the event the test proved encouraging, with nothing adverse showing up. I was however given a further appointment and more tests. 'Just relax' said the nurse, as the electrodes were placed around my head. 'There will be flashing lights and I'll ask you to tell me if you feel anything different.' She seemed positive about my responses and said I would be informed about returning to see the consultant for the results of the test. As I told her about our plans for New Zealand, the nurse wished me well and said she felt sure we'd be very happy. As I left the hospital I hoped my next visit would be the last.

The wait for the hospital results seemed interminable. One day an eye-catching envelope came, bearing a stamp with a Kiwi on. It was from the motor firm in Dunedin who were sponsoring our emigration. 'Read it out' said Patricia. 'It's a long letter' I replied, and picked out the important points. I would have to agree to work for them for a minimum period of one year. Tradesmen averaged $89.88 gross or around $71 after tax 'but competent men can command a wage well above this…'

'That could be you…' interrupted Patricia. 'Let me finish' I said, '…a good furnished flat can be obtained for around $25 a week…the British pound is currently worth approximately $1.79….' The letter went on to state that work for women was plentiful, with weekly wages averaging $45 to $55 gross. 'That's not bad' commented Patricia, quickly doing the sums in her head. 'If we're interested in joining the firm they ask for my qualifications and full personal details as soon as possible' I said. 'I shall send them today!' 'And what about the medical form?' said Patricia. 'I'll contact the hospital and see if they can speed it up. You know, after the first year with this firm I could start my own crash repair business' Patricia said 'You wouldn't do that after they've been kind enough to sponsor our passage out there?' 'It's just something to bear in mind' I said, 'The wages they quote only work out at about £50 a week – I was earning £160 in Donaghadee.' Patricia replied 'That's water under the bridge now.'

10

Deja Vue

'I have already arranged for you to have another ECG' said Dr Walls, 'this time under Professor Lanigan at the Richmond Hospital in Dublin, the leading centre for your condition. What do you say to that?' What was I supposed to say? And what was my condition? No-one seemed sure. I nodded and asked when this would be. 'You should have already received the appointment details' I replied that I'd heard nothing about it. 'Perhaps it's the post' said Dr Walls, and consulted his notes. 'As a matter of fact it's for next week' Well that was something, not too long to wait. Two days prior the day of my appointment in Dublin I received the definite offer of a job with Brown and Wells in New Zealand. One had to smile that letters could go around the world with such speed yet my hospital appointment get lost. 'You know our passports are out of date' I said 'We'll have to go and get some photos taken for the new ones. We could all go to Dublin next Wednesday and have them done after my appointment. We'll go to that studio at the corner of Henry Street and Moore Street' 'The one we went to when we first met?' asked Patricia. 'That's the one. It'll be two birds with one stone.' Aileen chipped in, 'But Daddy we shall miss school' I said 'I'm sure the teachers won't mind you being off one day – you need photos if we're to go to New Zealand' Patricia added 'We can see Aunt Nora and Uncle Christy while we're there too.' This did the trick and there were no more objections. Arriving at the Richmond hospital Aileen, Philip and Brenda waited in the car and amused themselves with their books, while Patricia came with me into reception. When I emerged from the test she asked anxiously how it went. 'Professor Lanigan will send the results to Roscommon hospital. Now let's go and say cheese for the camera!' After the photos were taken the studio owner said 'Don't I know you both from somewhere?' Patricia replied that we'd often called in to have pictures done, though not for some years. 'Yes' I said, 'when we were first going out' 'I thought so' smiled the man, 'I never forget a face. Good to see you again.'

At home it was back to the same old ding-dong days, with nothing to look forward to but getting away. I knew that Patricia was equally dejected about our life at the moment, but suffering in silence and putting a brave face on things for the sake of the family. At least I was feeling a little stronger since the fever, and could do a bit of repair work to keep us ticking over. When the photographs arrived I signed them together with all the documentation and sent everything off by registered post to the British Embassy. I thought back to the photographer's kind remarks and how he'd recalled Patricia and me after so many years. It had been a nostalgic reminder of more carefree days, perhaps a hint that in spirit we might once again be those two innocent souls, looking to the future with hope and excitement in our hearts. I was glad we'd gone to Dublin that day.

At my next visit to Roscommon hospital the consultant announced he had 'some good news and some not so good news.' The good news was that the EEG done in Dublin showed no major sign of epilepsy. The bad news was they wanted me to return to the Richmond the following month for a brain scan. 'It's just in case you sustained any damage during the explosion in 1971' he explained. Patricia and I sat speechless. Would this hospital business never end? 'And the glandular fever you had will leave you with fatigue for some time yet' he went on. 'I've a job offer in New Zealand, that won't be affected I hope' I said. The consultant gave me a stern look. 'My advice would be to wait until you're well enough to work again before taking your wife and children half-way across the world.' On the way home Patricia and I had little to say to one another. It was true I had recently had some dizzy spells, which my father maintained was the spray-paint fumes in the confined workshop, but I maintained it was side effects from the increasing levels of medication I was now on. I went back to Dublin alone for the brain scan. They told me the same day the test was clear, and that I had nothing more to worry about. Halfway home I stopped off and enjoyed the sandwiches and flask of tea Patricia had packed for me, feeling more relaxed than I had in a long time. Our passports soon arrived, much to everyone's excitement. All we required now was my medical certificate, which since the scan put me in the clear, should have been sent on by now. Despite the reassurances after the scan this delay was rather worrying, and when one day I collapsed suddenly at home and was taken into Roscommon hospital, the doctor advised that anxiety had certainly played its part. In his opinion my mind was still being affected by the stress and shock of the bomb. I did tend to get muddled. With the medical certificate holding everything up my concentration began to drift, and instead of trying to work I would stroll off to the village pub, sit over a couple of pints and let my thoughts wander. No nearer a solution and with little money coming in, it wasn't long before I was obliged to return cap in hand to Mr Green the welfare man and ask to go back on Home Assistance. While in his office I had an asthma attack, and had to use my inhaler. Mr Green was all kindness, and asked how Mrs Coogan was. I replied that my wife was as well as could be expected given the circumstances. The truth was that Patricia was now displaying every sign of unhappiness. We were in a in a state of desperate inertia, and there just seemed no way forward. I wrote to the employers in New Zealand and explained the situation about the form. A letter came quickly back stating that the job would be held open pending the full medical information. This was swiftly followed by a letter from New Zealand House, also wanting the medical report. They also said I might be required to go to London and have a further examination by their own doctors, before final plans could be made for the family to depart.

Patricia and I finally agreed we could not let everything rest on the medical, which may or may not give me the all-clear.

Almost at our wits end in the damp and overcrowded cottage, which had already been declared unfit for habitation by our GP, we decided to approach Roscommon Housing Department to see if they could find us alternative accommodation. Roscommon Council wrote back to say that their own medical officer had not closely inspected our dwelling, but agreed it was small for a family. However, it went on, the roof did not appear to be leaking. It seemed therefore that our case did not warrant attention and if we wanted to move it was our responsibility to arrange it. This made me very annoyed, and Patricia also was upset. It wasn't as though we hadn't tried to do things ourselves. We felt at the end of our tether. 'I wouldn't mind if they'd come and had a proper look at the place before passing judgement.' I muttered, throwing the letter down on the kitchen table. I seemed to spend my whole life getting angry over letters. 'I don't blame you for being mad' said Patricia, 'between the North and here they have brought me to my knees, and look at you, not to mention the children all squashed into this tiny place.'

As the days passed I became increasingly withdrawn, and when I did speak my stammer being noticeably more pronounced. Some mornings I would begin work on a damaged car I had purchased and, overcome with fatigue would return to the house to make some tea, sometimes falling asleep while sat at the kitchen table as the kettle boiled. I was aware I was now very ill, and tried to hide this from the family. Having drifted from my faith over the years, I now made frantic efforts within myself to find hope, praying silently each day for guidance, believing it was God's will we were where we were.

Summer arrived, bringing Nora and Christy to us again. This time they came all the way on the bus, getting off at the stop right outside the cottage. Christy's company gave me a good excuse to get out of the house and spend several evenings down the local pub, where by now I was a familiar sight. I was drinking along with my medication, something I knew I shouldn't do, but I couldn't help it. The alcohol and convivial air had made the pub a place of sanctuary for me. When the time came for Nora and Christy to go back we went out to the road to wave them off.

Even as the bus departed I could see the sparkle had left the children's faces. And I knew Patricia would miss the companionship of her sister and the sharing of her burdens woman to woman. The bright interlude was over and now we just had each other for company. And having me for company then was not ideal for any family. For from that point on, as the futile weeks turned into months and life went on its dreary way, my awareness of what was happening around me seemed increasingly cloaked in a mist of confusion. I gave up working almost entirely, just tinkering with an engine for a few hours on odd days to pass the time, but with little profit from it. I was admitted to hospital again, this time with a gastro-intestinal complaint. I remember being put under anaesthetic and surrounded by doctors as a tube was inserted down my throat. '…it's very inflamed…' I heard one man say as a pad was placed over my face. I was later discharged but never received any results from this examination. Patricia was now obliged to shoulder all responsibility for the family. Late in the year she obtained an appointment for me at the Regional Hospital with a Professor McCarthy, who taking account of my personal history and current lethargy and depression, suggested I admit myself for observation to the psychiatric unit at Galway hospital. Apart from the fear and stigma associated with such a place, I was now quite disillusioned with hospitals of any kind and felt they could do nothing for me.

Back home I remained in a world of my own, and one day while lying down under a car adjusting the clutch I fell fast asleep, only to be woken by my father and a neighbour pulling me out from beneath the vehicle, much to everyone's relief. Our faithful gun dogs Patch and Scampy were barking about too, as happy to see me safe as everyone else. Apparently I had been under the car for several hours and Patricia and my father, alarmed at my disappearance had summoned help for a search. They had harboured the terrible fear that in my present state of mind I may have gone down to the river to take my own life. But low as I was I would never have contemplated such an act. Though I had lost faith in everything and life seemed merely a burden it was still life. Far more importantly I knew that for me to commit suicide would cause my family an unimaginable pain, one which time would never heal. For this reason alone I could not countenance it. Even on my darkest days I felt there must be some kind of future awaiting me, but what would it be? I simply could not envisage anything to look forward to. I clung to the thought that if I put the past behind me things might improve, but I had neither the strength nor will to bring it about. One thing in particular had begun to haunt me. I had heard that after my own tenancy, Brookspeed Motors in the Crumlin Road had reopened under the name of Edenberry Filling Station. It was to be no garden of paradise for its new occupants. The new manager, 24 year-old John McLean and petrol pump attendant Heather Thompson aged seventeen, had been there just a fortnight when one Saturday morning two IRA men burst in, forcing them to kneel in the inner office. One gunman emptied his weapon into John the other fired nine bullets at Heather. She was just seventeen. The bodies were found later by a customer, the room still full of smoke from the gunfire.

11

The Blood of the Lamb

'Aileen, Philip – bring the flash-lamp, quickly!' called Patricia urgently.

'I have it' said Philip, as he and his sister followed their mother out into the darkened yard.

'Shine the light over here!' yelled Aileen, 'I think I see something.'

'Where?' said Patricia.

'It's Daddy!'

Patricia walked towards the motionless figure illuminated in the torch beam. As she drew closer she could see his face was white with fear and though the night was bitterly cold, perspiration was running from his forehead.

'Philip' said his wife, 'are you able to talk – what's wrong?'

'I don't know – there's someone out there…'

I had just gone out to fetch some more coal for the range when I'd heard the bang. It was this that made me cry out. A piercing and terrifying cry as Patricia described it. She and the children had heard the bang too.

'Come and sit by the range' said Patricia, as the children struggled into the kitchen with the heavy bucket of coal.

'Your colour is coming back.'

'I couldn't move' I said 'it was a strange feeling, it's never happened to me before.'

'You gave us a fright' said Patricia as she put more coal on the range.

'I'm sure it was a gunshot' I said.

'Well we couldn't see anyone in the yard.

'The dogs didn't bark…' I said.

'No, and if there'd been anyone prowling about they'd have let us know right enough.'

'That's true' I said, feeling a little more composed 'The bang could have been a car backfiring out on the N5…'

I had now been put on Home Maintenance Disability Benefit by the Western Health Board. My father, seeing the deterioration in my health had taken me along to the doctor who diagnosed high blood pressure, which with treatment was soon under control. As the cold, early months of 1976 passed and the hours of daylight increased, my fears and anxieties were eased a little by the vivacity of springtime as it opened up all around us. The daffodil bulbs I'd planted when Mrs Law had given her consent to the workshop were blooming again, song-birds chirruped in the dew-drenched branches in the early morning and new-born lambs began to appear like little dots of pure white cotton wool in the faraway fields. Our dogs Patch and Scampy could smell the warmth of coming summer in their nostrils, and raced around full of the innocent and carefree excitement with which only children and animals are blessed. Coming home from an appointment one early afternoon I was surprised that the dogs were not in the yard to greet me. I called them, expecting any moment to hear the clatter of paws on the cobbled alley as they hurtled toward the cottage. Yet after loudly calling both their names again several times there was no sign of either animal. Patricia came out and said 'I've seen some stray dogs around again. I hope ours have not gone off with them'

'Yes' I replied 'I was shouting at those strays to go on home all last week, if they have homes. They looked well fed. Someone told me a ewe was killed last week, which might explain it.'

'But where's Patch and Scampy?' mused Patricia, 'they've never been off like this before.'

'No – when they get back we'll keep them locked in the yard for a while. We don't want them out causing any trouble.'

Later that day, after the children had returned from school, a Gardai vehicle drew up outside the cottage. The officer, who knew me, came into the yard. 'I see your dogs are missing' he said immediately, looking around the yard. I nodded warily. 'We've had a farmer report some of his sheep have been mauled and they're to be put them down. It is believed your dogs are responsible. I'm afraid they'll have to be destroyed.'

'What do you mean?' I snapped. 'I mean they'll have to be shot' he said flatly.

'Wait a minute' I protested, 'how do you know it was my dogs…'

'And if you don't do it, I shall have to.'

As calmly as I could I tried to reason with the officer. 'Listen can we not lock them up till we're sure which dogs have caused the problem? There's been some strays around…'

'The complaint has been made against you and your dogs' said the Garda resolutely. 'They have to be destroyed.'

'That's very unreasonable!' I protested.

'It's not' retorted the officer. 'Are you going to see they're put down or shall I shoot them for you? And another thing – the farmer wants full compensation from you for his sheep' I took a breath as the officer waited for my reply.

'I shall put them down myself' I said quietly.

When the officer had left, the children, who had heard everything, were in a terrible state. They ran up to me, pleading with me to let them hide Patch and Scampy away.

Patricia was the first to see the dogs loping home across the fields, whereupon she immediately caught hold of the two youngest children. 'Come children, let's go next door and see John and his wife, come now…' Closely followed by Aileen, Patricia led them quickly away. When the dogs entered the yard they were very quiet, as if knowing they had done wrong. I looked at Patch and saw there was blood on his coat. I took both the dogs' leads and put them gently around their warm necks. I was now in a terrible state myself, close to tears. For the children the two dogs were their friends and companions to be cuddled and cared for. Aileen, Brenda and Philip had played joyfully with them from the moment the cute little puppies had arrived in our home, and watched them grow as part of the family into our affectionate and much-loved Patch and Scampy. Where would I find the courage to do what must be done? I fetched my Browning shotgun and returned to the yard. Wiping the tears from my face I fired two shots in quick succession. The dogs' lay quite still. They had barely made a sound. It had been swift and painless for them. Concealing the bodies, I went out to the field and prepared their graves. The deed done I wiped the gun clean and hid it away. Patricia and the children did not return till the evening, when the Garda officer made a brief visit to check the order had been complied with. Next day John told me that other dogs had been involved in mauling sheep, but their owners had not been named. Patricia heard something similar in the village. Patricia, whose pride and honesty would not allow us to owe money, insisted I call at the butcher's shop owned by the farmer and settle up for the dead sheep. As I paid him he said 'If you wish I can cut the lamb up and you could freeze it.' I agreed to collect the meat the following day. Patricia didn't take kindly to this. 'I would have told him to keep his sheep' she said sharply. Nevertheless, money being short it was no use cutting off our nose to spite our face, so we agreed to purchase a chest freezer and take the meat.

With the dogs gone there was a gloomy atmosphere about the house. Everyone to me seemed sad and depressed. I pottered about with repairs, my thoughts dwelling on what had happened and blaming myself for not challenging the Garda officer's orders more robustly, at least until there had been a fuller enquiry. It seemed to be yet one more thing I had failed at. My physical and mental deterioration had become a matter of concern to the whole family, prompting my brother Pat to invite me to stay with him for a while. Pat was now living at Cricklewood over in London, and it was felt the change of scene may do me good. He would also arrange for me to see his own family's physician, a Dr. Copeland of Regents Park, if I were willing. A change is as good as a rest they say, and for all I knew it might be for the better. Dr Copeland welcomed us both in his smart surgery. 'How are you Pat – has your brother seen anything of London yet?' I told the doctor I'd lived here in the 'swinging sixties' and run a business too. The short stay in London turned into three months of medical appointments arranged by Dr Copeland. A letter from the senior registrar of a Professor Frankerd at University College Hospital London made this assessment of me:

Dear Dr Copeland
Thankyou for sending this man to the clinic. He gave a history of sudden onset of hemiplegia with no loss of consciousness last year, since then he has been unwell. Over the past year he has been having attacks of loss of consciousness with no convulsions. He has a stammer and suffers from asthmatic attacks. Neurological examinations were completely normal. However blood pressure measurement shows a difference between the two arms, the right arm 120/80 the left 85/60. I have asked for fasting cholesterol and lipid studies and will see him in three weeks.

I'd received letters of my own, fond ones from Patricia and the children asking how I was. I felt anxious about how they'd be managing without me. I spent much of the time walking the London streets gazing into the shop windows, yet despite all the exercise I was losing my appetite, which worried me. All I really wanted to do was go home. Further tests followed, and in mid-July Pat took me to see a Harley Street neurology specialist Mr William Goody at his home consulting rooms, number 12 Connaught Place. After lengthy examination Mr Goody gave me his firm opinion that I did not have epilepsy. In a letter to Copeland he stated that I had been under very severe strain since the bombing of 1971, and was arranging an ECG at University College Hospital. Before leaving Mr Goody I asked him that, since I did not have epilepsy, would the bombing really have caused all my illness, including the shakes and fainting. 'What you are suffering from Philip is a major psychological trauma. I have seen patients before with your symptoms, anxiety and tremulousness. Soldiers sometimes develop this condition – what was once called 'shell-shock' or 'battle fatigue'. 'Doctor, I'm returning to Ireland in a few days. What shall I do?' Mr Goody sat back and looked at me sympathetically. 'You live in the West of Ireland, it's a beautiful place. I myself often visit County Mayo for the fishing' 'But about the treatment?' I said, hoping he would give me some guidance. 'Try to keep to what has been prescribed to you. Relax in the West of Ireland and stay away from the rat race of cities. I strongly suggest what you need more than anything now is counselling. It would be a great help towards your recovery. If anything does show up on the ECG this afternoon I'll contact your doctor. Take care of yourself and try to avoid the stress. It's important.' I thanked him and paid the receptionist on the way out. It was good to know the epilepsy was ruled out, and that I would soon be going home.

12

Final Straw

Back at the cottage the family had arranged a great welcome. But though nothing was said I could tell from their reactions that I must look less well than had been expected after the break in London. I had lost a lot of weight, which I suppose was very noticeable to them after such an absence. As I sat by the range the children began telling me some of the things that had happened while I had been away. I felt listless and unable to focus on anything that was said, paying little attention to the efforts they had made to brighten the place up for my return. What I did notice was how drawn and underfed Patricia and the children seemed to be. There was a timid look about them, and my mind now connected this and all the lack of sustenance, hope and joy in them with that terrible night of the bombing. The children had never received any counselling or help after seeing their father led in a daze from the burning building, and I felt a sudden searing pain of remorse in my heart for how fate had scarred their young lives. After dinner, of which I ate little, I went to my suitcase and fetched some small gifts I had purchased in London for everyone. They were only small but everyone was so grateful and gave me a hug. They all seemed so pleased to have me home. When the children had gone to bed I talked to Patricia about London and the various medical men, about Mr Goody and his advice for how I might best recover, and particularly about Professor Frankerd's firm opinion that I did not have epilepsy. If I could now relax and just get well, the doctors would sign the medical form for New Zealand House and we could yet be on our way. Once again, this was a case of easier said than done. Over the weeks that followed I finished a car I had been working on and sold it, giving the much-needed cash to Patricia. But living again in the pokey cottage the walls seemed to be closing in on me. I slept little, and when I did would frequently have nightmares and flashbacks to the frightening events in the North. When I did venture out I got the impression that some of the locals seemed to be talking about me. My weight plummeted, soon reaching just seven stone. My clothes hung off my gaunt frame like those of a tramp, and seeing my thin face and parchment-like flesh in the mirror I knew I was a woeful sight to behold. There were rumours in the village that I might not have long to live. Overhearing such talk was deeply upsetting to Patricia, and I knew from the sorrowful looks of the children that they too had heard such things, which pained me immensely. My mental health went from bad to worse and I became very depressed. One day I went into my bedroom in a terrible mood, and would not answer when Patricia tried to speak to me. Something I had received in the post that morning had profoundly upset me. I did not want to be disturbed, and since there was no lock to the bedroom I pushed a heavy press against the old door to keep everyone out. 'I want to be left in peace' I called out. I was now on large amounts of medication, my old doctor having been replaced by an ex-army medic who had upped my dosage considerably. I sat on the bed and must have dozed off a while. The next thing I remember is shouting at the top of my voice that I was about to be blown up. Vivid and horrific flashbacks had appeared in my dreams, and I was reliving the experience of the burning building and the men coming to kill me all over again. Hearing my tormented cries my father, who was staying with us, came and helped Patricia push open the door. Patricia made me a mug of hot tea, and my mother took the children down to look for fish in the river. When I was calmer my father asked what had upset me so. 'It was a letter he got this morning' said Patricia, 'I don't know what was in it' 'What was it son?' asked my father. 'Just a letter' I muttered, 'from North Down Council, informing me they have taken over the site at 23 Warren Road and offered me payment of £120 for the land. 'Here, take a look'. My father took the letter I had drawn from my pocket and shook his head as he read. 'Quite apart from the true value of the land, I cleared that site of rubble at my own expense; that alone cost far more than £120' I said. 'It's the last straw, now they have everything!' 'This is very unjust' said my father gravely. 'There is no justice in the North' said Patricia. 'Never mind' said my father trying to console me, 'we'll see what can be done.' 'I shan't accept their money now' was all I could find to say. With my disturbed state of mind only seeming to worsen, Patricia's elder sister Maura paid a visit to offer what comfort she could. Both sisters talked with me, and arranged a consultation with the GP who had treated me before I had gone to London. He maintained that what I most needed was to have my tablet intake regulated, and the best place to do this was in a psychiatric hospital not far from our home. This sounded alarming, but being close by I could have visitors every day. Patricia and Maura both felt that with my health now so desperate it might be the only way. Though muddled and feeble in my mind I still felt the will to do whatever it took to get better, and therefore agreed to admit myself to the hospital as a voluntary patient that same evening.

The journey didn't take long. Patricia had prepared a light meal for me before we left home, then she and Maura had come along in the taxi with me. As we drove up the long avenue St Patrick's Hospital, which had formerly been a TB sanatorium, looked very impressive lit up against the evening sky, beautiful almost. We got out and walked up the steps of the handsome building surrounded by flowerbeds and lawns. I carried my own small case which Patricia had packed. The doctor we had seen that morning was waiting at the reception to welcome me and oversee my admission. I signed myself in the book and turned to Patricia. 'I'll see you the day after tomorrow' she said 'then every day after that. I can come over with your friend Canon Flynn' 'Oh sure' I said, 'I had forgotten about the Canon – he comes over to Castlerea every day for a few hours and has a meal, that's right, I'm sure he'll gladly give you lift' A male nurse then appeared at the reception and picked up my case, asking me to follow him. After kissing Patricia goodbye I was led away. Turning once more I saw the sadness in Patricia's eyes as she left with Maura. I knew there would be talk in the village, and felt a sense of shame at the unkind or thoughtless looks and wagging tongues that may be awaiting her and the children. Meanwhile the nurse had taken me through a series of heavy doors, locking each of them behind him.

13

Night Falls

As I was escorted from the brightly furnished reception area of the hospital and into its inner chambers, a shiver of fear passed through me. The change in surroundings came as a shock, like being suddenly plunged in darkness into ice-cold water. Passing down long corridors, the bare, pale painted walls and echoing cries of the inmates gave me the same feeling of nauseous desolation and despair as when I was incarcerated in the Crumlin all those years ago. Like then I knew I had to follow the rules, or be in trouble, and felt very uneasy about what might be in store. I was taken to a large open-plan ward where single beds were set in several long rows. This was not like the Crumlin with its small cells. Rather it reminded me of the inside of the Nissen Huts at Arboe, when my brother Pat and I had taken our parents eggs for the GIs, who'd been so friendly and generous with their chocolate. The nurse showed me to my bed and departed. Some patients were already lying down, while others waited till some of the lights were switched off. I seemed to settle down rapidly, I supposed I must be tired. It had been a full day, and events had developed very rapidly. I'd been told that my medication would be completely changed to ant-depressants within a few days, and then I could go home. All seemed peaceful, till I was woken sometime in the middle of the night by angry shouts and bumping sounds. Opening my eyes I made out a large figure clambering across the beds, waking each of their occupants in the process. Before I knew it the figure was close by and had sprung at my own bed. He was hurling verbal abuse at me for apparently preventing him sleeping. I realised I must have been snoring. Male nurses had by now rushed over to break up the confrontation, and lead the man back to his own bed. As he was taken away some other patients confided that I should 'take no notice of Vincent' as he was an epileptic, but also a bully and no-one got on with him. I felt shaken after the scuffle, and slept little more that night. If I had to endure this kind of fighting, I would rather go home I thought.

Next day I kept well away from Vincent, and at dinner-time moved to another table when I saw him approach. I viewed the prospect of bed-time again with apprehension, and sure enough as the lights went down Vincent shouted across 'I shall be down to you again if you don't stay quiet!' It wasn't just the snoring. The man had clearly taken a particular dislike to me, and I was now feeling very anxious. I sat on the bed, reluctant to get undressed, then walked over to the duty nurse, who was positioned behind a high security counter. 'I want to be allowed home' I said. The nurse looked up for a moment but made no reply. I tried again. 'Will someone phone and ask for my friend Danny to come and collect me please.' Again the nurse remained silent, as if not hearing me. I was now very agitated and repeated my request. Eventually another male nurse appeared, a young man whom I knew as Thomas. 'We have a new bed for you' he said. 'Somewhere you won't be disturbed. Come with me' Thomas led me to the far end of the ward and indicated a vacant bed. I sat down, but still felt unwilling to sleep till Thomas came back and persuaded me to undress and lay down. He then sat in a chair close by. After a few minutes another nurse called Francis came to take over, passing as he did so a remark which I found very upsetting. I was about to get up again but was immediately restrained in the attempt by Francis, and each time I stirred or made some sound, he would put pressure on my upper shoulder. When I tried more earnestly to get out of bed, he took hold of my left arm, forcing it behind my back. The sharp pain made me scream out 'You are hurting me!' Half the ward was now awake as two nurses suddenly descended upon me with some sort of jacket, grabbing me about the arms and head. Panicking, I began to struggle desperately but pain in my shoulders and face was so intense that I started losing consciousness. My fierce resistance overcome I was aware of the jacket being fitted about me, my arms bound and immobilised. After this everything went dark. I woke to find myself lying alone on the floor in a small room. I still could not move and dimly perceived thick leather straps with large metal buckles encasing me. I shouted for help. No-one came. I shouted again, my voice strained and hoarse. All I could hear were my own words reverberating inside my head, my own voice mocking me. Although in pain I tried to recollect everything that had happened to me and my family over the past years, and to think why I was now imprisoned here in circumstances of such woeful ignominy far from my dear wife and children. There had to be some reason for it all. In the silence and isolation of that windowless room, lying like a trussed animal, I endeavoured to work it all out. But I was drained, a mere empty shell into which no proper thoughts would come. Soon, tears began to fall from my eyes and I cried myself bitterly to sleep.

Keys turned in the lock. I opened my eyes to see a nurse enter the room. He knelt over me, unbuckled the jacket and handed me a cup. I sat up and drank clumsily, my arms stiff with cramp after the hours of restraint around my body. There was also a severe pain in my jaw. I did not speak apart from asking to use the toilet, and was shortly taken for a medical examination and given some drugs. Over the next few days I received several injections in my left arm and the pains in my arms and face gradually eased. I cannot recall any other details of where I slept, or indeed what else I did, for about a week after this. It was only one night, after the doctors and nurses had left me and visiting hours must have been long over, I heard a voice, trying to wake me. The voice was familiar, and after a moment or two I realised it was that of my father Patrick. I could not see my father but as if through a blanket of fog heard him say quietly to some other person '…he is finished…'

The following day I was given extra helpings at dinner. 'You could do with putting on some weight Philip' said the nurse 'so eat as much of this as you are able...' My only real awareness or desire now was to go home. If eating more would do it then I'd eat more. 'Thankyou' I muttered, 'I'll try.' Another day I was taken before a woman, a doctor of some sort I supposed, who set me some mental tests, asking me various questions of arithmetic and suchlike. When I could not answer anything she became very irritated and flung her sheets of paper about on the desk. 'You'll have to go back to school!' she said crossly as if addressing a naughty and backward child. Oddly I knew the tests were simple, and felt distressed and humiliated at my failure. My harsh interlocutor with her snide criticism gave me the sense I was stupid rather than unwell, wicked even. Perhaps that was why I was here.

'Would you care to attend mass?' I looked up from my chair to see a nurse looking enquiringly down. It was the day after the tests.

'Mass?' I said sleepily. 'Yes, there is a small chapel in the grounds. I'm about to go over if you'd care to come.'

'I would like that.'

'Then please follow me.'

It was the first time I had been outside the hospital walls since my arrival. The air smelt sweet and fresh, the smell of freedom. The service was comforting, though I still felt drowsy, with all the sights and sounds and rituals of the mass coming to me as if in a dream, a memory of other occasions, in another life I had once lived. That same afternoon the nurse came to me again. 'Come along with me Philip. You have a visitor' I felt surprised, then expectant.

'Who?'

'Your wife.'

Patricia. Mistily I remembered the plan for her to travel over and visit with Canon Flynn. Which days had been mentioned? Struggling with the dates I tried to recall how long I had been in the hospital. Why had she not come sooner? From the door to the visitors room I saw Patricia seated and waiting patiently. Our eyes meeting with a rush of affection and delight we fell immediately into each other's arms.

'I thought you were going to get a lift with Canon Flynn' I said.

'I have' said Patricia, 'he's here now.'

'But before…you never came to see me till now…'

'We've called over several times….' she was querulous with emotion as she spoke.

'But how…?'

'Philip, they kept telling me it would be too upsetting for you to see me, I pressed them but they wouldn't allow it, every day the same story…oh dear…'

'But that's a lie – I wanted to see you, I asked to go home after the first day!'

'I felt sure of it – your father…'

'He came, I heard him…'

'Yes, yes, he was very angry with the hospital, he warned them he'd get a habeus corpus writ against them if they refused to let me see you…oh Philip…!'

14

The Kindness of Neighbours

Aileen, Brenda and Philip were all thrilled to see me home. At the same time they appeared to me to be lonesome and dejected. It was the 4th October 1976, and I had been in St Patrick's Hospital for just under three weeks. It had seemed like a lifetime, and I realised the days of my absence must have stretched slowly for the children too. Various neighbours now began to rally round. Molly from the village lobbied the council in an effort to get us re-housed, another great friend old Mrs Cassidy kept us supplied with eggs, since the foxes had picked off most of our own hens. Trying to get my mind onto the future I wrote to New Zealand House and the firm in Dunedin again. On the 17th December a reply came from the High Commission that the assisted passages scheme had now been abolished, closely followed by a letter from Dunedin reiterating this change. We had now spent most of our savings and paying the full fare for all of us to New Zealand would be impossible. Gone were the bright hopes of starting a new life in a new land. New Zealand was not to be and we had no choice but to accept it. We would have to stay put and find some other way to improve our living conditions.

Meanwhile my health remained poor. I had been placed on the outpatients register at St Patrick's where I attended regularly for medication. When I had the energy I would attempt to work, but these days became fewer. When attempting to lift heavy objects they would simply fall from my hands after a few minutes, and I would then sit around for long periods feeling sorry for myself. From an early age I had relished hard work, and to be so restricted left me feeling miserable and inadequate. I had put on weight now, but too much of it. The worst thing was there seemed no hope of my depression and physical weakness improving. I was like one of my own smashed cars, but one I could not repair. The doctor changed my prescription slightly, which enabled me to drive again, though anything more strenuous remained beyond my powers.

It was during the spring of 1977, just we were coming out from second mass, that our neighbour little Mrs Cassidy came up and spoke to us. 'Come along with me Patricia' she said smiling, 'and you Philip, and bring the children too.'

'Where are we going?' I asked.

'Why, I want to invite you all to the pub of course!' beamed Mrs Cassidy.

'Thanks but we have to ...' I began.

'We'd love to accompany you Mrs Cassidy!' broke in Patricia

It was in fact very pleasant to sit down as a family that day in the well-known surroundings of our little pub. After a few drinks, and as Patricia and Mrs Cassidy talked of local affairs, the old lady made a suggestion.

'I was wondering' she began, 'I'm going over to Knock next Thursday, when there's a day for the blessing of the sick. And I was thinking...' at this point the old lady and Patricia seemed to exchange a glance '...you might like to accompany me.'

'Oh' I said 'I didn't know they had a special day...'

'There is one each month' said Patricia, 'Mrs Cassidy and I have often talked of taking you to Knock.'

This remark explained Patricia's ready compliance when Mrs Cassidy had suggested coming to the pub. The invitation was not 'out of the blue' at all, the two of them had obviously decided to broach the idea with me. I knew about Knock of course and its history, and had joined a small pilgrimage to the shrine when I was a young man in 1952, taking a bus all the way from my home in Lisnaskea.

'Shall we go then?' said Mrs Cassidy, her bright eyes twinkling at me like those of an eager bird. The proposal was something of a surprise. I was about to thank her and say I would think about it, when Patricia said 'Yes, we shall all go.'

Little Mrs Cassidy had her answer and the following Thursday myself, Patricia and the children together with Mrs Cassidy set off from Roscommon shortly after midday and motored the thirty miles to the little village of Knock in County Mayo. On arrival we parked the car and made our way slowly into the grounds of the shrine. I had remembered parts of the main thoroughfare from my visit of some twenty-five years ago, but much was changed too. The stalls which had lined the streets were now relocated, leaving a large open area around the old church and at the south gable wall where, in 1879, the Blessed Virgin Mary, St Joseph and St John the Evangelist had made their appearance. To the right was an altar with the figure of a lamb and angels hovering. Hundreds of walking sticks left by pilgrims had accumulated ever since the 1879 Apparition, when Archdeacon Cavanagh the parish priest at Knock had been confronted with all the dreadful disease and starvation brought on by the Great Famine of that year. The walking sticks, being so many were now stored away. I gazed around appreciatively at the newly built Basilica, now large enough it was said to accommodate ten thousand pilgrims. People were already filing in for the mass, to be followed by the sacrament for the anointing of the sick. Mrs Cassidy showed me to a seat in the front row. At the end of the proceedings we all agreed that it had been a rewarding experience and that we had enjoyed seeing the wonderful new building and also the opportunity of showing the children such a historic place. I knew what Patricia and Mrs Cassidy were hoping for of course, but in truth I felt no sudden sense of a cure or transformation. Yet at the same time the afternoon of prayer had been comforting and I had found solace walking in the beautiful gardens. A deep feeling of peace came over me in these wonderful grounds and I had felt able to pray. On the way home I thanked Mrs Cassidy for the trip.

'We are all very grateful to you for our visit to Knock. It was very thoughtful of you to make the suggestion that we pay a visit.'

'Not at all' said Mrs Cassidy, 'I am only trying to assist, and prayers are helpful.'

'That is true' said Patricia.

A couple of days' later, feeling a pain in my teeth, I realised some of the back ones were loose and made a mental note to pay a visit to the dentist. Meanwhile the weather was warm for the month of May, and coming out of mass one Sunday Patricia, Aileen, Philip and Brenda decided to walk home from church while I went ahead with the car. It was whilst I was settled down in the cottage peacefully reading the papers and having a cup of tea, that I heard through the open window the sound of laughter. Looking out I saw Patricia and the children returning home, and with them a neighbour of ours Mrs Moran. It was a long time since I had heard Patricia laughing, and I was curious as to the reason. I then heard her call out 'Tell your daddy we want to see him!' Brenda and Philip then immediately ran in shouting gleefully 'Daddy, daddy come quick, mother wants you…' Laying aside my newspaper I went outside and greeted our neighbour. 'Good day Mrs Moran, it's a lovely day'. Mrs Moran nodded cordially and looked at Patricia, who was clearly bursting to tell me something and could contain herself no longer. 'We have news for you Philip' she said, 'Mrs Moran has offered us some of her land to build a home on!'

'What? Where…?'

'On that three acre field the other side of the bridge.'

'Oh really….?'

'Mrs Moran heard about us being so over-crowded here and it being so damp and all – and the let-down we had over the other site' said Patricia, full of excitement.

'It's a serious offer' smiled Mrs Moran

'Well…' I spluttered, 'that'd be a lovely spot for a home…and if you're willing Mrs Moran…'

'I am.'

'Then it's the greatest news we've all had in a long time!'

258

15

The Kindness of Families

Mrs Moran was indeed serious, and there were no vague agreements or false promises. Her son Martin contacted their solicitors and formal arrangements were made for us to buy the land. At my suggestion we purchased the whole three acre field, giving us the option to also build a business premises at some future date. The price settled on was very reasonable, and Mrs Moran welcomed the possibility of my parents building an additional bungalow of their own on the site. A deposit was paid, followed soon after by the balance – we still had a little money in savings, and a loan from the bank took care of the rest. By this time it all seemed too good to be true. I was half expecting everything to go wrong any day, and from past experience we all knew that obtaining planning permission was the one hurdle which could see us come tumbling back down to earth with a painful bump. Drawings were quickly made and submitted to Roscommon Council, and each day Patricia and I would sit anxiously over breakfast waiting for the clatter of the postman's bicycle. 'It could be months yet before we hear' I kept telling Patricia, nonetheless remaining as hopeful as she for a letter sooner rather than later. In fact the planning department's reply arrived in a few weeks. Opening it with trepidation I was amazed to see that the council had granted us full planning permission for the two bungalows. In jubilant mood I thought of submitting further plans for a petrol station and business straight away. However my health was still poor and I decided on reflection this might be putting the cart before the horse.

With the flurry of activity about the land I had not had time to get to the dentist, and the increasing discomfort in my mouth reminded me an appointment was now long overdue. The offending tooth was removed and I thought no more about it till a few days later the pain returned. This time I went to see a specialist doctor, who on examining my mouth promptly asked 'Who broke your jaw?' I told him about the bombing and my going into the burning building in 1971. 'But I've had x-rays since then' I said 'and they'd have shown up a fracture wouldn't they?' The doctor agreed. 'I'd like to run some x-rays round the corner if you don't mind, then we'll know for sure. Take this letter to the hospital and then come back and see me. As the x-rays were being taken I sat racking my brains for some explanation. As muddled as I'd been on occasions over the past few years I would have remembered sustaining a fracture of the jaw. The doctor must surely be mistaken. When I was given the x-rays I took them back to the doctor. Opening the envelope he showed me the photograph of my facial bones and exclaimed heartily 'You poor bugger! Your jaw has been broken – who did it eh?' At a complete loss I said, 'I really don't know – I've not been in an accident and I don't fight.' The doctor smiled. 'Well don't worry, jump back in the chair and we'll soon ease that pain for you!'

As the doctor worked on me, his expert hands putting right whatever it was that was damaged in my mouth, I remembered in a flash what must have inflicted that damage. That night in the psychiatric hospital it had been unskilled and unkind hands which had held me, forcing the straight-jacket about my arms and over my head. That's when I had felt the severe pain in my face, pain which it now seemed certain could only have come from being punched in the head. When I told Patricia she agreed there was no other explanation for the fracture of my jaw. It also dawned on us that this criminal injury was the reason the hospital staff refused to let the family see me for nearly three weeks.

We now had land to build on, but as yet lacked the resources to start work on our new home. My health and strength were still fluctuating wildly, and at one point I was hospitalised in intensive care for two weeks with severe blood pressure problems. Immediately upon being discharged I wrote to the council to see if they could assist us financially with the building of a new home. They replied that regrettably no grants or special schemes were available. We seemed so near and yet so far. It was finally our families who came to the rescue, with both my parents and Patricia's family giving us the money we needed for building. Materials were ordered, some willing tradesmen found and foundations were laid in the three acre field. Wherever we were able, the whole family assisted with the construction, and there would be myself, Patricia and the children side by side filling stones into sub-floor and carrying the blocks for the bricklayers – it all helped to keep the cost down. Whilst this was strenuous labour it felt satisfying to be taking part in creating our new home.

16

Return to Knock

Keen as we all were to raise our bungalow, Sunday is the day of rest, a time for prayer and devotion with one's neighbours. The fellowship of our own church service usually carried over into the pub on a Sunday lunchtime, and one particular Sunday after mass we found ourselves once more sitting and having a few drinks with little Mrs Cassidy. Her presence reminded me of something I had been meaning to ask.

'Will you be going to Knock again Mrs Cassidy?' I said.

'I should like to visit before the winter yes' she replied. 'The Sacrament for the Sick is to take place again on the last Thursday of this month.'

'Shall we all go together?' suggested Patricia. It was readily agreed.

Arriving in Knock this time we had difficulty finding a parking space.

Pilgrims had travelled to the holy shrine by plane, coach and car from all over Ireland, and many had come from overseas for the special sacrament. 'Just look at the crowds!' marvelled Patricia gazing round at the throngs of people and vehicles weaving their way slowly along. I had been looking forward to sitting at the front again, but when we entered the Basilica the first few rows were already full. I contented myself with a seat a little further back, reflecting that it made no difference where one sat. I could already see something like a hundred priests, bishops, handmaids and stewards in attendance around the Basilica, all bearing oils for the anointing of those in need. The priests were already making their way among the congregation, and looking round I could see that Mrs Cassidy who was sat with Patricia and the children, was now receiving the blessing. While waiting my turn I closed my eyes and listened to the beautiful singing of the choir. After being anointed I devoted the remainder of the day to prayer and meditation, in the hope that my ailments, both bodily and spiritual might one day be healed. When mass was over I met up with the family again. 'How do you feel now Daddy?' asked one of the children. They had obviously been hoping for some miraculous cure, to see a magical change in their dear daddy that would make him happy and well. I wished I could have given the answer they all longed to hear – that divine providence had lighted on me even as the anointing oil touched my body, and that I had been made whole again.

But it had not happened. As on the previous visit to the shrine, I did feel touched by a sense of peace, but it went no further than that. In truth I didn't know what I expected, but there had been no blinding light. The crowds were now making their way slowly towards the 'Apparition Gable' of the old church, where the Bishop was to give the Blessing of the Sick. As we made our way across the square I had occasion to pause halfway, as a most peculiar sensation had come over me. The nearest thing I could describe it to would be that of weights being removed from my feet, weights to which I was so accustomed that I had forgotten they were there. Being now as it were, suddenly unshackled, I felt my whole body as surprisingly light. Yet I also felt larger, elongated, and supplied with a sudden rush of energy from I knew not where. My steps across the square became instantly effortless, and with this came an almost giddy sense of dexterity and power. At that moment, I felt really and truly as if I were walking on air. Once on the other side I stood calmly with the others and listened to the blessing, not daring to speak lest on opening my mouth this remarkable sense of invigoration should exit my being as swiftly as it had arrived.

On the way home the family and Mrs Cassidy enquired once again how the visit to the shrine had gone for me this time. 'I greatly enjoyed it' I said, 'the singing and the services were beautiful. It was very good to have gone again, thankyou Mrs Cassidy' I made no mention of the extraordinary feeling that had come over me in the square. There was a very good reason for this. The experience, the inner feeling, had reminded me very much of my childhood vision. Not since that long ago morning when, as a boy I had witnessed Our Lady manifest herself before me in the fields of Arboe, had I felt such a strong and particular emotion as today. I had not seen the Blessed Virgin again, but the resonance of the two occasions, between which so much had happened in my life, was unmistakable. And that day in Arboe when I had run home to tell my mother she had, understandably, not believed me. I had been kept indoors for several days for fear I would go around telling the neighbours. Now I was a grown man, though clearly one still learning, and as regards what had now happened to me at Knock, I decided to keep my own counsel for a while.

17

A New Beginning

'You've been looking better this last few weeks' said Patricia one morning over breakfast. It was of course Patricia who had noticed the first gradual signs of change in me. I still hadn't said anything much about the occurrence at Knock.

'I do feel a bit improved lately' I replied casually.

'And you've been doing some work on the cars again.'

'The bricklayer's almost finished the walls on our bungalow' I said changing the subject.

'I thought so' said Patricia. 'I was having a look from the road yesterday. Does that mean we can get some of the grant money?'

'Yes, the first part is payable once the walls are up.'

Our finances for the building work had been stretched to the limit even with help from our parents, but luck had been with us and there was a government scheme to help families after all.

'After that it's up to us to get the roof on and the rest of the work done, hopefully in the early part of next year.'

'So we could be in by the spring!' said Patricia, as a spontaneous smile lit up her face. It was good to see her smiling again. After the years of anguish which had worn my wife down it was heartening to know that a major cause of the family's distress, lack of a decent home, would soon be cured. As for my own cure, the mental scars were still there but the pain which had accompanied them now showed signs of easing. On the physical side, the excess weight I had accumulated was causing problems, and I thus embarked on vigorous walking routines of several miles a day, together with cutting down my drinking. Gradually this paid off, and I felt fitter and more energetic as the months passed. By agreement with the hospital my medication was decreased. There were still black days, but now I learned to see depression or anxiety on the horizon, to prepare myself and to cope. Things did not change overnight for me. My spiritual and mental state might be best likened to a car which had been travelling down hill for a long time. I hope it will not be thought a sacrilege if I say that that day at Knock the Good Lord got in the driving seat and steered me around. From then on, though I moved slowly and may sometimes have stalled on the steep gradient, I have been heading always towards the top of the hill, towards the light.

The day our bungalow was completed was a great event, and Patricia and the children were all thrilled at the event of moving in. To think we had planned to travel to the other side of the world, and were now setting up home a couple of fields away. It felt just as much of an adventure. Everyone was content in the smart, spacious new living space, and the children still had their friends and relatives close by. As well as taking up work again, I became more active socially, as secretary of the local gun club and forming a branch of the Irish Music Society named after Douglas Hyde. One morning our postman Paddy issued me an unexpected invitation.

'How would you like to become a steward at the Knock Holy Shrine Philip?' he asked. I was amazed, as I had no idea he was connected with the place.

'Well, I...' I spluttered 'what would I have to do?'

'Nothing' replied Paddy 'I'll call for you at 9.30 Sunday morning. It is our autumn day of recollection for all the handmaids and stewards. I'll introduce you to our chief steward'

When Paddy and I arrived at the Shrine it was a bright, clear October day in 1980.. The St John's Centre was already half-full and soon the crowd had swelled to over a thousand. I was introduced and welcomed and asked to supply two character references. After these had been submitted with an application form I received a letter stating I had been accepted as a steward and giving an address for obtaining my uniform. In the spring of 1981 I attended for the first time as a steward at the Knock Holy Shrine.

Meanwhile there remained many unresolved issues, most significantly the so-called "vesting order" by which the Ards Borough Council had taken away our rightfully owned property in Donaghadee. The day we drove up and revisited the place we'd worked, prospered and finally been driven out of, was an emotional one. Particularly when we saw that the council had already carried out its plan to turn the Warren Road site into a recreation ground. It was now very pleasant for the people who were enjoying it, but that didn't alter the fact that an unjust act had been carried out. Over the next few years I made further attempts to seek legal redress but without success, and in 1996 decided to take the £120 the council had offered for the land. I received a polite letter back, and a cheque, which included interest, and amounted to £381.25. The interest was more than the original paltry sum! It still seems extraordinary they should have been so scrupulous in calculating interest to the penny like that after stealing my land. To add insult to injury the letter informed that 'legal costs have been discharged on your behalf by Ards Borough Council'. Was I supposed to be grateful! The hypocrisy was, and remains, truly boggling. I also wrote several letters asking why I had been turned down for service in the RUC all those years ago. They all went unanswered save for one to the Fair Employment Tribunal for Northern Ireland, who informed me my enquiry fell outside the statutory time limit for complaints.

Whilst such unfortunate matters must be placed on record, there were many positive events in my life after Knock, and it is important I should remind myself of them. Recalling the remarks of the psychiatric nurse in St Patrick's Hospital that I 'should go back to school' I eventually did just that, and in 1992 after studying with the Open University I was awarded an MBA, a degree in Business. My pride at the achievement was offset by a great sadness that my father was not there to see it, having passed away only a few months previously. In 1994 I was given the opportunity to serve the community by being appointed as a Peace Commissioner. I continued working, and though still needing some medical support (I was eventually awarded a disability pension) managed to wean myself off the anti-depressant drugs. I trained as a healer myself, gaining qualifications of MNFSH (Member The National Federation Spiritual Healers) worldwide membership. I set myself to work in this capacity, volunteering locally via the church and at Knock. I later obtained a further degree as a Reiki Master, and more recently Patricia and I have been blessed with grandchildren.

Since that remarkable day at the Knock Holy Shrine I have seen and experienced many wonderful things there. These, together with accounts of healing and other reminiscences and thoughts I hope to commit to paper at a later stage. For now I want to say thank you for staying with me and reading about my experiences. Many of them I would not have wished for, but as we all know God works in mysterious ways his miracles to perform. Not that I am a remarkable man or one who can perform miracles. I am just an ordinary person who, like most of my compatriots, has lived through some extraordinary and troubled times. I have been far more fortunate than many. What I call the 'lost years' of my past, years muddled by depression and drink and medication in which I cannot recall the first Holy Communion of my youngest child, for example, and in which my dear wife heroically shouldered the burden of keeping our family's bodies and souls together, are of course to be regretted. But whilst the past must be accepted in all its aspects it should also be learned from and built upon. This way the present and the future are not sad echoes of what went wrong before, but reveal themselves as a time full of opportunities for creative living with one's family and friends and in society. Knock gave me back my life. Once, my soul was poisoned by fear and resentment at those who threatened me and took away material things, forcing me and my family into poverty. It is now freed to use what gifts I have to serve the community and help God's work. That in itself is a blessing.